I0236693

Sandi Jacobs

Written By: Aaliyah Murphy

ISBN: 978-1-5356-1748-2

Contents

Chapter 1

"Smile! Say cheese! Cheese! Click!" the photographer said to us.

"Sandi, would you come here please?" Mother asked.

I couldn't walk or talk yet, but I could crawl like a soldier, sliding on my belly across the grass. Mother laughed. It seemed I could always make her smile.

"Oh, Sandi! You silly girl! What would I do without you?" Mother asked. I giggled and Mother picked me up as Jaycelyn walked in the door. "You're late, Jaycelyn! Your father will be quite furious with you!" Mother exclaimed.

Father walked into the living room from the kitchen. "Jaycelyn Marie Jacobs! You're half an hour late! We shall deal with you later!" Father yelled.

Thirty minutes later, we were all sitting in the kitchen, eating dinner. Mother, Father, and Jaycelyn were having lobster, peas, mashed potatoes with gravy, and green beans. I got to eat creamed squash. Father looked at Jaycelyn ever so fiercely.

"Why, hello to you, too, Father," Jaycelyn said fearfully.

"Why were you so late, Jaycelyn?" Father asked.

"I…I…I was forced to stay at school…"

"Why?"

"Well, earlier there was a fight between two kids in the parking lot. There was a stabbing. Dustin's dad and the other kid's dad got into a fight, but Dustin—"

Father banged his hand on the table, completely interrupting Jaycelyn's lies. He walked toward Jaycelyn. Mother hopped up out of her seat and ran toward Father.

"Lee! Please sit back down! Don't be so quick-tempered! Please, baby…sit down."

Father caught his temper and sat down. Everyone was silent. Then, there was a sound I only heard every so often. It was the doorbell. Jaycelyn ran for the door, and my parents picked up on why. My father ran for the door, too, and my mother ran after my father.

"Dustin!" Jaycelyn yelled as she ran toward him.

He knelt and hugged her.

"How many times have I told you to stay away from my daughter?" Father asked.

"Look, Mr. and Mrs. Jacobs, I don't mean no harm to Jessie!" Dustin exclaimed.

"Stop calling her 'Jessie'! That isn't her name!" Father growled.

"Lee! Calm down!" Mother yelled.

"Just stop it! Dustin is my best friend, and there's nothing you can do to change that!" Jaycelyn snapped.

With one quick motion, Father slapped Jaycelyn, and she fell to the ground. Jaycelyn screamed in agony.

"Lee! How could you?!" Mother exclaimed.

Dustin knelt on the grass where Jaycelyn lay and picked her up and laid her on his chest. "Jessie…everything's okay. Your problems will go away someday. Jessie, sweet darling girl. Oh, Jessie, free without a care in the world. Where will you go? Through thick and thin, I'll be there when you cry. Oh, close your eyes…close your eyes…just close your beautiful eyes…" Dustin sang ever so softly and repeatedly until Jaycelyn felt safe. Dustin, a strong, tough, sometimes quick-tempered, muscular thirteen-year-old boy would stay out of all the trouble in the world for a nine-year-old girl.

The sound was so sweet that I wanted to find out what it was, so I got up and wobbled outside. When my mother gasped with excitement and said to my father, "Look, Lee!"

My father smiled. Dustin and Jaycelyn laughed. I walked over to Dustin and Jaycelyn and pointed at Jaycelyn. "Jessie, Jessie!" I said and everyone laughed.

Dustin looked at me, picked me up, and laughed. "Sandi, you're so silly. What would we do without you?" Dustin asked.

I giggled, put my finger in my mouth, and pointed with the other one at Jaycelyn and said, "Jessie!"

Later that night, Dustin stayed the night, and Mother was helping me keep my balance on my feet. Upstairs, Dustin was helping Jaycelyn with her homework.

"One times one is?" Dustin asked.

"One. Come on, Dustin. I know all my ones. Start from…twos?" Jaycelyn replied.

Dustin laughed and replied, "Oh, all right, Jessie! Two times two?"

"Four."

"Two times three?" Dustin leaned in to kiss Jaycelyn, caught himself, and said, "Well?"

"Six."

"Jess…w-we should g-g-go to b-bed… now," Dustin stuttered.

"Uh, yeah."

"What's the matter, Jessie?"

"Nothing…you're right. We should sleep…"

"I swear you're the best liar ever, but I know you too well. C'mon, Jessie. You're my best friend."

"Well, umm…okay…it seemed like you wanted to…" Dustin leaned in to kiss Jaycelyn hesitantly. He caressed her face instead.

She looked at him confused by the sweet gesture, her eyes gleaming with innocence.

Dustin was close, too close. As he sat there in awe and temptation, the bedroom door opened. Dustin stopped a few centimeters away from her lips. "Princess, I promise I will turn into a handsome prince if you kiss my forehead and tell me what fifty times sixty is. I SWEAR!"

Jaycelyn played along. She kissed Dustin's forehead.

"Now what's fifty times sixty?" Dustin asked.

"Three-thousand!" Jaycelyn exclaimed.

Dustin laughed and said, "Oh, smart, beautiful, graceful princess! Will you tell me what forty times sixty is?!"

"Well, of course! That's easy! Two thousand four hundred!"

Mother laughed. "Oh, princess, what shall I call thee?!"

"You shall call me Princess Jessie!"

"And we lived happily ever after, after Jessie told me what five hundred times six is!"

"That's too easy! Three thousand!"

"The end!" Dustin said.

Lucky for Dustin, he was a pretty slick guy.

"Very well done! A bit too close for the kissing scene, but she learned a lot!" Mother said.

When Mother walked back down the stairs, Jaycelyn closed the door and fell to the floor laughing.

"Glad that worked!" Dustin said.

They laughed. Jaycelyn got up off the floor. Then, she leaned against the door. Dustin walked over to her and put his hands on the wall and stood in front of her. "Dustin," Jaycelyn hesitated, "I think you know but in case you don't… I kind of like, like you. Like a lot." She stared down at her feet shyly. He ran his fingers through her hair, "When you're older Jessie, I promise."

Dustin leaned in and kissed Jaycelyn on the cheek, his lips lingering there for a moment. "You can't tell anyone this, but, you're my first kiss, Jess."

Jaycelyn's eyes grew. "But…a guy like you?"

"A guy like me would turn down all the girls in the world for my princess."

The very next day, I woke up to people yelling words at me. I had never heard these words before. "Happy birthday!" everyone yelled.

Happy birthday? Okay, I guess.

We were all watching television when that sound came again. Mother went to the door, and the police barged in. They picked up Dustin and cuffed him then walked out. Jaycelyn ran outside, screaming. Mother ran outside after Jaycelyn. She wasn't quite fast enough though. Jaycelyn grabbed hold of Dustin's waist and screamed, "Let him go! Please! Let my best friend go!"

Dustin exhaled, holding back tears in his eyes. Dustin inhaled sharply and said, "Jessie! C'mon, Jess. You gotta be strong for me. I can't see you cry."

"Okay. I'll try."

Dustin was forced to push Jaycelyn off, or they would have used something called the Taser on her. Mother detained Jaycelyn as Dustin was pushed into the cop car. Jaycelyn's heart broke as she watched the car leave. Dustin sat quietly in the back of the cop car until they were at the police station and inside the interrogation room.

"All right. I swear to tell the truth and nothing but the truth. So, you wanna know what happened? Well, sixty minutes before school ended, I decided to leave early and walk my best friend home. Plus, she was getting picked up for a family photo. I went to get her, and we walked out the back door. I heard a voice say, 'Terrorist.' I turned around and charged for the guy. I didn't think what they said was all that funny. These tenth graders making fun of a nine-year-old girl because of where she came from. Jessie always said I was one to be quick-tempered. But, knowing me, I never listen. I walked up to them and said, 'I don't think what you're saying is funny. In fact, I don't find it funny at all!' The lead person who I was referring to pushed me and said, 'I do.' I got up off the ground and punched the guy in the face. I walked away, toward Jessie. The guy ran past me and pulled a pocket knife out of his pocket. So I looked at where he was headed, and it was toward Jessie. I pulled out my blade and stabbed him. Then, the dads came, and yeah, that's about it."

"Okay. I want a lie detector test pronto, and this Jessie boy—"

"Hey! Jessie is a girl, and she's my best friend."

"Was that the little girl back there?!" the interrogator asked.

"Yeah, she's a witness to what happened, and I'll take the lie detector test. I just wanna get outta here."

Dustin went to take his test.

As we walked into the strange building, we saw Dustin taking his lie detector test. Jaycelyn ran up to the window and watched. An hour later, Dustin was back inside the interrogation room, and they asked Jaycelyn to come inside as well. She ran for Dustin, but they held her back. They thought Dustin was a bad guy. But I knew he was not. I got out of my stroller and slid through the cracked open door. I crawled under the table and popped out and hopped on Dustin's lap. Mother looked around for me and said, "Lee, look!"

Father and Mother ran for me. I put my finger in my mouth and patted Dustin on his head and, with all my strength, said, "D-d-d-u-stin…Dustin. G-g-ood boy…Dustin. Good boy!"

Hoping I said it right, I gave Dustin a big hug. Everyone laughed, and Jaycelyn hugged Dustin. He picked her up and sat her on his lap. "Thank you, Sandi…" Dustin whispered.

The police escorted us home and wanted to keep a close eye on Dustin; however, his father would go to court.

Some people came to the door. They were called the CPS. They came to talk to Dustin; they went into the living room. After fifteen minutes of talking, Dustin looked beyond upset. He started using words I'd only heard when Mother, Father, and Jaycelyn watched PG-13 movies, words that our parents forbade us to say. The CPS worker looked shocked and said, "Why I've never heard such foul language in my life!"

"Well, get used to it if you're dealing with me! I'm not going anywhere! I ain't leaving Jessie!" Dustin snapped as he stormed out of the room. He picked up Jaycelyn and walked out the door.

Mother opened the door quickly, but Father stopped her. "Lee, what are you doing?! He just walked off to God knows where!" Mother snapped.

"Janessa baby, calm down. It's going to be okay," Father replied. "Let him cool down, baby." For some reason, Father had had a change in attitude.

"Jessie, can I talk to you?" Dustin asked.

"Of course, we tell each other everything, don't we?" Jaycelyn said.

Dustin lay down on the grass at the field they were at. Jaycelyn lay on his chest, and he kissed her forehead. "They want me to go to Tennessee and live with my godfather. They're gonna talk to your parents because they don't think I should be around Sandi…and you…"

"Dustin, they can't do that, can they?!"

"Funny…they're the CPS…they think they can do whatever they feel like doing!"

"Dustin, calm down please," Jaycelyn said. She looked him in his eyes and held his hand.

"Jaycelyn Marie Jacobs," Dustin said as he leaned in and kissed her on her forehead again. After kissing her, he said, "Wait for me."

By the time Dustin and Jaycelyn made it home, it was six in the morning. Mother and Father were furious. Dustin knelt down and hugged Jaycelyn tightly and said, "Go upstairs and get ready for bed. I'll be up there soon."

"Okay," Jaycelyn replied.

"I'm in big trouble, huh?" Dustin asked.

Mother and Father nodded and pointed to the living room door.

"Where did you go with Jaycelyn? You just took off with her. Why? What is it about Jaycelyn that just soothes you?" Mother asked impatiently.

"Nothing. It's nothing, really. She's my best friend," Dustin replied.

"Let him leave, Janessa. Dustin, you're free to go," Father said.

Dustin left a month later.

Chapter 2

When I turned seven, Jaycelyn was fifteen, and she was never home during the day. She was always out, doing homework or other things. She had over 236,849 letters from Dustin, and she had one thousand that expressed her feelings for him, but she never sent them. Okay, maybe not that many but it was a lot, a lot. She kept them in a trunk that she hid under her bed with the key in the lock. No one went under the bed but me. I'd read every note in that trunk.

One night, at midnight, Jaycelyn came through the window. I had some letters in my hand when she came fully in the window. She stared at the chest, then looked up at me "Ha! Reading them over?" she asked.

"Yes, they're so sweet. Why didn't you send them?!"

"He doesn't even feel that way anymore!" she replied.

Mother walked in. She looked at Jaycelyn, set a new letter down on our dresser, and walked out. Jaycelyn ran over to open the letter, and I took out my clipboard and acted like I was writing the number 236,850. I teased and giggled.

"Oh, hush, Sandi!" she said.

I laughed and ask her to read the letter out loud.

She hesitated for a moment. Then, she said, "Okay."

Dear Jessie,

I'm glad to know that you're okay. Still, I miss you terribly and can't wait to see your darling face again. I'm coming back in two days. This is the last letter I'm gonna write you.

See you soon,
Dustin

"Wow! He sounds like he has feelings for you…like really. You think he'll kiss you for real this time?" I asked eagerly.

"I dunno. He's nineteen. Although I really want him to…" Jaycelyn sat on her bed and pulled out her clipboard and started to write. I sat on her bed and watched her write her letter.

Dear Dustin,
I can't wait to see you. You're going to have thought I lost it, but here I go.
I miss you, Dustin, terribly. You're my best friend, and I couldn't live without you. There's something I want to say to you, but I know you don't feel the same way about me anymore.
Jaycelyn Marie Jacobs

Jaycelyn went to the post office and had the message sent right away. Dustin received the letter at five in the morning, right before he left. He got his plane ticket and flew down right away. He brought the letter with him, and he wrote one on the plane. He arrived at our house at 5:45 a.m. He came in through the window that Jaycelyn always left cracked open, and put the note on Jaycelyn's chest and tapped her. Then, he crawled under her bed. He saw the chest and unlocked it. Then, he began to read the letters. Jaycelyn woke up fifteen minutes later and saw the letter.

Jessie,
When you open this letter, call my name, but lay back and close your eyes. Call my name five times.
Dustin

She did as he instructed, and he took off his jacket and lay in bed. He wrapped his arms around her and whispered the song he always sang to her. Jaycelyn opened her eyes and looked to her right. Dustin stopped singing and whispered, "Don't be so surprised. So, Jess..." He held up the last letter Jaycelyn wrote and read it out loud. "Jaycelyn Marie Jacobs, when you were nine, I said to wait for me. I never mentioned emotional things between me and you because I wanted you to know that, no matter what, I'd love you then, now, and forever." He kissed Jaycelyn and looked at her deeply. "You should've sent the letters in that chest to me," he said.

"But I thought th—"

"You thought wrong, really wrong...uh...if I asked...never mind..." Dustin interrupted.

Jaycelyn decided not to ask, so they went to sleep.

A few minutes after they'd fallen asleep, Mother walked in and screamed. She woke Father up, and he went into the room with his hunting rifle. He walked toward the bed and held the rifle up to Dustin's head. "What do you think you're doing in my daughter's bed?!" he yelled.

Jaycelyn and Dustin woke up, and I woke up shortly after them. I yelled Dustin's name and ran toward them. He sat up quickly as I ran into his arms. Then, he said fearfully, "We didn't do anything, Mr. Jacobs. I swear. I came early this morning, and Sandi let me in."

He gave me a look that said "play along," and I replied, "Yeah, Dad. I mean, yes, Father. I let him in. It was cold and raining last night."

"Okay. Breakfast will be ready in an hour," Father said coolly. It was suspicious the way he gave up so easily.

Then, Mother and Father left the room, and Jaycelyn and Dustin hugged me and laughed.

"You're a smart girl!" Jaycelyn exclaimed.

When breakfast was over, Dustin took me and Jaycelyn for a walk...I mean, Jaycelyn and I. I decided I needed to talk to Dustin, so I asked if he could sit down with me for a second, while Jaycelyn went to buy ice cream. Yummy!

"Dustin, pal o' mine, when are you gonna ask Jaycelyn out?" I asked impatiently.

"Don't tell…but soon," he replied.

"How soo—"

Jaycelyn came back, and I abruptly cut my sentence short. Soon after, we went home and Dustin sat on the couch nervously. Something was wrong with him. We didn't know what though. Jaycelyn walked over to him and sat down. They stared at each other, and without words, she knew what he wanted.

"Go into my suitcase, Jessie, and get my mom's jewelry box. Don't open it at all. If you do…" Dustin said.

Jaycelyn went upstairs and followed his instructions. She didn't want to hear Dustin's threat, but he wouldn't threaten her. She came downstairs and gave it to him. Dustin always looked at his mother's jewelry box when he missed her and wanted to cry. The thought of him crying made him nervous. "I wish my mom was here. I miss her," Dustin said sadly.

Jaycelyn kissed him on the forehead.

"Jessie, your eyes are beautiful," he said as his gaze locked with hers.

"Thank you. What?" Jaycelyn replied nervously.

Dustin ran his hand through her hair, and he caressed her face. Then, he gently laid her on the couch. He stared at her for a minute, before he lay on top of her. "Jaycelyn, can I ask you something?" Dustin asked.

"Make a move already before you get caught. You've kept me waiting long enough," she said.

Dustin started to kiss her, but he pulled back. Then, he did it again, two more times.

"Would you stop teasing me?!" Jaycelyn retorted.

"Okay, baby," he replied.

Dustin was a few centimeters from Jaycelyn's lips when our mom came downstairs.

"Oh, my God! What the —! Lee!" Mom said.

Dad and I came running down the stairs. When we got there,

Mother explained what she'd seen, and Father was furious. He yelled all kinds of curse words I'd never heard before. Dustin got up and tried his hardest to explain what happened, but he couldn't. Father charged at him, but with all my might, I ran in front of Dustin, and when my father got too close, I held my fists out, and well, let's just say I hit him where it hurts.

"Sandi!" Mother exclaimed.

Now, Father was upset with all of us, and he was ready to kill Dustin.

"Sandi, why the hell did you do that?!" Mother asked.

Chapter 3

"Well, okay. I'm just gonna tell it to you straight! I'm tired of all of this! Why do Dustin and Jaycelyn have to hide their feelings for each other? They've been in love since Jaycelyn was nine..." I said. I spoke for, what felt like, an hour, and when I was done, everyone was astounded with me.

Little did we know what our dad had in mind for Dustin.

Later on, when they left the kitchen, I went upstairs with Jaycelyn and watched TV. Dustin, after getting permission, went into the bathroom and took a shower. He decided that he and we were too cooped up in the house. When he came out, he was fully dressed in his best from head to toe.

"Look at you!" Jaycelyn said with a wide smile on her face.

"Yes, I have to say you look outstanding, Dustin," I agreed.

"Thanks, ladies, but I have a question for you, Sandi," Dustin said.

"Yes, Dustin?"

"Where in the world did you learn all those words?"

"Oh, well, I don't know exactly. Guess I'm just smart like that, huh?"

Dustin took us girls out to eat. Then, he took us to a carnival.

Dear Diary,

Today was the best day ever! ☺ Dustin took me and Sandi out to eat and to a carnival. I don't think I've ever had that much cotton candy in my life! Actually, Dustin was pretty surprised I'd never had cotton candy before. Well, until today that is! Ha-

ha! ☺ Dustin is sooo, sooo, sooo sweet to me. I just don't know what to do with him! Uh! Okay. So, I know what I want to do with him, but I can wait just a while longer. ;) Sandi tells me she can't wait to see the day when me and Dustin get married. To tell you the truth, I can't wait either! Well, I better go to bed now. It's like five in the morning, and we just got home. My mom and dad will be ***furious*** with us, but hey, they'll have to learn to live with it! Ha-ha!

Good night

"Babe, wakey, wakey. C'mon, girl. Get up for me." Dustin said softly.

"What? Huh? Oh, hey. What's the matter?" Jaycelyn asked.

"Nothing. It's just…I wanted to talk to you about something," Dustin replied.

"Oh, okay. What's up?" she asked.

But Dustin didn't reply. He just stared at her for a moment. Then, he started to kiss her. He hesitated.

"What's the matter, Dustin?" Jaycelyn asked quietly.

Dustin became too nervous and shook in his skin a little bit. He got up and went for the door, but as soon as he did, Jaycelyn got out of bed and pushed his back against the wall. She stood on her tiptoes and kissed him as many times as she could before she thought Dustin would pull away, but he didn't. He picked her up and put her legs around his waist. He slowly made his way to the bed and lay down on top of her. Dustin unbuttoned his shirt as quickly as he could and took it off. He looked at Jaycelyn and took off her shirt.

Five minutes later, Dustin pulled away and looked at Jaycelyn with concern. "I ain't pressuring you, am I, Jessie?" he asked.

"No, I'm fine…really," she replied.

Dustin laughed. "Look at you. Are you *sure* you're ready? I mean, because if you aren't, I *can* wait…"

"Dustin, I think the question is, are *you* ready?" Jaycelyn replied.

He laughed again. "What do you mean by that? I'm nineteen. I'm ready when you are."

"Well, it just seems like you're hesitating and nervous."

"Oh, it was just because I didn't want to do anything that made you nervous or anything. So yeah, kinda made me nervous because I didn't know," Dustin said with contentment.

"Well, then I guess you know now, huh? So quit stalling! Look, if I was nervous or uncomfortable, I wouldn't have gotten out of my bed and came after you. Please stop hesitating."

"Okay. But you need to let me know if I'm hurting you at all, okay, Jessie? I don't wanna do anything that's gonna hurt you."

Jaycelyn smiled, and Dustin kissed her. Then, he finished undressing her.

It was 6 a.m., and Jaycelyn and Dustin lay down and looked at each other. Dustin had a glowing look of fulfillment all over his face. Jaycelyn kissed his cheek, and when she turned over to go to sleep, he leaned over her shoulder, kissed her on the cheek, and whispered, "I love you."

At 7:37 a.m., I was up. I had already gone downstairs, and I was eating.

"Where are Jaycelyn and Dustin?" Mother asked.

"Oh. They're upstairs sleeping. We were up all night talking and laughing," I replied.

"Well, what were you all talking about?" Mother asked.

"Oh! We were talking about the carnival last night! It was lots of fun! There were games and food and candy!" I replied full of excitement.

"Well, they need to wake up, or else they'll miss breakfast. Janessa, would you go and get them please?" Father asked.

"No! I'll do it! I needed to go to the bathroom anyway! Be right back!" I said nervously. Dustin was supposed to be sleeping in the guest bedroom across from ours. I ran up the stairs and woke them both up.

"Jaycelyn, Jaycelyn, Jaycelyn! Hey, you guys! Wake up!" I shouted.

"What is it, Sandi?" Dustin asked.

"Mother and Father are looking for you two, and if you don't hurry up, get dressed, and go downstairs for breakfast, you'll be in trouble!" I said firmly.

They hurried up and put clothes on. Dustin went downstairs first before Jaycelyn and said that she'd be down as soon as she could. Jaycelyn and I went downstairs together. Dustin was staring at Jaycelyn with such satisfaction that our father noticed.

There was glee all over his face. He couldn't hide what he was feeling for her inside. Jaycelyn mouthed for him to stop staring at her like that, but no matter how hard he tried, he couldn't. So Jaycelyn started a conversation. "Hey! Dustin…uh…thanks for taking us to the carnival yesterday!"

"Yeah! That was a really fun time!" I replied.

Dustin laughed and replied, "No problem. Really anytime honestly. I had fun last night, too."

Jaycelyn looked up at the ceiling and smiled. There was glee all over her face now, too. I looked down at my feet and laughed. Soon, all three of us were looking around the room, laughing.

"I mean…isn't that right, Jessie?" Dustin said.

Jaycelyn and I looked at each other and laughed. I found myself distracted by Jaycelyn's bright eyes. Maybe it'd be weird for some, the way I was too old for my age, the way Jaycelyn and I were so close. She caught me in my trance.

"Two bodies, one heartbeat, right Sandi?" She said and held my face in her hand.

Then, Jaycelyn answered his question, "Oh, yes." She winked at him and finished her sentence. "Yes, that was really fun. When can we do it again, Dustin?"

I giggled. "You guys are so lame. Yeah, Dustin, I'd totally enjoy the sight and sound of that again!" I said sarcastically. I should've been asleep, but I was far from it, and I had pretended to vomit before I fled to the guest bedroom.

Then, everybody, including our parents, laughed.

"What on earth are you three talking about? You three just keep laughing and laughing." Mother asked.

"Oh, Mother. They're just inside jokes. You wouldn't get them at all. They aren't even funny, unless you were there. More of a rude sort, especially if you wake people up at night," I answered sarcastically.

Dustin tried to hold in his laugh, and Jaycelyn looked up at the ceiling. Then, she answered, "Poor Sandi. We're so sorry because, if you rode that ride too…" she started, putting extra emphasis on the rode. Then, she finished, "All you could do is make noise. You're not having fun, unless you're waking people up." I gagged at her comment.

Dustin snickered. "Yeah, especially if you're like Jaycelyn and love to scream," Dustin said under his breath.

The three of us laughed.

Then, I said, "Yeah, I *can* wait to ride that ride. It was way too scary and out of my league for my age."

The three of us laughed again.

"Yeah, it was way out of Jessie's age range, too, but she insisted on riding it, so that's what she gets." Dustin looked up at the ceiling.

We forgot that our mother and father were in the kitchen. They all sat quietly looking around until our father and I broke the silence. "So, children, what exactly did you three do at the carnival?" Father asked.

"Sandi and I played as many games as we could, and we ate popcorn and cotton candy. Then we met up with one of Dustin's friends. Her name was Clarissa. She was very pretty, and she started getting flirty with Dustin. It was hilarious, so we made an inside joke about it," Jaycelyn replied. "Yeah, and then, we saw this really big ride, and it was called Pedal to the Metal. It had lots of loops and went up really high. I wasn't old enough or tall enough to ride. I didn't want to anyway because it seemed scary. So Jaycelyn and Dustin got on, and Clarissa watched me. I heard that Jaycelyn almost peed on herself and was screaming the whole time. Even when they were done, she woke up these babies in a stroller, and they started crying," I said.

"Oh, Dustin, sounds like the girls had a very fun time. Many thanks to you," Mother said and laid her hand over father's.

"Oh, no problem. I love the girls. They have fun with me all the time," Dustin replied.

I giggled and mumbled under my breath, "Yeah, especially Jaycelyn. Isn't that right, you two?"

Dustin and Jaycelyn laughed.

After breakfast, Jaycelyn, Dustin, and I went for a walk. Dustin and Jaycelyn held hands, and Dustin put his other free arm around me.

"Babe, can I ask you something?" Dustin said.

"Yeah, sure. Anything. What is it?" Jaycelyn said.

"Would you get married at a young age?" he asked.

"Yeah, I would actually. Why do you ask?"

"Oh, just because I wanted to know...me being nosy...again," he replied.

She looked at him with a gleeful look on her face.

"Don't look at me like that, Jessie. That's all there is to it...nothing more," he said.

She kissed his lips lightly, grabbed my hand, and walked into the house.

Dustin was thinking too hard to even realize where we were or that we were even back at the house at all. Dustin walked in two minutes after us, and our dad was sitting at the table with a suitcase underneath him.

"Dustin, come here for a few minutes. I have a proposition for ya," Father said.

Chapter 4

"You making fun of the way I speak, Mr. Jacobs?" Dustin asked angrily.

"No, no, no, Dustin. I just think that, for all of our predicaments, we—"

"I ain't stupid. I know what that means. I went to school, a'ight? I ain't dumb. I know how to speak, and just 'cuz I choose not to speak the way you do, don't mean I ain't got no home training. I hear the way you speak to me…you talk to me like I'm a dog…like I'm a child…like I don't understand you…like you have to break down all your syllables and watch how many words you say to me at a time. I'm not dumb, okay? I can speak full sentences. Just 'cuz I'm from the country, don't mean I'm stupid, so quit treating me like it. I was schooled then, and I'm good and schooled now!" Dustin snapped.

"Oh! Well then. I guess you understand where you and I stand. Dustin, I am not fond of you. You are a…a hoodlum and a risk taker. I doubt that you do not act like that out there in your…world. Honestly, cutting to the point, I don't want you around Sandi," Father said sternly.

"Look. Cut to the chase 'cuz I think we both know, by now, this ain't got a thing to do with Sandi. So just tell me straight up. You don't want me to be around Jaycelyn. Then, you'll lie and say, 'It's best if you love my daughter from afar because it helps the love grow stronger.' You'll say, 'Jaycelyn is more of an upper-class citizen.' Well, I'm one who has to fight for what he wants. Just like that. That's all you had to say," Dustin snapped back making sure to lay his accent on heavy.

"Well, fine. Then, I'll give you the honest truth. You took the words right out of my mouth. All accept one. I'm willing to give you ten thousand dollars to stay away from my daughter. There's a lot you could do with that. For instance, why didn't you go to college, Dustin?" Father asked with slight tension in his voice.

Dustin took in a deep breath and looked at Father with intensity. Then, he said, "Because I didn't have the money, all right?"

"Now, Dustin," Father started while chuckling. After he finished, he said, "I think we both know what this money could help with. Your room, board, college, and hey, if you don't want to stay on campus, then you can have your own apartment and pay rent!"

"You have all this money. Why don't you use it for your family's better good? I do not want it!" Dustin said sharply.

"Well, I have a backup plan, just in case you said that," he said while opening up another suitcase. "How does fifty grand sound to you?"

"Sounds like you're trying to bribe me out of love with your daughter." Dustin's phone rang, and he answered. "Hello? Yeah…oh…okay…bye. Well, Mr. Jacobs, I need to go to Tennessee for a while…" Dustin got up.

"I will let Jaycelyn know you're leaving," Father said with a smile.

"No, you don't trust me. Then, I don't trust you. I'll tell her myself."

He went upstairs to our room. Dustin knocked on the door, and Jaycelyn walked out. They stared at each other, and within that minute, she knew what was wrong. "You can't go! You can't just leave again! What am I supposed to do while you're gone?! You can't just drop everything and go! Are you crazy?!" Jaycelyn exclaimed.

"Will you quit yelling at me like you've lost your mind? I don't want to go, but I have to, Jaycelyn. I'm coming back. I promise," Dustin replied.

"That's what you said last time, and it took you forever to come back," she replied.

Dustin breathed in sharply, trying to hold back tears and put his forehead to Jaycelyn's and kissed her. "But I came back, didn't I?"

Jaycelyn started to cry. Talking through her tears, she said, "But what if you don't come back? What if you fall in love with someone else? Or you forget about me?"

"Jessie, I won't forget about you. I'll only be there for a month or two. I love you, Jaycelyn. Wait for me."

"Okay. I love you, too."

"Good because I don't know what I would do without you," Dustin said, breathing in sharply and slowly, trying not to cry. He wiped away Jaycelyn's tears, kissed her on the cheek and walked away. Jaycelyn watched him walk away until she heard him leave out the door. She closed our bedroom door and walked away.

"Jaycelyn? Why'd he leave?" I asked.

"I don't know. I don't know."

Dustin called Jaycelyn a month later. When she answered the house phone in her room, she was sobbing.

"Jessie, what's wrong? Jaycelyn?" Dustin asked, concerned.

"S-S-Sandi," she stuttered. "They sent her away! To a boarding school for girls. I don't know why…they cleaned the room out, and I don't know where any of her things are. They took down all the pictures of her and everything. They barely even mention her name! It's been this way ever since you left."

"Okay. Okay. Where is it?!" Dustin said, enraged.

"It's in Montgomery, Alabama. It's called the Boarding School for Girls, and in parentheses, it says 'With no Talent or Manners.'"

"Okay, babe. I'm gonna go and get her. That doesn't sound like a good school to begin with. I need the address."

"Okay. It's 3212 N. 79th Street. Please, please keep her safe with you."

"Okay. I love you."

"I love you, too."

They hung up, and Jaycelyn got dressed. Dustin got in his father's blue pickup truck and left. An hour later, his cell phone rang. It was his father. "Dustin, your fiancée is here! Why didn't you tell me you were getting married?!"

"Dad? W-w-w…huh?"

"Clarissa is really beautiful. Wow!" his father said in amazement.

"Dad, I'm not getting married. Put Clarissa on the phone," Dustin replied angrily.

"Hey, sweetie! I always knew you'd come to your senses. Jaycelyn's dad told me that you wanted to marry me," she said with excitement.

"Clarissa, I never said that. He said that because he wants me to stay away from Jaycelyn."

"Oh, that makes sense, but you can still come to your senses and fall in love with me instead of that little br—"

Dustin hung up the phone and looked at his map. He was finally off the freeway and in the city. While looking around for the building, he saw two guards walking down the street. He pulled over and asked if they knew where the building was. They laughed.

"Are you blind, child?!" the first guard said. He looked about forty-two years old. He was wearing a gray uniform, a black tie, old worn-out and faded black boots, and he had gray hair. He was African-American, and he was wearing glasses that turned into tinted sunglasses when he was outside.

The other guy looked very young. He was wearing the same suit, tie, and worn-out faded boots. He looked about twenty-nine and had as much maturity as a thirteen-year-old boy. His hair was black and fading to a light brown color, as if he had dyed his hair.

"No, I ain't blind. I need to know where the building is. I ain't from around here," Dustin replied.

"No wonder why…you drivin' downtown with a map…" the second guard said.

"Well, look, dull eyes…" the first guard said while chuckling. "It's the big building down the street."

The building way down the street was huge and gray. It had the name of the school written on it in black, and its windows were tinted black, as well. The street was a T-shape in front of the building. Dustin walked in slowly, looking around. Soon, the school principal walked toward him. "Uh. I'm looking for my daughter. Her name is Sandi Jacobs. I'm here to pick her up," he lied.

"She is in room 222. That's down the hall, to the right, up the stairs that way," the principal said, making fast, sharp, stiff hand motions, then walked away.

"Yeah. Thanks."

When Dustin got to the room, I was giving an Italian presentation: "*Io nascevo," I started.*

I gave the required five minutes of my presentation, then I sat down.

The teacher walked over to the door. "May I help you?' she said with a funny Italian accent.

Dustin laughed. "You have very beautiful eyes," he said.

She laughed. Then, she shot Dustin a smile.

"Wow! And what a pretty smile you have. Well, I need Sandi," he said nervously.

"Sandi. You're…umm…leaving."

I jumped up and down out of my seat and ran for the door, yelling, "Dustin!"

"Hey, kiddo!" He kissed me on my forehead and picked me up. "C'mon. Let's go."

We walked out the school building, but once we got outside, we couldn't find Dustin's truck.

Dustin shouted a string of profanities.

I looked around. "There! Over there! I see some guys!" I shouted. I looked harder. "Dustin! They're about to smash your car!"

Dustin and I ran over there. The guys dropped their tools, rocks, and logs and looked at us funny.

"Yo, yo, yo! Aye, MJ, look at what we got here!" one of the thugs said.

The other thug said, "What you wake'n me up fo', fool?!" His voice was very deep.

"There're crackers ova here, lookin' like they need sum from us," the first thug replied.

"So take care of it. I'm busy," MJ said.

"A'ight, G. I got dis. Look, fella, y'all kind ain't wanted ova here, so go on!" the thug said.

"Huh?" I said.

"Did I stutter, b—" the thug replied.

"Hey! I don't appreciate you callin' my sister outta her name. So back off," Dustin interrupted.

"What you gonna do about it? That's what you are little girl, a good for nothing, white b—"

Dustin stepped up and punched the thug in his jaw and told me to run to the car. I got in and looked down by the pedal and saw another man under there. "Where do you think you're goin', little girl?" he said.

I kicked him in the face as hard as I could three times. Dustin opened the door and pulled the man out and hopped in.

"Dustin, go! Go! Start the car!" I yelled while I locked the doors.

He started the car and drove off. He looked back and saw the thugs throw an old lady out of her car. They were behind us now.

"Oh! Sandi, they have a gun! Get down!"

Glass shattered as the shots came through the back window of the truck. I screamed.

"God, Sandi, close your eyes!" Dustin yelled as he turned the corner. He saw a police station and drove as slowly as he could. He yelled out the window. "Sir, please stop them! They're shooting at my car. My sister is in the car, and I think she's hurt!"

The police officers signaled for him to come inside the garage, and they stopped the thugs.

Dustin got me out of the car and looked at me. "You okay?!" he asked.

"Yes, I'm fine. Some glass just cut my cheek, but I'm all right," I replied.

"You sure? We can take you to the hospital if we need to," Dustin replied.

"No, no, really, Dustin. I'm fine."

"Okay. We're gonna go now," Dustin said to me and the police officer.

"All right, sir. Everything will be taken care of," the police officer said.

"Okay. Thanks," Dustin replied.

We soon left the police station and took the car to a repair shop, and I looked like I was getting tired of sitting and waiting.

"Hey! Let's go for a walk," Dustin said.

"Have you forgotten where we are?" I replied nervously.

"No, but I just thought you looked annoyed from sitting here all day."

"Very much so. We can get something to eat after this, right?" I asked.

"Yeah. Sure why not," Dustin replied.

After we left and got something to eat, we traveled to Tennessee and stayed at Dustin's father's house. Dustin and I both passed out on the couch. We were *exhausted.*

Chapter 5

"HELLO?" DUSTIN SAID WHILE ANSWERING his phone.

"Dustin, I'm sorry," Jaycelyn said.

"Sorry about what, Jessie?" he asked quietly, trying not to wake me.

"About calling so early."

"Oh, no problem. Is there something you need? It's like 6:30 a.m. down here, and it's pretty hot."

"Oh. No, I just wanted to make sure you're okay," she replied.

Dustin laughed. "Yeah, babe. I'm fine and so is Sandi. How about you?"

"Oh, I'm good. I've been sick a lot, but I'm good."

"Oh, you okay? You want me to come and get you? Do you need anything?" Dustin asked.

Jaycelyn laughed. "Dustin, calm down! I'm okay."

"I'm sorry. I can't help it. I've been away from you for too long."

"Yeah. Hey, Dustin?" Jaycelyn asked nervously.

"Yeah?"

"Would you come and visit me?" Jaycelyn asked.

"Here I come," he replied.

In the background, Jaycelyn could hear Dustin waking me up.

"Dustin!" Jaycelyn said with a chuckle.

"Seriously, I'm coming. See you when I get there, all right?"

"Okay. I love you."

"I love you, too."

"Hey, Sandi! We're going home," Dustin said with a wide grin on his face. "It's a long, long trip by car, and I know how you hate sitting in one spot for too long, so we better get going quickly," he said.

"How long, Dustin?" I asked anxiously.

"Oh, I dunno 'bout fifteen…" He paused and thought about how to make the trip sound shorter. "Nine hundred fifty-six miles," he said with a devious smile on his face.

"Dustin, hours. How many hours? You know we're originally from Wisconsin before New York it was Wisconsin. We have to know everything in hours," I said.

Dustin chuckled, knowing I wouldn't like the sound of it.

"Fifteen hours and thirty-one minutes, Sandi," he said and looked back at me as he was changing his pants.

"Dustin, I have some very important things I want to discuss with you," I said.

He paused and looked at me with his pants halfway up his legs. "You sound just like your father." He looked nervously around the room. "Well, go on, Sandi," he said as he continued to dress himself.

"First of all, why are you changing in front of me? Do you think that is appropriate?"

"Sandi, you remember the night of the carnival when Jaycelyn and I—"

I interrupted him, "Enough said!" I exclaimed with a giggle.

Dustin laughed and went into the bathroom, pulled out a female's brush and gently brushed my hair. I looked at him curiously; he was a very caring gentleman for his age, as if time made him grow up too soon. We studied each other carefully as if we waited all this time to truly get to know each other. Then, I realized what happened. I made him feel as if he still had a piece of Jaycelyn with him. A piece of his mother and lover all wrapped up into one. Jaycelyn was actually my age when he fell in love with her, and he was around my age when he lost his mother. Yet, somehow, all of this that he saw in me made him joyful.

I watched him head for the door and I, like a helpless puppy, followed him. He was no longer just my sister's really caring lover; he was my brother. He became my family, my mother, and my father tied into one. He let me know that, no matter what happened, I had a new family who would take care of me. Him.

"Jaycelyn Marie Jacobs!" Father said as he stormed up the stairs. Jaycelyn tried to hide, but it was too late. "You! This was all you!" Father yelled. The sound of a slap and Jaycelyn's scream startled us.

Dustin started for the room, but our mother stopped him. Jaycelyn ran down the stairs with tears in her eyes. "Dustin! You came! Please, please take me away from here! I hate it here!" Jaycelyn yelled.

"I will. I swear to God I will!" Dustin said.

"I am ashamed. I hate this family. Why are we this way?" I said.

My mother looked at me as my father ran for me. His hand was a lightning bolt, too fast to catch.

I had courage and strength. "I hate you," I said. This time, I was quick and tense. Violent and angry, I do not want to be the whipping girl anymore. I ran into the kitchen as my father chased me around and around. He grabbed a bat, and I grabbed the knife. A hit to the head pushed me to the ground. I was bleeding a river across the floor. My own weapon stabbed at my neck. I turned around and faced this man. I drew my knife through his abdomen. The poison leaked out. He won't last long, I thought as my mother yelled and screamed.

Dustin and Jaycelyn ran to me and pulled me toward the door. I looked back at my mother, lying in what was now my father's little pool of blood. I thought, He was once a man, then a father. Now he is Lee, a stranger who makes a rapist my greatest friend.

Dustin started his car, and I was no longer bleeding.

"Dustin, where are we going?" Jaycelyn asked. She was worried.

"We are leaving the state for a while. We are going to the airport, and I will return the car I rented and get us plane tickets to go somewhere away from New York," Dustin replied.

I looked out the window. The Toyota had black leather seats. There were five seats, counting the middle one, which held small picture frames with letters in them. Jaycelyn sent the entire set, the ones in the chest, to Dustin. That chest was in the back of the car. Dustin looked at me through the mirror, and Jaycelyn followed his gaze. Jaycelyn grabbed my hand and held it tightly. Then, she whispered, "Everything will be okay. I love you, Sandi. Thank you for speaking out. That was very brave of you." Her face was very pale and was still red from Lee.

I started bleeding again, and my pulse rate was dropping, but I didn't care right now. My sister was hurt, and we were fleeing the state. We reached the airport, and I did not feel sane at all. When we got on the plane, my uniform white tank top was soaked in blood, and Dustin called for help. I was very faint. Within twelve minutes, the ambulance came, and I passed out. When I woke up, I was in a hospital bed in Washington, D.C. "My throat hurts. May I have a glass of water?" I asked politely.

"Yeah. I'll go and get it for you," Dustin said with contentment.

An hour or two later, I was free to go.

We went to rent another car and drove past seven statues that I knew nothing of at all. We stopped at a hotel called La Ramona, and it was expensive. The lobby was amazing. There was a huge fountain in the middle of the room. In the far-right side of the room, there was a replica of the Mona Lisa on the wall, and underneath it were blue chairs along the wall. The walls were a pretty caramel brown, and at the top of the wall, there were twenty inches of thick white paint smoothly painted across the wall. The tiles on the floor matched the wall with a diamond pattern. White, then brown, white and then brown again. The front desk was made of black granite top and mahogany wood. It was smoothed out to perfection and carefully painted white with an artistic design that ran the length of the heavy countertop. Behind the desk, there was a thick gray stone wall that fit oddly into the scenery. The wall was one-hundred and two inches, and the desk met each start of the wall. The wall and desk were perfectly aligned. On the desk, the words of the hotel were engraved and filled with fancy gold paint. We signed into a room and walked up the stairs that were covered in red velvet. Our room number was engraved in black on a gold palate. Dustin pulled us into the room and locked the door.

"Why did you do that?" I asked.

"I thought I saw a CPS worker," Dustin said while catching his breath.

"And?" Jaycelyn asked with a confused look on her face.

"We would have been questioned," Dustin said.

There was a moment of silence and then a loud bang on the door. We just stood quietly, without making a sound. Soon, the banging stopped, and we continued on with our day.

Dustin pulled Jaycelyn over to their bed, laid her down on her back and kissed her. She wrapped her arms around his back and kissed him repeatedly. I decided to go and take a shower. When I came out, I dried myself and got dressed. When I went back into the bedroom, Jaycelyn and Dustin were asleep, so I decided to go for a walk. I took the key off the dresser and Dustin's wallet and went into the hallway. I walked down the stairs. I couldn't breathe. Life was flashing in and out and all between. I prayed faintly in my head. We had never been religious, but a tug of my heart dropped me to my knees.

A faint voice was coming closer. I couldn't see, only hear. The feeling in my hands went numb, but I felt something cold. "White, brown, white, brown." Blank pages ran across the blackened screen. "Sandi? Are you focusing?" Blank pages faded, and a woman appeared. "Her health is failing. Doctor! Her umbilical cord is wrapped around her neck!" Fade out…fade in… and back again. "Aww! She is so cute! Mommy, Mommy, Mommy! Can me and Dustin…I mean, Dustin and I name her?!" Tension entered the room. A man's voice shaped up the spine holding Jaycelyn's back. Fade in, fade out…

"Hey, little girl! What's your name?" "You know she can't talk yet!" A chuckle, a man spoke but not for the first time. A response, a mocking clap, a slap, a yell…blurs of people's faces and traces of map drawings, turning into figures made of numbers and letters.

"Okay, Sandi, can you repeat after me?"

No response, a repeated question, no response. An abusive slapping sound made by someone older and given to the face of someone young. "Beating her for not talking in school won't help her or her grade..." Fade in...fade out...and in between. Something from long ago... a picture...no ring...a commitment...no ring. A picture of a proud man holding a little girl with soft, long black hair, now lightened by the sun, chemicals, and lemon juice. That man is a man no more but is beneath everyone, whoever was supposedly below him. Fade in...

"Sandi! Sandi!" a woman yelled, but this was no woman but a pale-faced girl. Scared for her life and yelling from the other side of a mirror. "Sandi!"

No answer. I was afraid now and unresponsive.

Chapter 6

"How dare you take my child away from me?!" Mother yelled.

"We will take this to court!" Lee yelled sternly from a far corner where he was placed in his wheelchair.

I was pushing myself to wake up. I woke up thirty minutes after our parents arrived.

"Sandi Jacobs!" Mother said.

"No, do not touch me. I cannot see you," I replied.

My vision slowly returned with the silence. I realized they had transferred us back to New York, and we were in a hospital there.

"Why are you here, Mother?" I asked.

"They needed blood for a transfusion, insurance, and such. They needed parents, which Jaycelyn and Dustin aren't," Mother replied.

On that note, Jaycelyn stepped out into the hall.

"Jaycelyn?" Dustin said as he followed her.

"Yeah, Dustin?" Jaycelyn replied.

"You look so worried."

Jaycelyn burst into tears.

"Wha-what's the matter?!"

"I-I-I'm…" Sobs interrupted Jaycelyn's sentence.

"Jaycelyn, breathe!"

"Dustin, I can't tell you," Jaycelyn said, sobbing.

"You're my best friend, Jaycelyn. You mean a lot to me."

"I-I-I don't mean enough."

"What? Jaycelyn, we pretty much go out. C'mon. Tell me."

With heavy hesitation, Jaycelyn replied, "I'm…I'm pregnant."

"Jaycelyn, that's so sweet. Are you serious?"

"Yes."

"I love you. I would never leave you, Jessie. Never."

"Okay, I guess I believe you."

"It didn't take much convincing," Dustin teased.

I'll be back later," He said while walking away.

He didn't look back. He just kept walking. Jaycelyn watched until his absence was a fond and distinct memory. If he didn't come back, she'd be sure to remember the last time she saw him. She walked up the stairs to meet me in my new room. She sat down on the floor and watched people leave the hospital parking lot.

When Dustin came back, he stood outside my glass window door. Jaycelyn looked up, and he motioned for her to come outside. He held a bag in his hand; it looked like it came from the pharmacy downstairs. She ran out the door to meet him. He waited until the door was completely shut before he began talking.

"What's in the bag?" Jaycelyn asked.

Dustin pulled out a One-a-Day magenta box. It had the silhouette of a pregnant woman on the box.

"Pre-natal pills? It took you half an hour to get a nine dollar box of pills?"

"I did have to wait in line. What's wrong with you?"

"Nothing much. I'm just really tired and hungry…ugh."

"Can I get you anything? Wait. Didn't you just eat fifteen minutes ago?"

"Really? Are you really gonna ask me that?" Jaycelyn asked with tension in her voice.

"Calm down. What do you want to eat then?"

"Anything really. Okay, a salad with chicken, garden tomatoes. Mandarin oranges, bacon bits, cucumbers, carrots, and pineapples with ranch sauce."

"All right. That's kinda specific. Anything else?"

Ignoring Dustin's comment, with a grin, she said, "A root beer soda and a brownie and ice cream. Oh, a fudge brownie!"

"Okay," Dustin said while laughing. He kissed Jaycelyn on the forehead and went to the cafeteria to see what he could find. Jaycelyn took a pill out the bottle and held it in her hand. Hesitating, she put the box in her purse and walked into the room.

"Jaycelyn?" I said faintly, turning my head slightly to the right.

"Yeah, Sandi?"

"You okay? You look sick."

"Oh, I'm fine. I'm just hungry and tired and hot. Can I open the window?"

"Yes, if it helps you feel better."

Jaycelyn went to open the window, and Dustin knocked on the door. Our mother, like lightning, hopped out of her seat and opened the door. Dustin had Jaycelyn's salad in a bag that he held with his teeth. In his right hand, he held her soda and straw between his fingers. In his left was her fudge brownie and ice cream in a bowl. Mother just stood there, glaring at him. Jaycelyn looked over. She walked toward the door. "Move." She pushed our mother to the side and took her food from Dustin. She opened the top on her salad and practically shoved her face into it. She didn't care what the salad had on it at this point.

"How dare you push me like that?" Mother yelled.

"Whatever," Jaycelyn said, pacing the floor and eating.

"Excuse me?" Mother retorted.

"I'm trying to eat, so can you please leave me alone?"

Lee then stood up, but Dustin walked in front of him. There wasn't much he could do in his condition. Lee sat down. For once in his lifetime, he felt intimidated. The room was silent as Jaycelyn finished her ice cream. She put her pill in her mouth quickly, so no one would see and swallowed it down with the last of her root beer.

"Jessie," Dustin said, "it's ten o'clock. We should get going."

"Oh?"

"Yeah. C'mon," he said as he walked for the door.

Jaycelyn got up, and Dustin held the door open for her and smoothly walked out behind her.

"Where are we going?" Jaycelyn asked while entering the elevator.

"To the fifth floor. We have a doctor's appointment," Dustin said with a grin on his face.

When they made it to the ER waiting room, they waited a full two hours before being called in by the nurse. "Okay, Jaycelyn Jacobs. When is your due date?" the nurse asked.

"Oh, I don't know. I just confirmed with…my boyfriend…today," she said hesitantly.

Seeing her nervousness, Dustin walked over and held her arm.

"Interesting. All right. When was your last menstrual cycle?"

"It was the night of that carnival," Jaycelyn started as she looked at Dustin who was counting with his fingers. "So about five months ago…"

Dustin kissed her cheek and whispered in her ear, "Calm down, Jaycelyn. I'm right here." He rubbed her arms lightly, trying to make her goosebumps go away.

"Oh! So you could have an ultrasound if that is about right," the nurse said excitedly. "Okay."

"Now, how old are you?"

"I'm…" Jaycelyn paused.

"It's okay. You can tell me, honey. We don't judge here. I was younger than fifteen when I had my little girl."

This reassured her. "I'm…fifteen years of age. My birthday is May 17th, 1988."

"Okay, honey, Dr. Stephonie will be in with you shortly."

"Okay. Wait. How old are you now?"

"Twenty-three," the nurse said. She smiled and walked out the room.

"Wow! Her little girl is eleven now," Dustin said in amazement.

Fifteen minutes later, the doctor came in. He shook Dustin's and Jaycelyn's hands. "Charles Stephonie, I'm going to be your OB-GYN. Now, sir, how are you—"

"I'm her boyfriend and the child's father," Dustin interrupted.

"Good, good. Most guys don't come to these kinds of things. How old are you?"

"I'm nineteen."

The doctor cleared his throat.

"Dr. Stephonie, I know what you're thinking. Please don't report this. My parents don't even know. I really love him, and I've known him since day one. Literally," Jaycelyn said.

"All right. This will be our secret for now, only because I don't know how your situation is at home. I heard about your sister. However, you will begin to develop a stomach to fit your growing child. The hospital isn't allowed to disclose information with others anyway." He paused before finishing. "So, your secret will be safe until then. Now seeing as you're still in school, you may or may not be able to complete your high school education. So, you are about five months or a little over. So about twenty-two weeks into your pregnancy. How about we take a look, shall we?"

"Sure. Why not?" Jaycelyn replied a little dumbfounded by his last statement.

The doctor got the ultrasound equipment ready, and finally, there was a pretty picture of Jaycelyn's baby on the screen.

"Awe, Jaycelyn! It's so cute!" I said.

Jaycelyn laughed. "Thank you. It's his first picture," she replied.

I gasped in amazement. "It's a boy?! I'm going to be an auntie!"

"Hush down now before someone hears you, child!"

"Oh, right! Sorry."

We were back at "home." I would be going back to school when it was in session. Jaycelyn, on the other hand, was back in school and making up a lot of work. Normally, she was a straight-A student. Right now, it was straight Fs. The new semester was around the corner, and she only had five days left to complete the missing work before the school board piled on the next week's work. We'd been gone for almost six weeks. With all the school work, it felt like six years. Jaycelyn stayed up late for three nights, alternating assignments she needed to complete.

She finally finished at the last moment. At the end of eighth period, she ran back and forth to teachers turning work in and getting the next week's work in return. She went to the office and got a nicely typed document that her teachers, parents, and she had to sign in pen. When she completed this week's assignments, she had to return it to the office signed and with an excused absence note card stapled to the front of the document. Since today was a Friday, Jaycelyn only had the weekend to do this week's work. Our laptop had been taken from us, so Jaycelyn had to take her things to the library.

She walked miles to the library, but by the time she got there, it started raining, and Jaycelyn ran for the closing door. "Ma'am, the library is closed," a dark-skinned African-American male, wearing a Miami Heat shirt and black pants said to Jaycelyn calmly.

"No, sir, you don't understand. I walked five point two miles to get here, and I don't have a ride. Please, sir, let me in." She stressed.

"No can do. Unless you're taking the job offer, I can't help y—"

"I'll take it!" Jaycelyn yelled. She cleared her throat. "I'll take the job offer."

The man stepped aside and let Jaycelyn in. "All right. The library is yours to use until three a.m. By 3:30 a.m. the floors, tables, and bathrooms need to be clean on the first, second, and fourth floor. You need to be out of here before then because the doors automatically lock. Do all that and be back here at four p.m. to discuss your pay, schedule, and work hours."

"Okay. Thanks." Jaycelyn went straight to the bookshelves and got the books she needed to write the final essay drafts for her classes. When she finished, she went straight to work on the chores she needed to do. She looked up at the clock and saw it was 2:25 a.m. She went back to the first floor to type her final drafts for her English, citizenship, and linguistics classes. Each of her papers had to be 250 to 320 words, and she could type eighty-two words per minute. Jaycelyn looked up, and it was three in the morning. Her linguistics paper was the last thing she needed to type, and it was exactly 320 words long. She figured it would take her approximately three minutes to type it and seven minutes for spell check and printing the papers out.

When she was finished, she walked over to the phone and called Dustin. She called nine times and left three messages, but he still didn't answer. It was pouring outside, and lightning struck light across the sky. Jaycelyn signed out on a clipboard and started walking home. She was soaking wet and was two and a half miles into her walk when Dustin rode by. He rolled down his window; her blonde streaked black hair covered her face, making it harder for him to decipher who she was. She kept walking, shivering in her purple pencil skirt, black laced heels and her halter top.

"Babe!" Dustin shouted.

She turned to her left and desperately walked toward the truck and opened the door. She got in and kissed him on the cheek.

"I am so, so, sorry babe. I didn't know it was you callin', and I—"

"It's okay. I was almost home anyway. And you didn't know. It is fine."

Dustin drove the rest of the way home. Jaycelyn saw Lee in the door; she kissed Dustin good night, got out of the car, and slowly made her way toward the door. Lee opened the door in silence. When Jaycelyn walked through the door, Lee pushed her onto the stairs and slapped her in the face. "Where the hell do you call yourself coming home at five in the morning?" he yelled.

He hit her again, and Jaycelyn screamed. Dustin ran out of his car, and Lee kicked the door shut behind him before Dustin made it to the door.

I woke up at the sound of a door slamming shut and ran halfway down the stairs. I jumped over Jaycelyn and ran for the door. Lee grabbed me by my waist and flung me into our dining room table. The glass broke, and I had blood on the right side of my face. I couldn't move, and I struggled to scream. I managed to crawl to the back door. I rolled off the back steps and on to the wet and muddy grass.

"Help!" I cried, yelling over the thunder. "Help! Help us! Please, somebody!"

Lee came to the back door. Dustin ran and hopped over the wooden fence.

"Dustin!" I yelled.

Lee hit me. Dustin ran toward me.

I shook my head. "No! No!" I pointed to the opened back door. It was pitch black inside.

Lee stomped my arm into the ground. I screamed.

"Sandi!" Dustin yelled.

I shook my head again. "Go in the back door!" I yelled while crying.

Lee punched me in the jaw.

Dustin ran inside, looked back, and proceeded through the house, stepping on broken glass. "Jessie!" Dustin screamed while looking around in the darkness.

"Dustin!" Jaycelyn cried.

He walked toward the sound of her voice. He saw Jaycelyn lying down on the floor. She was crying. He instantly fell to his knees, and he held her in his arms. He rocked back and forth, kissing her on her forehead. His tears landed on her face, and instantly she stopped crying and looked up at him.

She sat up and hugged him tightly, so tight that her barely noticeable bump pressed against Dustin and he felt the baby kick. He picked her up and walked out of the front door. He opened the truck door and put Jaycelyn inside. "Wait in here. I'll be right back, okay? When I close this door, lock all the doors and hide on the floor in the back seat. Understand?" Dustin said.

"Yes," Jaycelyn replied.

Dustin left, and Jaycelyn did exactly as he said. He ran back into the house and through the house to the back door. Lightning lit the sky and struck a tree in the yard. Down came the tree and smashed into the side of the house. Dustin looked for me in the yard, but I wasn't there. He ran back into the house and turned left into the kitchen. He walked down the hallway. It was pitch black, and water was up to his ankles.

He walked into my parents' room. My mom was sleeping on her side of the bed with headphones in, and her music was too loud for her to know what was going on. He kicked open their bathroom door. Water flew out the opened door and pushed Dustin onto the floor. Dustin couldn't find me in there either. He ran and turned off the water, but the water was still growing. By the time he walked out of the hallway and closed the door behind him, he heard a crackle and a beam of light came from a small hole. He walked toward the beam. Before he made it to the door, white wood broke off in pieces, letting out more and more light. Finally, the door broke and crumbled down. Our room was full of water, and the water was sparking things that were plugged in. Water that was pushing Dustin against his will out of the room was flying everywhere. He grabbed hold of an unplugged lamp and pushed it through the rushing water with him; he made it to the bathroom in our room.

The shower and the bathtub faucet were on. The tub was plugged to hold all the water until it overflowed. Dustin turned off the faucet and shower, but he still couldn't find me. Those were the only bathrooms in the house that he ever knew of. He looked out the bathroom door and saw things sparking even more. He unplugged the tub and let the water drain out. Water flew out down the hallway and rushed into the open door. Dustin was thrown through the closed window in our room and two stories down, landing onto the concrete walkway. A rush of water followed him, cushioning the blow.

Jaycelyn ran out the car. A woman driving a Mercedes Benz stopped her car in the middle of the road. She left on her headlights and opened the door. She was listening to the radio. There was a flash flood warning.

"Miss!" the woman yelled through the heavy rain and wind.

Jaycelyn turned to face her.

"Did he just fly out of that house?!" the woman asked over the thunder.

The weather was so obscure that you could feel God's wrath through the thunder and hear it with the violent, blinding lightning. The lightning was so powerful that it seemed to take the sound away from the thunder. Jaycelyn nodded in shock. Dustin rolled over and laid his head on Jaycelyn's folded knees. He spoke quietly and faintly, "I-I-I'm fine. T-Th- There…a girl…a little girl being drowned somewhere. I tried…I couldn't find her." He coughed.

"My sister! You have to help me find my sister!" Jaycelyn screamed.

Dustin sat up, then stood to his feet. Lightning struck a tree Dustin's car was parked under. It lit on fire and fell over and smashed Dustin's car.

"Was that your car, sir?" the lady asked.

"Yeah. Don't worry about it! Can you help us?" Dustin asked.

"Of course!" the woman yelled.

They ran back into the house. Water was falling out of a huge gap in the house and was falling by gallons. Jaycelyn grabbed her backpack and threw it onto the couch, away from all the water. They ran back into the kitchen. When they made it to the hall, water was rushing at them, Jaycelyn and the woman started swimming in the water.

"Jessie! Your mom is asleep in her room!" Dustin yelled.

Jaycelyn went down the hall and opened the door, but when Jaycelyn got there she was gone. Jaycelyn went back down the hallway, fighting the water.

"She wasn't in there!" Jaycelyn yelled over the sound of thunder and rushing water. They followed the rushing water into the living room. "The guest bathroom is over there!" Jaycelyn yelled, pointing to the right. Instead of taking Jaycelyn's directions, they swam to a wall with an unlocked door. They were puzzled as to where all the rushing water was coming from.

Chapter 7

"THERE ISN'T A BATHROOM IN here!" Jaycelyn yelled.

The woman looked around. She spotted water that seemed to be leaking from the closet. She swam to the closet door and tried to pull the door back, but it was hard to pull open. She held her breath and looked at the door. It was locked from the inside. Dustin swam over to her, and Jaycelyn followed.

"This door is locked from the inside!" the woman yelled.

"It's a closet! Why would it be locked from the inside…or any side?!" Jaycelyn asked.

"That's just it. It's not what it looks like!" Dustin yelled. He opened up the windows in the room to let water flow out. It was a difficult task with all the pressure, but he managed to do it. When Dustin could stand, he kicked the door, and the lady joined in. Jaycelyn went underneath the bed and pulled out a hammer and smashed the door open. Water broke down the rest of the door, pieces of wood dancing in the air; the closet was a newly renovated bathroom, a master bathroom to be exact. They finally found me. Jaycelyn screamed and cried. I was pale-faced. My lips and ears were violet. I had been underwater for four hours and thirty-nine minutes. What they thought to be fifteen minutes of searching was not. They picked me up and ran downstairs to the lady's car. Jaycelyn ran back in to get her bag. Water followed their footsteps in gallons down the stairs. She got inside the car. Dustin sat in the front seat with Jaycelyn on his lap. I lay on the back seat, and I was leaning over some.

The sky had shown its vibrant colors of pink and golden yellow. The clouds were perfectly shaped and the right shade of white. The air was crisp, clean, and sweet-smelling. Water splashing onto the car as we passed drained into sewers of every kind. The rose gardens in the back of yards bloomed quickly, dancing to the brisk feeling of the air. They breathed heavily with the excitement of the first day of spring approaching as fast as we were driving.

Panting…I could feel someone breathing on me heavily. I could see black figures moving over me and away repeatedly.

"Two thousand watts!" a woman yelled.

A loud buzzing noise and a rubbery noise, and then it hit me. A zapping feeling that was filling me with a rejuvenating energy. I sat up and screamed; the doctors comforted me. I threw up water all over the bedsheets. I kept gagging and puking up a nasty, slimy, and yellow substance. It did not taste good at all. Jaycelyn ran into the room, and Dustin and the lady followed.

"Dustin, she's okay!" Jaycelyn cried.

The lady stopped walking.

"What's wrong?" Dustin asked.

"I just…I've been away from my son for so long," the lady replied.

"Oh, I'm sorry. What was his name?"

"The same as yours. D-U-S-T-I-N. I haven't seen him since…he was…six," the lady replied with an ocean of sorrow splashed across her face.

"A… Ad-dilene… Adilene Cervantes," Dustin stammered.

"Yes? How do you know my name?"

"You're Adilene Cervantes. You're forty-five years old. You were born on October 5, 1967."

"Dustin? Is that really…oh, my gosh!" Adilene ran and hugged Dustin tightly, crying and thanking God for giving her baby boy back to her. Dustin hid his face inside her neck, mumbling how much he'd missed her.

"Oh, gosh, you've gotten so big! I haven't seen you in thirteen years!"

she cried.

"I know. My God, Mom, I've missed you so much!" Dustin replied.

Adilene wiped away her tears and sniffled.

"How have you been? What's going on? What's new?" Adilene asked with curiosity, knocking at the door of every single question.

"Well, I have a baby boy on the way in about four months," Dustin said.

"Oh, wow! That is wonderful, even though you're young. Who's your wife?" she asked excitedly.

"I'm not married. My girlfriend is pregnant. Mom, this is Sandi," he said while introducing me to her. "She's Janessa and Lee Jacob's second child," Dustin said politely. He was trying to make a point.

"How nice to meet you," Adilene said with a smile.

"Mom…"

Jaycelyn walked back into a dark shadow.

"Mom, Sandi is going to be an aunt in four months."

Adilene looked at Jaycelyn with eyes wide open. "Oh, Jaycelyn! Come here," she said. Jaycelyn rose to her feet and walked to Adilene. She hugged Jaycelyn and looked her in her eyes.

"Jaycelyn honey, do your parents know?" Adilene asked. Jaycelyn shook her head. "Poor thing! And it's too late for an abortion, isn't it?!" Adilene said.

Jaycelyn gasped and covered her mouth. "No. Never. I can't do that. It's not fair to do… and it's not just my kid."

"Too much, too much to do," I said. I was dizzy and absentminded now. I was not okay. I woke up too soon. I threw up more nasty liquid. My fingertips turned a magenta color. I leaned back, feeling the odd brick-like hospital pillow hold my neck and the shape-shifting foam hold my back. I kept blinking my eyes more and more, slowing, falling, and shutting tightly. A loud beeping noise occurred out of the blue; it stopped all conversations in the room and control room. Doctors rushed in and rushed family out. Slowly, my heartbeat was dropping; I was trying not to fail. I had no other choice but to go down with my heart. I was losing this battle between my heart and myself.

It was 3:59 in the afternoon. Dustin drove up to the library door and stopped. Jaycelyn hesitated to open the door.

"Jessie?" Dustin asked.

"Yeah?" Jaycelyn replied.

"Are you all right?" Dustin asked.

"Will you come inside with me?" she asked fearfully.

Dustin kissed her for a while. Then, he kept to himself. "Yeah, I guess," he replied.

Jaycelyn quickly shot him an upset look.

"What?" he said, angered by her look.

"Nothing. You don't have to. I changed my mind. I'm not going in," she replied with an attitude.

"All right. Fine. Be stupid. It's your loss."

"Excuse me? So I'm stupid now! Wow! Thanks so much, coming from my boyfriend. Gee! It really warms your heart. You're the one who didn't go to college!" Jaycelyn retorted.

Dustin laughed. "Yeah, right. I totally forgot! But no! I'm the stupid one! You're the one who's knocked up, single, and gonna be a high school dropout." He looked at her fiercely and said, "Get the hell out of my car now!"

"Fine," Jaycelyn said while opening the door. "Dustin, you're just damned to hell!"

"Funny. I was already there when I started this relationship with you!" he yelled back. He started his car and drove off.

"You're damned for getting a fifteen-year-old pregnant!" she yelled as the car drove off.

Dustin flipped her off while making a left turn at the corner.

Jaycelyn walked inside and saw the man she was looking for. "Hello!" he said and shook Jaycelyn's hand.

"Hi, sir. How are you?" she replied.

"Great. Just great. You did such a fantastic job yesterday. It was just…fantastic!"

Jaycelyn giggled. "Thank you very much.

"Now, your pay is two hundred and fifty dollars by the hour, and you--"

"What?! Two hundred and fifty dollars an hour?! That's insane!"

"How so? This is a high-class national library. Is it too much? Because we can take some away, of course?" He said with a smile on his face.

"No! I need it!" Jaycelyn said eagerly.

"All right. Now, you must work a total of six hundred hours every twenty-one weeks for two terms to earn a raise or promotion. Understood?"

"Yes, sir! I heard every word," Jaycelyn said with a smile.

"All right. Then, here is your schedule. Let's get to work!" he said while walking away.

Jaycelyn had worked for twenty-one hours total so far for that day.

"Hey, kiddo! Time for your break! You get a one-hour break, so I suggest you sleep!"

Jaycelyn went to the employee lounge and went straight to sleep. Another employee from the bookstore on the second floor woke Jaycelyn up. For an entire two weeks that was Jaycelyn's routine. She had nowhere else to go besides the library. She was way ahead on her school work and kept an A-plus in every class. Dustin didn't call, text, email, or check up on Jaycelyn.

Jaycelyn worked five more weeks straight and then took a break and left the library.

"Hey!" someone called from behind her.

"Oh, hey, Darrell," she said sleepily.

"Here's your pay in cash, just like you asked," he said while handing her the money.

"How much is this?" Jaycelyn asked curiously.

"It's seven thousand and two hundred dollars," he whispered.

Jaycelyn shrieked and covered her mouth. "Oh, God. Thank you so much!" she said and kissed Darrell on the cheek. She put the money in her pocket and walked to the hospital.

"Jaycelyn?" the nurse said.

"Oh, that's me!" she replied.

"Oh, my gosh! Look at you!" the nurse smiled, and Jaycelyn giggled.

"What?" Jaycelyn asked.

"You're getting bigger! Aww! It's so cute!" the nurse said.

Jaycelyn laughed. "I'm fat! That's cute?!" Jaycelyn replied while laughing.

"When you are pregnant, it is absolutely adorable. Plus, it's baby fat," she said as she winked and smiled at Jaycelyn.

Doctor Stephonie came into the room and told Jaycelyn about her health and the baby's health. Jaycelyn sat quietly, thinking about how Dustin wasn't there with her. "Is there anything I can help you with, Miss Jacobs?" Dr. Stephonie asked.

"No. This problem can't be fixed," Jaycelyn replied as she walked out the door. She walked upstairs, down the hall and to the right. While on her way to my room, she saw a woman walk past her.

"Callum?" she said. She walked past my room. Then, she came back and said, "Callum?! What are you doing in here?! The nurse is looking for you, sweetie!"

Jaycelyn ran to my room. "What are you doing in here, ma'am?"

Jaycelyn asked. "My..." she started and cleared her throat. "My son..." She pointed to a boy sitting next to me on my bed. "His name is Callum. And I was coming to get him. He has been visiting her a lot. He says that they are friends," the lady said.

Chapter 8

I COULD FEEL WARM, SOFT, gentle hands caress my face and my arms. Warmth was slowly going to my cheeks and fingertips. My cheeks turned a rosy pink and the color ran to my lips. My skin seemed to come alive again as it faded from a colorless gray to a creamy white. Dead skin fell off at the seams, and my skin became smooth. I slowly shook myself awake. The first thing I saw was the blurry image of a human figure leaning over my body.

"Hello," I said with a very scratchy voice. I still couldn't make out who the person was. My eyes uncrossed, and I realized it was a boy. "Hello," I said again, trying to gain my vocal strength back. He still didn't answer. "Hel—" I started.

Before I could finish, he said "Hi, Sandi," with a smile on his face.

"So, you can talk?" I replied.

"Yes, I'm Callum!" he said excitedly. I giggled at his eagerness. "I couldn't wait until you woke up. I was getting so impatient!"

"Callum," I said with a smile on my face.

"Yes?" he responded.

"Oh, no, I was just saying your name for the first time. Very unique," I replied.

Callum smiled at the sound of a compliment. He was an adorable kid.

"Hey, Callum!" Jaycelyn said.

I turned my head so fast I gave myself whiplash. "Jaycelyn!" I screamed excitedly while holding out my arms for a hug. It felt like music to my ears to hear her voice again. She hugged me and Callum's mother walked by the side of my bed. "Hi, Sandi. I'm Callum's mom. I was wondering if you and your sister would like to come and stay with me for a while, just until you all get back on your feet. So, what do you think?" she asked quietly.

Callum looked at me with a huge smile and nodded his head. There was something about him that made my stomach flutter and my heart skip a beat. I turned to Jaycelyn as she desperately checked her phone for any news from Dustin. I looked at Callum's mother and nodded with a smile.

The excitement and curiosity went to my head, and I couldn't wait to get there. Jaycelyn looked at the door, and the nurse walked in. Callum looked at the nurse with a sad look on his face. "Callum, you are supposed to be on the fourth floor! You need to be hooked up to your machine!" she chastised.

Callum's face was a deadly purple. He collapsed onto the bed. He was having convulsions. His mother put her hand over her mouth and let out a short whimper. My hair, which seemed a dull orange, began to brighten with life as it stood up with my fear as if someone rubbed my hair with an orange balloon. My hair had sucked the color out of the balloon like a vampire drains the life out of his victim. I touched Callum's chest. I couldn't feel a heartbeat. He pulled on my hair until my face was next to his. The nurse ran out of the room to get help. Callum squeezed my head really hard against his chest.

"Pressure! He needs pressure! Where is the doctor?!" Callum's mother yelled.

Callum started to cough up blood, but he still would not let go. He held on to me tightly. I wanted to help him. His mother had to pry his grip away from my head. My IV needle ripped out of my arm, but I did not scream. I went through more pain than that tiny needle. It felt like a pinch and nothing more. Callum began to throw up violently. Blood spewing out of his mouth like a waterfall and spread across the floor like a lake. It did not just soak but saturated the bedspread until most of it looked like a tie-dyed shirt. It dripped quickly onto the floor. The sheets became like a cloud, releasing all the precipitation it could no longer hold on to the earth. Callum was everywhere, not just blood, but Callum. He began to choke on his vomit; it was as if he had been hit with mustard gas. The nurse came back with help after she idiotically left the room, putting Callum's life in danger. I took my IV and jabbed it into his arm. I did not care if I did it right as long as it helped. Callum's eyes began to roll to the back of his head and the muscles in his eyes began to show.

The nurse ripped Jaycelyn and I from the room. She yelled at the top of her lungs, "Do not ever do that again! You do not stick people with medicine or blood or anything that another patient has used! If he dies, you'll get a lawsuit!"

"Oh, right, but you won't get a lawsuit for running out of the room while a patient was having a problem beyond a seizure?! Or go to jail because you risked his life to get help?" I snapped back.

"It's my first day!"

"Yeah, and it is my first day being awake again, and I still did more than you, so if you sue, I'll counter sue," I said with a sarcastic smile on my face.

After some hours, we could go into the room again if we chose to do so. I ran into the room and jumped onto the bed and lay next to him. The bed was soaked with blood still, but I didn't care. Callum opened his eyes and looked at me with a smile on his face.

"I am glad you survived and all, but how did you?" I asked him. I was both curious and shocked.

Callum laughed. "I am superman. It's easy. It happens all the time. We just don't know if the last time will be my last time here on earth. So that's the only scary part." Callum kissed my cheek and blood stained my pale cheek like lipstick, but I didn't mind. I rolled onto my left side and laid my head on Callum's shoulder. He looked at me and said, "This is the start of a beautiful friendship."

I laughed and held his hand, and for the first time in my life, I felt safe. I drifted into a deep sleep for an hour, but it only seemed like five minutes.

When I woke up, Callum and his mom were talking in a language I'd never heard before. "May I ask you a question, without offending you?" I asked quietly trying to regain my voice.

Callum's mother looked at me and smiled as if she knew what I was going to say. "Yes, you may," she replied softly.

"Umm." I stopped and took a moment to think about how to state the question. "What's your ethnicity?" I asked.

She looked at me and then responded, "Andamanese. Do you know what that is?"

"No, I haven't heard of that before, but it sounds very pretty," I said with a smile.

"Well, I will have to explain it to you some other time," she replied with a smile. "Right now, I have to get Callum cleaned up and to the correct room," she said as she stroked his hair.

I got up and walked around the second floor of the hospital. Barefoot, I walked down the cold marble stairs. I was waiting to be checked out of the hospital as it was my day to leave. Walking down the stairs made winter seem like another warm season. Then, everything started shifting and moving. I saw hallucinations of birds flocking through windows. Glass cracking and spiders hiding in the heat were falling from crevasses in the ceiling. One look up and Mother Nature told me something important that day. "Sandi," she said, "it's not your day to leave."

"Sandi! Sandi! Sandi, where are you?" voices shouted in the distance, but they sounded very loud, very close. Maybe it was me who was drifting off far into the distant darkness to a place of no return. I could not tell if my eyes were opened or closed, but there were times, if I really focused, I could tell my eyes are closed because when they were opened it was so dark that it made closing my eyes seem like lights. In my mental breakdown, I saw the light, but you never go towards the light... So, I went toward the dark, and in the dark, there was a thunderstorm in my heart.

"Revive her! Revive her!" distant voices screamed. They had to rip Jaycelyn from the room because she was having painful contractions and bleeding, but she wouldn't voluntarily leave.

When I finally woke up five hours later, Jaycelyn was there. She waited with me until I woke up. Her face was red and wet from crying so much, but I knew it wasn't because of me. They knew I would wake up; otherwise, they would not have left me. I turned to my left and my head started throbbing. She rubbed my head and stroked my hair out of my face.

"Hey," she said with a stuffy nose and a smile.

"Tell me what happened," I said.

"Well, there was an earthquake, and you were found under a heavy pile of rubble and—"

"Not that. What happened with you, Jaycelyn," I said, cutting her off from her sentence.

"Well, I have triplets. Excuse me. I had triplets," Jaycelyn said. "Sandi, she says it's not *your* day to leave."

I found myself lost within the basement. I don't remember how or when I got there except that I was there. It was dark. I had no flashlight, and I was constantly mistaking my long, untamed orange mane for thick spider webs. Then, all of a sudden, I was falling, face first, onto the blistering cold concrete floor. It sucked the heat out of me, and I was unable to move at certain moments. What happened, and how did I end up down here? I felt for any kind of support with my hands, so I could pull myself up before I became frostbitten. I wasn't supposed to be in the basement anyway because there were no lights and there was just an earthquake. But how did I get down here? I wondered. I started to anger myself thinking and thinking just to never find an answer.

"Well, I'd hate to be the bearer of bad news, but you're stuck and hopelessly lost, dear friend," I said to myself as I began looking around like I could see in the dark. Then, I felt something. It was a flashlight, a small flashlight. It was good enough to light a path for my eyesight. I flipped the switch back and forth trying to turn it on. "Damn. No batteries." I, then, became afraid of the darkness. It was too quiet, too eerie. It brought out a side of me I had never seen before.

In a fit of rage, I threw the flashlight, and it sounded like it hit something made of glass. I heard a dark roar and groan. Then, I felt glass all over the floor. I sat there completely frozen in silence for what seemed like hours but was really five minutes. Then, I heard footsteps being skid across the floor and something metallic being dragged across the ground. Papers began flying everywhere and what sounded like heavy books being thrown onto the floor. Then, a loud deep groan. I whimpered as quietly as I could while trying not to scream and take off running. Then, there were flashes like when you turn on an old projector. It was the flashlight. A big, old, glass bookshelf had been hit, and glass was missing. I could only see that path. Then something blocked the light, and I heard heavy, deep breathing. I looked up as it was walking across the light. Then, it paused and stood to face my direction. It was holding a long metal rod with blood in a pack attached to it. Its hair was wild and had an orange-red looking color to it and piercing green eyes. Blood was splattered across the face and arms from the IV needle ripping out of its arm.

It chuckled and tilted its head. The neck cracked and broke, and it screamed. "This is where you should be," she said, and it flew on top of me quicker than a lightning strike. She beat me and screamed at me, choking and breaking my collarbone. Blood started seeping through my skin and stopped underneath the surface because it had nowhere to go. I stiffened my neck, trying to stop her from shaking me, but it only made the impact worse when the concrete met my head. I felt around and found a book and began beating her with it. She started to look familiar, but I couldn't pinpoint her face yet. Then, I was sprawled across the floor again, being beaten by the same beast, but this time, there was some chain around my neck while she was trying to choke me. She took the book and threw it and the flashlight came rolling creepily toward me. I grabbed it and held it to her face, so I could see before I whacked her with it, but I couldn't hit myself. She became more than familiar. She became a reflection, a clone, a replica. She became me. She was me. Then, she grabbed a book the size of more than two volumes of books combined, and it was lights out for me. But then she paused. In a rough and raspy voice, she said, "Tell me your name..." When I didn't answer right away, she repeated herself, but this time, she yelled, "Tell me your name!"

"Sandi. My name is Sandi."

She hit me with the book and laughed maniacally.

"Wrong, wench! What is our name?!" she yelled even louder, provoking me to scream with the last few breaths I had left.

"Sandi!" I yelled as loud as I could. Then, I heard footsteps running to reach the basement. She looked at me and giggled quietly as I blacked out.

"Schizophrenia," she whispered.

"Sandi! Sandi! Someone help her! She's having a seizure!" the lady doctor yelled.

"When will she come back? When will she come back?" I asked the first time I woke back up.

"When will who come back?" the doctor asked.

"Schizophrenia. She hates me," I replied.

"What are you talking about?" she asked with a worried look on her face.

I explained the whole story, and the nurse just cried and nodded her head. She walked out, and she never told me why she started crying, only that she was sorry. I just lay there in silence, wondering what was going on. My thinking led to a conclusion. Only certain kinds of people ended up down there, people like me. I felt my neck, the chain around my neck ended up being a key. I looked to my left, and there was a book with a lock on it. It was dusty and old-looking as if it was passed down generation after generation. It had been signed by a woman named Santa María and in parentheses was Sam for short. I couldn't move without feeling sore, but I still tried to reach for the book. A helping hand gave me the book and sat on the bed with me.

"Whatcha got there, kiddo?" Dustin said nervously.

"Whatcha doing here, sir?" I said in an angry and mocking tone.

"Aww! Hey are you mad at me, too, Sandi?" he asked.

"Jaycelyn is not mad at you, though," I replied.

"Huh? But I haven't seen her. Plus, I wasn't talking about her. I was talking about my mom, but I guess she counts for something." He ended his sentence awkwardly and looked out the window. There was an uneasiness tiptoeing up his spine, and he turned around. Jaycelyn was standing in a corner, quietly listening to the awkward conversation. He turned away quickly as tears rolled down his face. He felt so ashamed that he couldn't even look at her. He quickly excused himself from the room without a word. Jaycelyn turned her head to the corner and just let him walk by. Tears were streaming down her face as her nose turned red from crying. She put her hand over her mouth and tried to cry quietly, but she broke down from holding the weight of the darkness on her shoulders. Dustin looked at her through the glass window and then walked away. For the first time there was nothing he could say or do to make anything better.

Chapter 9

I LOOKED AT JAYCELYN WITH a look that told her she didn't have to let him get away like that. "I can't let him back in, Sandi. I just can't...I don't know why, but something just doesn't feel right anymore," Jaycelyn said through tears as if she were a foreigner speaking broken English.

"I know, Jaycelyn. I know. I'm just so tired, so tired," I replied.

Jaycelyn got up and looked at me. "I'm sorry, Sandi. You've done a lot for us, for everyone. You can rest now. I'll be here when you wake up," she said with the fakest smile she could possibly find.

"I don't think I'll wake up this time, Jaycelyn. I just can't anymore. I can't keep fighting," I replied weakly.

Jaycelyn looked at me in a way she never had before. I was all she had left, and she couldn't lose another soul since she already felt like she'd lost her own. She walked out of the room and exited the hospital.

Soon after that, Dustin came back to see me. "I don't want to be hostile with you, or you to me, Sandi," Dustin said nervously.

I couldn't sit up because of the brace the doctors had put on my collarbone to put it back in place. "Okay, Dustin. I forgive you, but you have to talk to Jaycelyn. You can't leave her by herself, dude," I replied.

Dustin didn't say a word; instead, he looked at me with surprise.

"What is it?" I asked.

"You've never said 'dude' a day in your life," he replied.

I smiled and slowly turned my head into my pillow.

"Hey! Don't suffocate yourself now," Dustin said.

Jaycelyn smiled from outside the door. She wasn't showing before since she was so small. Oddly, she didn't start showing until her sixth, almost seventh month. I looked at Jaycelyn and smiled as she slowly and quietly walked into the room.

Dustin turned around to face the woman he was in love with as if she were some inner demon he could never get rid of. She backed away, but he held her arm and got down on one knee. He pulled out his mother's jewelry box and opened it. Inside was a beautiful black sapphire ring with diamonds all around the silver band. It was a size six, the perfect size for her ring finger, and it had the date of an engagement proposal engraved on the inside of the band. The date was 4/12. Jaycelyn carefully examined the ring as Dustin put it on her finger; she looked at him in shock as he stood up and put the jewelry box away. I smiled and, as painful as it was, let out a slight giggle because of the moment. Dustin walked closer to Jaycelyn and looked at her intensely. "Why do you look so surprised, Jaycelyn? I told you I'd never leave you," he said.

"Yeah, but you did. I thought you weren't coming back, Dustin. Please don't ever do that to me again," Jaycelyn said nervously.

"I promise I will never do that again, Jaycelyn. I promise," he replied. He looked at me and smiled. "Thanks for the advice, Sandi," he said.

"No problem." It felt like the shortest sentence I'd ever said in my life.

Everyone else was happy, so why wasn't I? I asked myself over and over, but I couldn't find an answer, so when Jaycelyn and Dustin left the room to talk quietly and were far enough down the hallway, I made my decision. I decided to let my heart go, to rip it out, and leave it on the table for spare parts since it was too beaten to be used as a whole. Slowly, one by one so as not to startle anyone, my heartbeat dropped, and the monitor beeped. It got louder and louder, but no one could hear it because I would come back to life for a minute and then die all over again. It was life, not death, that would kill me and death, not life, that would save me.

Thirteen. My face was pale and blue. Twelve. My eyes rolled to the back of my head. Eleven. The left side of my body was numbed. Ten.

My best friend jumped on my bed and saved my life. I looked around angrily to find out I was in the same place I was in before, but it was darker outside now.

"Sandi, are you okay? You can't die on me! Please don't…" Callum pleaded.

"All right. I guess I won't," I replied.

"So, something is wrong?" Callum asked.

"When is anything not wrong?" I retorted.

Callum gently sat me up and hugged me. I looked around for Jaycelyn and Dustin, but they weren't there.

"You and I will be leaving from the hospital soon, Sandi, okay?" Callum's mother said.

I turned and looked at her and shook my head.

"Jaycelyn will be back soon, honey. We aren't leaving without her," she said.

"Callum, are you coming with us?" I asked.

He looked excited but shook his head and held on to me tighter.

"Callum has to stay in the hospital for a few more months before he is released," his mother said with sorrow in her voice.

"I want to walk before I need to learn how to do so all over again," I said randomly.

Callum helped me out of bed, and the nurse came and took my IV needle out of my arm. She began cleaning up my room, and Callum's mom and I were packing up my things. There was an extra pair of clothes in a bag for me and a toothbrush. I cleaned myself up and walked with Callum up the stairwell to the fifth floor. He held my hand and smiled at me. "Ya know, Sandi, I think I have a crush on you," he said randomly.

"That's how you decided to break the silence, huh?" I said while smiling at him.

He laughed and looked at me. Then, he stopped in the middle of the stairs.

I tugged on him. "Come on, silly!" I said.

He laughed and continued walking up the stairs.

We were allowed to enter the hospital room with Jaycelyn. She was getting another ultrasound and an update from the doctor. I touched the side of her stomach and felt a baby kick; it was a beautiful thing to feel my nephews in there, kicking in unison, excited to see the rest of the world. Almost as if they were tired of being in Jaycelyn's belly, caged in. Now I knew that there were two other people who knew how I felt. Then, it happened, that weird feeling you get when you are between life and death. Deciding…forever deciding…never able to forget the past because the past sculpts your future. A suicidal seven-year-old that grew up way before it was time. Jaycelyn looked at me and my intense thinking habits. I was piercing the skin on her stomach harder and harder.

"Sandi! Sandi, stop!" Dustin said as he ripped my hand away.

I screamed, while holding my head, and ran to the door. "Go away! Go away!" I yelled frantically.

Dustin held me closely and examined me. "What, Sandi? What is wrong with you? It's me! Dustin!" he replied, but I just stood with a wide-eyed look on my face.

I pointed to the window, toward the left side of the room that was off-center from everything else. A black shadow of Schizophrenia appeared and masked me all over again. My bones met the point of no return and flesh seemed to eat away at itself. I swung and flung my body around, trying to get away from the terrible dark shadow, but it pushed me to the ground. Flying around the room, I spun and bashed my head into the window. My body fell limp over the edge of the window. Half of my body was inside the window, and the other half was out.

Then, there I was, stuck in the psychiatric ward. It was too much like a prison down there in the renovated basement where they kept all the patients until the day of the earthquake. I was lucky enough to see the new and improved psychiatric ward. I couldn't be more miserable in hell than I was in there, but at least, the floor was soft. At least, the walls were okay to bash my head against when I got angry. At least, the sharpest object was my toenails which I couldn't reach due to the straightjacket and the fact they cut them every two weeks. I turned into a different person at night, and here I was, in the midst of my darkness, stuck in a light room.

"Miss Jacobs, you have a visitor," the lady said and put a wire around me as if I was some horse pulling a plough.

"I don't want to see anybody!" I screamed and yelled, banging my head on the floor, but she tugged at the wire, and I got up from being choked constantly.

Callum was on the other side of a window, and he slid something underneath it. I jumped onto the table and grabbed the diary with my feet and put it into my lap. The lady tugged on the wire, making me stumble in my chair. "Let's go, redhead!" she yelled.

I got up and carried the diary in between my legs. She took it from me and put it into a drawer with all my other things. She threw me into the room before I threw my fit.

"No! That was mine, you idiot! Give it back!" I said as I banged my head on the plastic window of the padded door.

"Shut up! You'll get it in the morning!" she said.

"No! You stupid jerk! I hope your husband leaves you for la morena he's been cheating on you with for twelve years! I'll be at that good for nothing drunk's funeral! You wench!" I screamed. Like I said, I was someone completely different at night. I yelled until my voice gave out. Turning my lungs inside out and my throat red, I passed out into a deep sleep.

"*Levántate, demonio*," the lady said.

"Kill yourself, wench," I said as I got up.

She didn't put the wire on me but took me out to the lobby of the hospital. The sunlight hit me, and it was as if the demon walked back into the darkness. I winced and whined and fell to the floor at the sight and feeling.

She took off the straightjacket and helped me stand up. "*Levántate, niña*!" she said as if I had been reborn. Even though she had done this for the past seven days, she still got excited every time she did it.

Jaycelyn and Dustin had me wait in the lobby until they arrived. I had been waiting for thirty minutes, and Dustin and Jaycelyn still hadn't arrived.

"Hey, birthday girl!" Callum said.

I laughed and hugged him. "Callum, my birthday isn't until the twenty-fourth of April, not the nineteenth."

"You might not be able to be out on your birthday," Callum said.

"Oh, come on! I'll be out for the whole day! I'll be a good girl! I'm getting better, really!" I said with excitement.

"Sandi, you aren't going to be getting out anytime soon," Callum said.

"I know, Callum. I just need a little bit of hope," I said and sighed.

Then, I saw Dustin and his fiancée walk through the door. Who would have thought that my sister would get engaged so young? I just couldn't believe it, and I was so happy for her, but just not for myself. I was the lost and mental child, the seven-year-old who went mentally insane. What I would do to get the time back, the time when I wasn't like this, the time when I wasn't playing God.

Chapter 10

"JAYCELYN!" I SAID AS I ran and hugged her.

"Sandi! How are you?!" Jaycelyn asked excitedly.

"I think the question is, how are you?!" I said, changing the subject. We all knew that talking about my feelings put me in a rage of anger that I couldn't control.

"I am fine. Hey! Guess when I'm due!" Jaycelyn said.

"Oh, yeah! I heard you got the day of conception wrong!" I replied.

"Yes, I did!" she said as she held on to Dustin's arm. "It's June eighth!" Jaycelyn said with anticipation.

"We thought it was earlier than that!" Dustin said.

"Wow! That's why you were so small!" I laughed. "Yeah! I'm thirty-three weeks pregnant and can't wait to get them out of here!" Jaycelyn said excitedly.

It was sort of an awkward reunion. We all knew that I could snap at any moment, but we tried not to care. The more we tried not to care, the more we thought about it. The more we pondered about what happened and where *we* went wrong. Even in this, I couldn't find sanity, and I took Callum and walked off. When Dustin and Jaycelyn wondered why, I told them I felt a breakdown coming. The people in the lobby watched me carefully. As if I were an untrained puppy that would pee everywhere, except on the newspaper they had set out, constantly being watched. That constantly made me want to get out of this place.

"Sandi, what's wrong?" Callum asked.

"I just can't... I can't act like I'm okay when I know I'm not... Callum,

I just don't know what to do. I want to get out of this place so bad. But they keep me here like a caged animal," I replied through tears.

Callum hugged me, and I fell to my knees.

One of the nurses quickly ran over. "Sir, it would be best for you to let go of her!" she yelled.

Callum looked very grown-up from a distance until you got closer, especially in the dark.

I quickly stood up and wiped my eyes. "No, ma'am. I'm okay really!" I said.

"Miss Jacobs, it'd be best if we got you back now," she said. Then, she looked at Callum and smiled. "Callum, I'm afraid Sandi isn't stable enough to—"

"Well enough to what, huh?!" I said as I snatched away from her. "You all think you know what's best for me, but you don't! Get away from me!" I said as I kicked at her.

Then, the Mexican lady who always had some joy of getting the "demon" out of me came. She held me and said, "*Cálmate, niña... Estas bien.*" She spoke Spanish to me because she knew only I understood it. It was so close to Italian I practically picked it up on day one. She took me and Callum to the front where all the light was, and I melted in her arms completely. The lady came back and took me to sit in my confinement. Jaycelyn demanded that I be taken out, but the nurse thought she knew best and said I needed to stay in there.

Why do I have to be stuck in here by myself? What did I ever do wrong to anybody? Geez. Can't I just be normal? Why can't I just be normal? I thought in silence. Now I had to act like a good girl and just seem like everything was okay.

It was five days later, and I sat in the lobby, quietly observing people. I went four days without a mental breakdown or a fit of rage, and everybody, including Callum, was testing me. They knew something was seriously wrong.

"Hi, Sandi! How are you feeling?" a random woman who had been sent by the know-it-all nurse asked me.

I turned over and looked in the nurse's direction, acting as if I didn't notice her, even though she and I both knew I did.

"Well, to be honest," I started. Then, I put my face in my hands and curled up in a ball.

The nurse ran over quickly with a smile on her face.

I looked up at the woman with a huge grin, and laughing, I said, "I've been amazing! How about you? How has your day been?" I asked the lady in return, but she just walked off with an attitude. I looked over at the nurse and silently mouthed the b-word. She stormed off, and I just laughed, thinking about how amazing my day was really going. Callum came over and hugged me tightly. It was the first human contact I'd had that I'd enjoyed in a long time, so I hugged him back and just held him there. I started thinking I was holding him for too long, but then he reassured me that I wasn't.

"You know I don't mind, Sandi. If they'd let me, I'd stay here all day."

"Ha! I wouldn't! I've been here long enough!" I said while Callum laughed.

I'd been in there five days more from the nineteenth…six days…ten days…eleven days…I was practically counting the seconds. They gave me some leave but not a lot. They let me keep my book, so instead of just waiting to get out, I decided to read it. Turned out that it was a book of my entire family tree. Well, most of it, at least. I really wanted to get out of this place, but that book was my only escape. Everything felt so real. I opened the book and could soak up information like a sponge for what seemed like an hour, but really it turned into days. The deeper I got into the book, days turned into months and months turned into years, but nothing would stop me from reading this book for this one hour of leave that the nurse allowed me to have.

* * *

Yolanda and Sebastian moved into a small, white, Victorian-style home at the ages of sixteen and eighteen. Yolanda had finished high school early and was eager to start a family of her own, a family that would be generations long and the best there was. Since Yolanda was a snob, she not only wanted, but thought that she had, the one hundred and ten percent best. Growing up, she was very athletic, so she became involved in a sports career. Sebastian loved everything about her, especially her cooking. She was a natural-born cook and was not only adventurous with her recipes but with traveling as well. She went to different countries to see the cultures and how she could work them into her foods. She never missed an ingredient and always had plenty to share. Food, that is. She was able to protect herself because she was highly disciplined and was able to learn martial arts as a way to build up strength and athletic skill, but it could also be used as protection.

Sebastian had always been into his music. He dreamed heavily of becoming a famous musician, and one day that dream came true. He was a virtuoso and had an ear for music. As a matter of fact, he had two. He would stop at nothing to perfect his music and his household since he was a perfectionist. He was also as adventurous as Yolanda and loved to travel to Egypt, China, and France. His little sister Isabella lived in France, but she bared no children. She died of leukemia at the age of eleven. When it was time for the funeral on December nineteenth of 1952, Yolanda was giving birth to their first child. A baby boy named Coyle and my eldest brother.

Coyle absolutely loved the outdoors. Growing up, he would sleep underneath the stars and come in with hives since he was allergic to practically everything. He made use of the two traits he took from our parents'. He was athletic like our mother and artistic like our father. He put his talents to work and painted for a living. He wasn't a major artist, but he made thousands from the artwork he created. He would have early appointments he needed to attend, but there was no sense in trying to wake Coyle up without a bucket of water because he was a very heavy sleeper and could sleep through anything. He'd gone to many art fairs at school and sold many of what he called his masterpieces. I just saw squiggly lines and tainted paper.

My other brother Caddis, who was a year younger than Coyle, watched and ridiculed Coyle for taking up art as a profession. Just like me, he never saw the point of it, but maybe that was because we didn't see what Coyle saw. Coyle always told us that art was a breath of fresh air, but Caddis was a very grumpy person. "How can you breathe fresh air when you are surrounded by all those paint fumes?" Caddis would say in return. Then, there were times when Caddis was not so grumpy and was fun to be around. He had the best sense of humor. I've never met a person funnier than Caddis. That was, until his grumpy side came out...then everyone was funnier than Caddis, but he wasn't all bad. He and my father were both master musicians, and they started a small family band together but soon broke up when they couldn't agree on what tone they should and shouldn't have. Many times, when we would go to the pyramids in Egypt, we found secret caves and tunnels. Caddis was not only adventurous but brave as well, and he led and forced me into the impenetrable darkness we faced each time.

The year after that, my first and eldest sister was born. My parents named her Caddy. She was so cute, cuddly, and fragile when she was first born to the age of seven. Our parents thought she would be the one they would have to sacrifice all of their yearly trips for, but luckily she was born just as adventurous as the rest of us, but when she didn't get her way, it was a disaster. Caddy had beat a boy at the lunch table for saying that she couldn't have his push pop and that she couldn't always get what she wanted. She was and still is extremely hot-headed and doesn't seem so cute and cuddly anymore. She would throw pots and pans at our father and brothers for making fun of her, and our father had to get stitches when he was play fighting with her outside and called her a loser. She loved being outdoors but hated being called a loser. She was sent to her room that night and for the rest of the week. She also got her allowance taken away, but since she was frugal, she didn't care. She saved up enough money to rent a place of her own for a few years. However, that would be a dangerous thing to let her do on her own because she was absent-minded and constantly forgot what she was supposed to do or was going to be doing.

Six years later, our mother gave birth to my second eldest sister, Carmen, and she was a lot to handle. She was very adventurous and had a keen eye for photography and took it up as a profession. Growing up, she was always taking pictures of the family and venturing off into the deserts in Egypt to find some rare and exotic animals and capture them in their natural habitat. When she was thirteen, she ventured off too far and got bitten by a snake known as the Horned Viper. It has been nicknamed the "sand viper" and with good reason. Carmen stepped on its tail without knowing it, and within a split second, it turned around and bit her in the leg. She tried kicking it off and fell on its back, and it bit her again in the arm and in the neck when she couldn't roll over and get up from the attack. Her scream alerted a nearby household and scared the snake away as she beat it with her fist.

The family found her and took procedures for the snake bites, but they couldn't for long because the snake was furious and on the attack. They quickly had to pick up Carmen and run to the house with the snake not far behind them. They scurried into their truck and drove to Cairo.

"What is your name?" a teenage boy asked.

Breathing heavily and slowly, she said, "Carmen."

"And where are you staying, Carmen?!" he asked while pushing on her chest.

"At the Cairo Marriott Hotel & Omar Khayyam Casino," she said and paused.

As he saw her begin to hyperventilate, he finished her sentence "On sixteenth Saray El Gezira Street, Cairo, Cairo," he said. "Keep her talking!"

An elderly woman who was driving said, "We are going to the Cleopatra Hospital on Thirty-Ninth Cleopatra Street, Salah El Din Square, Heliopolis, and Cairo, Egypt! Can you repeat that for me?"

He asked as he laid her back across the seats. He took a crepe bandage and wrapped it snugly around her forearm and leg. He took a splint out and put it on the bandages to avoid movement, she screamed with pain, but he had to keep going. When they reached the hospital, they carried her in on an emergency call, and the doctors saw her right away. Our parents, who were out sightseeing at the time, were contacted and rushed to the hospital.

She was released five hours later, and even though she was not a flirty person, she kissed the boy who had helped her and made him an exception to the rule. She was disciplined, like our mother, and because of this, she also was skilled in martial arts but had to take two years off. Her friendly side showed as she offered the other family dinner at the hotel, but it got canceled as she spoke because our mom was going into labor, and I was ready to be born.

It took only five painful hours for me to finally emerge from my mother's womb. I had deep red hair since my mother's was orange and my father's was brown. My eldest siblings all had an orange-brown hair color, except Caddy. I never amounted to much like my brothers and sisters. My parents believed I would be a disappointment, and I was looked down upon in school, too. I am an extremely finicky person and kept the house clean. Even at five years old, I would pick up toys and wash dishes. My father was sure I would make a great housewife, and I did, of course. My family was glad that I was adventurous like the rest of them and loved the outdoors but still no one was as adventurous as Carmen, but I was a huge daredevil. I went bungee jumping at ten when no one else would. It was an amazing experience, but my parents didn't believe I'd come back up. I don't think they cared either. I'd always been shy but outgoing, daring but quiet, sensitive but not too sensitive, and a party animal but only at the right time. I am sometimes even envied by my sister, but I always reassured her she had nothing to be jealous of, but as always, Carmen was stubborn and hot-headed. I normally sat in her room all day and wrote books and songs since her room was the warmest in the winter and the coolest in the summer. I dreamed of one day getting published and making good money. However, when the new neighbors moved in next door, which had always been more than walking distance, it changed everything.

"Paulo Arredono," he said sweetly.

It was as if my whole world as I knew it had changed. I knew he would be mine, but I just didn't know how, but fate did, and it would go about its own plan, not mine. Silently, I watched him, when he shook my hand, and I didn't respond with my name; instead of leaving, he just watched me. A piece of paper that was folded into tiny and neat little pieces flew out of my pocket and into the street. It broke the silence, and Paulo chased after it with me right behind him. It flew in all types of directions until it finally stopped at the park across the street from the movie theater. I watched him as he picked it up and held it without unfolding it. "Would you like this back, madam?" he said with the weirdest French accent I'd ever heard.

I shook my head. My tight ponytail with a bump in the front tugged at my medium-length red hair.

"Hmm…too bad I haven't seen it around anywhere," he said in his normal voice.

I tilted my head to the side and gave him a look. He knew I didn't believe him, but he wanted to hear my voice. He held the paper in front of me and waved it. I tried to catch it, but he just teased me by moving it out of my reach. Then, he ran in all different directions. I chased after him, and after twenty minutes of playing, I hid behind a tree, and when he walked around it, I tackled him. We fell on the grass, and I landed on top of him. It was as if we were in a movie and the perfect scene had just been made. We secretly both liked the way it felt, having someone to hold and look at. "Okay. You've earned it back," he said as he reached for the paper lying a few centimeters out of his reach on the grass. He handed it to me and then looked at me. I felt a sudden wave of unbearable weight and laid my head on his chest. It was as if fate was forcing us to be together. Instead of freaking out, he wrapped his arms around me and held me there gently, pressing me against him. "You know that seems kinda tight," he said as he slowly undid my ponytail, letting my hair slide out like fine silk unraveling from a dress. I still did not speak a word but gave a sigh of relief as my hair fell to my face, dancing like the flowers in the gentle breeze. Paulo looked at his watch and sat up with me in his lap, holding me with one arm. He wouldn't let me go for the world. He squeezed me gently and could smell my mango shampoo and ran his fingers through my hair.

"You wanna go see a movie? It's five o'clock, and the movie theater just opened," he said, hoping for an answer he could hear; instead, I looked at him, nodded my head, and smiled. I got up and pulled him up from off the grass, leaving the paper we'd desperately chased after behind as it fell out of my pocket again and fluttered in the wind, unfolded and landed on Paulo's doorstep. After the movie, I went over to the park and sat on a bench and waited for Paulo to come over. "That was a lot of fun. Thank you very much, Paulo," I said sweetly.

"Wow! You can speak English?" he replied teasingly.

"Yes, I can, Paulo. Is it surprising to you?" I asked sarcastically.

Instead of answering, he just stared at me. Then, he picked me up and carried me all the way home. He walked me up to my door and waited for me to pull out my key. When I finally got the century old lock unlocked, he opened the door for me. He hugged me and held me there for five minutes, but it seemed like seconds and then closed the door behind me as I walked in. When he walked to his house, he found my song, waiting patiently for him, resting up against the front door.

Morning came, and my parents were upset because I'd stayed out until about one in the morning on a school night. Any other night was completely fine as long as the cops on late-night patrol didn't find me. "I am sorry, Father. I lost track of time, but I know that is not an excuse because I should have known better," I said quivering with fear and exhaustion.

Mother let me off the hook, and I walked out into the front yard and caught Paulo's eye. He ran over and hugged me, picking me up and twirling me around in his arms.

"Hi there, neighbor," I said, while giggling and holding on to Paulo as he spun me in all different kinds of directions. I fell to the ground as if I were dizzy, and Paulo laid my head on his chest and cuddled me.

"You have a beautiful voice…you should use it more often," Paulo said. Then he laid me back onto the grass and kissed me. Kissing led to touching, which led to other methods of feeling, and things got hot and heavy quickly. He led me to his house where it seemed so empty and so quiet. His mother wasn't home, and as for his father… he never really had a father, just a sperm donor. He quickly pushed me against the wall and stripped me of my clothing and gently felt every inch of my exposed body.

He carried me and tossed me onto his full-sized bed. Taking off his pants and letting me do the rest as gently as I could. It was his way of making sure I wanted it as bad as he did, but he never asked me if I wanted the surprise I would get about a month or so later. When I finally started showing, my parents banished me from the house, and I went to stay at a motel for a month on my own. Since I'd met someone and gotten pregnant, my parents still believed I was absent-minded, but they couldn't believe I'd even known what to do. They always thought I was stupid. He lived next door, and my parents could talk to him anytime, and he was an amazing person, but of course, my parents didn't think so. It didn't matter, though, because I thought he was, and Paulo was still the fit, muscular, blond boy I fell in love with. I hadn't exactly told him that I was pregnant yet, but I knew he worried a lot since I'd disappeared and was never seen. Maybe I'll tell him...someday, I thought.

My younger brother, who was six years younger than me, always came in and asked about the baby when my parents allowed me to stay in the house for the weekend. Being a teenager was already hard enough, and he constantly asked when he could see the baby. "The baby will be born November seventh, 1985, then you can see the baby, okay, Chaim?"

He would always nod his head as if he understood me, but five minutes later, I'd hear, "When can I see the baby?" come from his mouth again after I'd given him an answer already. I guess that was only part of my punishment then, huh?

"What is today?" Chaim asked.

"Today is June eleventh, 1985,"

"When will the ba—"

"November seventh, 1985," I interrupted.

Chaim walked out of the room and went downstairs to tell everyone what I'd said. He was so happy, but I was scared. It'd been four months since I'd conceived, and I was watching Paulo from out the window. Paulo asked me to go with him and his family for a trip out of state for the Fourth of July, but I would be leaving on Sunday of this month, and he still didn't know about his soon-to-be child. My parents said the only way they would let me see daylight was if they knew, for a fact, that Paulo knew he was the father of the child. Paulo was seventeen and almost done with school. He would graduate this year since he was trying to finish school early to get a head start on college.

Chaim came into the room as I was looking out the window and thinking of what to say to him. Chaim was a bookworm and was very smart. He loved being athletic because he thought all the girls would run to him in elementary school, and he was artistic, so he always got straight As in art. He was also disciplined enough to take martial arts, which was something I didn't care for. He was small and thin and had that orange-brown hair I mentioned before. He came in asking so many questions since, in this house, nothing was kept a secret. I just wanted to give him some of my sleeping pills because, once he was asleep, there was little to no chance of waking him up. That was one of the advantages of being a heavy sleeper. Then, Paulo knocked on my door. Since my parents were asleep, I quickly rushed him in and upstairs into my room.

He wouldn't speak a word. He just stared for what seemed like an hour, but it was really only fifteen minutes. Then, he looked at me and asked me a question that I wasn't sure how to respond to, even though I knew the answer. "Is…is it mi—"

"Yes, it's yours," I interrupted, feeling a bit of shame in myself for ruining his life. He paced the room back and forth, back and forth, back and forth. So much that it seemed to move the room, and I was getting dizzy. Then he stopped and hugged me tightly. It felt as if he was clinging on to me for the safety of his life. I didn't care, so I just held him as tears of joy ran down my face. Fourteen and pregnant to my parents was something to be ashamed of, but for me, I could only feel joy. Even though I didn't know what Paulo was thinking, I was excited to know. He finally let go of me and kissed me; my parents walked by; instead of yelling, they knocked on the door. "You will be allowed to come back home after the baby i—"

"Carlos…" Paulo interrupted. "His name is Carlos," he said as he held my hand.

I hugged his arm tightly. After all, Carlos was a pretty adorable name.

"You will be allowed back into the house once baby Carlos is born," my mother finished.

She was pregnant again with another sibling of mine who was to be born in two months, and she didn't want two pregnant and emotional people in the same house.

Chapter 11

I WAS HAPPY TO STAY with Paulo and his mother, who was far more understanding than my family ever could be.

"You want to go play a game?" Paulo asked.

I looked at him curiously. "What game?" I asked as I perked myself up onto the guest bed.

"Twister!" he said as he kissed me.

I laughed and pushed him away before he could kiss me a second time.

Laughing, he said, "No, but your little brother is here again and he—"

"Oh, gosh! Don't tell me. I already know!" I said as I flopped back onto the bed and covered my face with my hands.

Paulo went to have Chaim come inside, and I could hear him running around, screaming "Where is the baby?" over and over until he had no more air in his lungs. If this is what the wonderful pitter-patter of feet sounds like I don't think I am going to enjoy it, I thought. Chaim came into the room and broke my thoughts and shattered them into multiple pieces. "The baby! The baby! Where's the baby?" he said as he ran around my room with his arms out, pretending to be an airplane.

"Chaim, I told you the baby isn't coming until November sev—"

"No! Mommy and Daddy went to the hospital, and I can't find the baby!" he said with nervous excitement.

"What?!" I said with shock since I didn't know.

Paulo and his mother both ran into the room. We got Chaim and went to the hospital; everyone had left and sent him over for me to babysit. When we showed up in the waiting room, everyone looked surprised. Carmen stood up and hugged me. "How are you feeling?" she asked.

"A little betrayed, but I'm fine," I said with a huge sigh of relief.

"You know," Carmen started but was never able to finish because Chaim started bouncing and tugging on her arm.

"Where's the baby?" he yelled.

"Chaim, you have to be quiet!" Carmen said.

Paulo grabbed my arm and took me to sit down. I had tears rolling down my face and was trying hard not to let anyone see, but nothing could ever slip past him.

"You're okay, Carmella. Maybe they just forgot to tell you out of panic," he said as he touched his forehead to mine, but right on cue to ruin a perfect moment was my father.

"Carmella, what are you doing here?" he asked.

Paulo turned around and his mother had a devastating expression on her face. "Returning your precious child to you. He felt left out and wanted to see the baby," I said and left without looking back to see if Paulo and his mother were following me.

Paulo came to the car about thirty minutes later to see if I was there. When he saw me sitting in the back seat, he waved and asked me to unlock the door. I giggled and turned my back. He crept to the other window. "Open the door!" he said with a creepy look on his face. He couldn't hold it for long since he was laughing. I pretended to be asleep on the seat and closed my eyes and started singing really loud. I opened my eyes and saw no sign of Paulo. "Open the door!" he said as he started banging on the roof of the car. I laughed and opened the door slowly.

"Please don't eat me," I said in a little girl's voice.

He hopped off the top of the car and closed the door quickly as he came inside. "I can't promise you that," he said with a deep voice.

"At least, be gentle!" I said as he pinned my arms to the seat.

"Maybe…if you're lucky," he replied as he leaned in to kiss me.

"Am I lucky?" I said as I pulled away. He moved in closer and looked at me.

"I don't think so," he said.

We didn't even realize that Paulo's mother was sitting in the car. We could see her weird facial expressions in the mirror. Paulo hid his face in my neck and started laughing.

I giggled and looked at Paulo's mom in the mirror. "I am so—"

"No! I don't want to hear anything for the rest of the day…please," she said while laughing as she interrupted me.

Paulo laid his head on my lap and looked at me. "You forgot to lock the door!" I said as I messed up his hair.

I lay back on the hospital bed, anxious and impatient. I am extremely nervous and can barely breathe. My contractions started, and I still had three more weeks to go. Paulo was rushing me into the emergency room, and his mother was right by my side. I just wished that my family would be there. We'd been arguing a lot lately. My father and mother got on me about everything, even though I lived next door; the food that they kept in the refrigerator was my fault for some reason. Since I'd moved out, my mother kept buying things that I liked and expecting me to eat them, knowing that I did not live there anymore. I came back from my flashback to the doctor screaming in the room for everyone to get out. "Are you okay, Miss Pickard?" the doctor asked. I could tell he was very panicked.

Breathing heavily, I managed to scrape up letters to make words but not full sentences. Then, I started to panic and passed out.

Carlos wasn't due for another two weeks, turned out the contractions I was having had nothing to do with the birth process. My health was deteriorating quickly, and I had to stay at the hospital for the last two weeks of my pregnancy. As it got near the time to prepare for the baby, the doctor insisted that I stay at the hospital. Carlos was born right on time, November seventh, 1985, at five in the morning. I was pretty much asleep during the whole commotion. Since I was already at the hospital, it made everything feel a lot more comfortable, until Paulo and his mom showed up. After that, I started panicking and the haze that I was in was no more, but Carlos was born healthy, and it was a smooth process. At least, that's what the doctor said; I had no medicine whatsoever to help out with the pain.

Eventually, when Carlos was born, I was allowed back into my parents' house without further persecutions. They had renovated the house and made another floor so that now it had three floors and more space. I slept up on the third floor with Carlos, and soon after my fifteenth birthday, I had another child, a girl named Serenity. My parents eventually stopped getting upset with me by the time they found out I was having another little girl a year after Serenity was born. By then, my mother had had three other children back to back. Carlos was three and Serenity was two, and they had a good education for their age. Every day, they went next door to see their father and spend some time with him while I did small talks with my parents. My little brothers and sister would always ask tons of questions. The newest editions to the family were Cameron, Collin, and Sherry. Not only were they helping make a mess of the house, but they invited my kids to join in on the fun, too.

Cameron was born in September, two months before Carlos, so he and Carlos were the same age, and so were Collin and Serenity. Sherry, however, was about to have her first birthday pretty soon. Since I'd waited two years before having Cairistiona, Sherry was a year older than her. Things started getting a little weird having to explain to your kids that every time Grandma had another baby, it was not their brother or sister, too. Instead, it was their uncle or aunt, and they had to show them respect. My mom finally decided to stop having children the year after Sherry was born because she was finally going through menopause and was done with all of her back-to-back births.

The following year, I had another boy named Santos, and Paulo and I also decided it was time to stop having children as well or else everything would get to be a little confusing. Two days after Santos was born, Paulo's mom died from a hidden tumor she had been dealing with all of her life.

Chapter 12

"PLEASE DON'T FORGET YOUR LUNCH box this time, Cairistonia. I can't take it to you today. I've got a doctor's appointment right after I drop you off at school!" Mother yelled across the room.

Summer finally came to its dreaded end, and I missed the summer trip to Italy that our family had. Even Grandma and Grandpa went! My grandmother was envied a lot in town for her "miracle eggs." Giving birth past age forty was a big thing, and God must have blessed her back in the old day. I was well aware of what menopause was, and I was all for it because I didn't ever want to have kids.

"Serenity, put the book away. It's time to get ready to go to school," Mom said calmly. I pretended to take the book upstairs, but once she wasn't looking, I ran back down the stairs and slipped it inside my backpack. Since our school went from first to eighth grade, we would all know the same people each year, except the occasional new kids we'd see now and again. Once there was a new kid, everyone jumped like frogs as if they'd seen a fly they wanted to catch or as if the new kid was a brand new amusement park that everyone wanted to go to.

"Momma, why can't we just take the bus?" I asked while smoothing out my uniform that I was neatly dressed up in.

"Because Grandmama says we're too good to ever be seen ridin' on any kinda public transportation, whether it be the city bus, a taxi, a train, a plane…" Then, she paused to look at me as we were quickly walking. "Even the big banana boat school bus," my mother and I both said mockingly.

"And the home...of the...brave!" the class said and then all sat down in unison. The teacher introduced herself as if she had never seen any of our faces before in the halls. "No running!" Mrs. London would always say. She'd even taken me and many others to the principal's office before. "Hey! Is it okay if I sit here next to you?" the new girl asked.

"Oh, yeah. Sure it is," I responded.

"Veronica Jolie," she said as she held out her hand.

"Serenity Pickard," I responded as I shook her hand.

"So what do you have in your lu—"

She was interrupted by Macy-Antonia and Hope London slamming their books down and taking a seat at the round, blue, twelve-dollar-looking table we were sitting at. The popular girls sitting at our table would definitely be the talk of the day, but I could not care less. They would always say that Mrs. London was their mother or aunt, but everyone knew they were lying, especially since Hope was the only one with London as her last name, but still, they continued to have popular reputations. Hope leaned onto the table and bent her elbow up as if she was going to lean her head on her hand; instead, she held out her hand to Veronica. "Hi, Veronica. My name is Hope London, and this is Macy-Antonia Stuart," Hope said in a snobby voice.

"Nice to meet you," Veronica said as she shook both girls' hands.

"The pleasure is all yours," Macy-Antonia said.

Then, they looked at me, and I just held my head down and looked at the table. This is going to be one extremely long day. I thought.

"This is my friend Serenity!" Veronica said as she slightly and aggressively shook my shoulder.

"Oh, yeah, we know 'Brownie,'" They both said as they laughed obnoxiously.

Once lunchtime came, I had my head pressed against the table.

"Hey there, buttercup. What's the matter?" Veronica asked as she sat down at the table with her lunch.

"Those two girls that sat at the table earlier," I said.

"Oh, yeah, them two. What about 'em?" Veronica asked.

I looked up at her, and for the first time, I realized her beauty. She was my age, a pretty white girl like Hope and Macy-Antonia, and was from Texas. She had beautiful dark, wavy, ash brown hair. She had freckles starting from the middle of her nose and stretching to the sides of her cheeks. Her eyes were pretty, shiny, and brown, and she had such cute curly eyelashes. Her nose was petite and neatly placed on her face. It didn't come out too far, and it wasn't too small or too wide. Her lips were small but plump and a rosy red color, instead of pink. She would never need red lipstick. "Hello?" she said as she broke my haze.

"Sorry. Anyway, they are just not nice to me," I replied.

"Oh, yeah, they seem pretty mea—"

"Hey there, Ver-Bear!" Hope said with overwhelming excitement.

Oh, great. She already has a nickname. It's just a matter of time, I thought to myself.

"Hi, Ho—" She started but then looked down at me. "Umm…what's your name again? Please pardon my memory," she said with a heavy but beautiful Texan accent.

"It's Macy. Macy-Antonia," Macy said as she glared at me. She was so angry that I could feel her glare burning a bald spot through my scalp. I sat up when Hope came to the table. I knew I was about to be in for some kind of treat.

"Hey, Brownie! How's your dad doing?" Hope asked. As she asked that, all attention turned to me.

"He's fine," I replied as I balled up my fists underneath the table.

Macy-Antonia decided it was her time to jump in. "Oh, are you sure that white trailer trash is your father? You're a brownie, you dummy. Your momma probably doesn't even know who your father is, just like the rest of your kind," she said with a snobby attitude.

I banged my fist on the table and got up and walked away with tears streaming down my face. This isn't the fucking 1920s, I thought.

"Have a nice day now!" Hope said as I ran out of the cafeteria.

Then, they turned their attention to Veronica. "That wasn't very nice of you to make fun of her like that," she said angrily, her accent getting thicker as she spoke.

"Oh, come on! She only got mad because it's true. If she really had her father at home, she wouldn't be so upset. Just a plain fact…obviously," Hope said.

Veronica stood up and slapped Hope so hard that her food flew out of her mouth and two tables down. Then, she pulled her hair and pointed at her. "You know it ain't polite to talk about black folks like that. They can be the wisest and some of the smartest people you could ever meet," she said with a stern voice. Then, she left the cafeteria and came looking for me. I didn't go far though. I was only sitting outside the cafeteria door.

Veronica and I walked home together early since we got suspended from school for three days. It wasn't fair since I didn't do anything, but I couldn't care less since Veronica had stood up for me. She came to my house and met the adults in the house since everyone else was still in school. My dad walked into the room, and Veronica looked really surprised when he kissed my mom. "They're real cute, Serenity," she said as she smiled and held my hand.

"Thanks, Ver—"

"My dad is white, but my mom is black and white," she interrupted.

Then, I looked at her differently. You wouldn't even know she had black in her since her skin was so vibrantly pale. Then, my dad looked at us and asked, "You guys wanna come with me to pick up the other kids?"

Instead of speaking, we nodded our heads in unison. I didn't know Veronica was such a curious person until we got in the car. She also had a very adventurous and free soul. "Is it hard pickin' up all them mixed kids? I know, sometimes, people look at y'all a lil strange," she said.

My dad was unsure of how to answer since she had so many questions. "Well, Victoria, I—"

"It's Veronica." She interrupted.

"Well, Veronica, umm…seeing as how you are still a kid and don't have to worry about things like that, let's not talk about it," my dad said as calmly as he could. We both could see how angry he was getting just thinking about it. He loved my mother to bits and pieces and hated how people thought of him for it. Especially with how much the times were said to have changed.

"I don't want to upset you, Mr. Pickard. It's just nice to know someone that goes through the same agony you do is all," she said while striking my father's curiosity. He glanced at her in the window, and she knew he wanted to know more.

"Well, my mom and I used to get picked on so bad in Texas that we moved. My mom is mixed with black and white, too, and my dad is white," She paused for a moment, trying to find the right words to say. "It got so bad that…my father stepped in front of a train. Then, people said that all the black folk were turnin' their white men into cowards."

My dad stopped the car and looked at Veronica with this intense and sorrowful look on his face. Instead of saying anything, he got out of the car and went into the school building. She grabbed my hand and looked at me. "I think he understood," she said as she looked out the window and sniffled her little red nose.

Those three days went by quick, and my dad dropped me and Veronica off at the front door. As we walked in the classroom, you could hear people whisper, "Good job, Ver-Bear!" with loud voices as we went to our seats. Of course, the table was surrounded with more popular people, and there was only one seat. Joana White took my spot and was talking to Josh Hinkle, who was also popular and a major crush of mine. Joana knew, for a fact, that he liked me, and that was why she made sure she took up all of his time every day.

* * *

Then, there I was, standing in the archway of Callum's beautiful vacation home in New York City. His family lived in the United Kingdom, but they bought a home here in order to travel to different places for some time. Boy, did they travel…a lot! They'd been as far as Canada and were already planning their next trip to Puerto Rico in the mid-winter of this year. I smelled sweet scents and aromas coming from the dining room. Beautifully scented peach candles on top of a ballroom white piano were swaying to their own melody. A frantic movement of twirls and mid-turns, they danced their fragrance into the air. The cherry hardwood floor shined brightly, as if it were just polished. A glass table had an intricate design engraved into the marble-finished table legs. The odd placement of orange furniture seemed to make the room oddly cozy and bright, with colorful spice jumping from brown wall after brown wall. Light bounced back and forth between the ember of the fireplace and the couch.

Callum's mom quickly led me to a door that seemed to have a large carving of a misshapen dragon on it. She slightly smiled and looked at me from the corner of her eye. "One of Callum's… unique ways of perfecting the house," she said quietly as Jaycelyn slowly followed behind us.

I smiled and touched the dragon as I opened the door. The kitchen had granite counter tops and white counters with carefully designed roses on them, some blooming and some not so much. I took a slight interest in the design but couldn't figure out why. They, too, had some misshapen figures, but this one was more intricate and harder to tell due to the distraction of the odd collection of flowers. The walls were lined with a cream-colored tile designed to be diamond shaped, with slightly gold-yellow and beige tiles standing out more than the average here and there. The flooring was granite with a honed-finish, instead of a polished one, but it took on a dark burgundy color that was slightly more than tinted. The refrigerator was of the best quality, of course. It could dispose of ice in a cube or crushed manner. It had the freezer on one side and the refrigerator on the other with some additional refrigerator space at the bottom. I learned later that I was going to fall in love with French-door refrigerators. It was cold-to-the-touch stainless steel with an odd blue tint that seemed to glow more than the sea-teal buttons. It was made by Samsung, a company that I observed didn't stick to cell-phones.

Later on, she taught Jaycelyn and me how to make a dish called curry. Now the stove I paid more attention to than how to make it. Jaycelyn's going to be the mother, not me, I thought. The brand was Maytag, and it had an extremely smooth surface that was thirty inches in length. It was an electric cooktop which everyone had nowadays, thanks to technology. I preferred the gas stovetop. It also had speed heating, which I guess was a good option to have if you wanted to burn something, which Jaycelyn almost did, of course, by playing with settings she had no clue about. The food still turned out good, but, my god, was it spicy. I guess all the extra heat from the stove amped it up a ton. Despite the immense pain, my throbbing tongue was giving me from the constant heat, I felt the need for a nice hot shower. If I could only find my way around the place before it struck midnight two weeks from now. I tried not to pay attention to every intricate detail there was, but then again, I was locked in a mental institution and a hospital for some time. This was the *closest* thing to home I had got and I didn't plan on giving it up too soon.

I walked to the upstairs bathroom in the "master suite." Since it was a vacation home, I guess that was what Callum's mom called it. The walls were painted burgundy with tiny white air-brushed flowers along the top and bottom of the wall. It kind of gave me that odd "welcome home" feeling that I knew I couldn't keep. I had to remember that, no matter what, I was just visiting. Nothing was mine. The floor, oddly enough, was a plush and comfortable-feeling carpet. I closed the green door to the bathroom and tickled my toes with the carpet, spreading them out to feel the soft material. A Whirlpool bathtub invited my body to relax and slowly tugged me underneath the water. I pretended to make a makeshift snow angel in the widespread tub. I opened my eyes and let the heat sting a bit before my eyes adjusted to the water. Instead of choking from a lack of oxygen, I took the oxygen molecules from the water, turning them into a weird red chemical. With a look like mercury, it took on an odd color. It slowly wafted over the water with an odd smell. Parts of my body were cramping in areas where they shouldn't hurt. I could feel water rushing inside me from some opening that wasn't visible to me. I closed my eyes and slowly took in the toxic and depleting oxygen from the liquid mercury. I could feel the beginning stages of maceration quickly take place as I relaxed quietly. The mercury solution seeping to every corner the water could hide, I would not choke, and I definitely wouldn't die.

* * *

A hand rushed through the water, feeling in the wrong places for my arm. "Sandi, Sandi, Sandi!" Callum said with urgency.

I rose up, and my long orange hair was now a dark brown color from being saturated for so long. Eyes bright green and face red with excitement, embarrassment, and urgency. I could have sworn I was seven just yesterday. Callum turned his back and went into the chess table-themed cabinets in the bathroom. He took out a makeup bag as I quickly cleansed myself with the aromatic soap. Peach… the woman loves peaches, I thought.

Callum's mom had grown up in Georgia for fifteen years, and peaches were a main dish. I knotted myself together, covering parts of me that shouldn't be revealed to the world…or a boy.

"What are you doing in here?!" I shouted with embarrassment.

Callum looked at me over his shoulder and gave me a crooked smile. Then, he continued on. A blue pack was ripped open and a teal-wrapped pad was handed to me. "You're bleeding, Sandi," he said with a look of amusement on his face.

My eyes grew with discomfiture. "Umm…" is all that seeped through the creases of my lips. Wishing I could omit this event from my memory, my face had *get out* written all over it.

When I got dressed in my white, tribal print leggings and my black tank top, I walked barefoot across the carpet and into the hall. Of course, my best friend was waiting outside the door.

"Just when you thought you were potty trained, huh?" he said with a devious smile that mocked my entire existence. Ha. Ha. Leave it to Callum to make a joke about the most embarrassing moments he could find.

"Very funny, bud," I said I punched him in his side. I hit his bone, but I wasn't going to show that it hurt me more than him. "Let's go downstairs," I said as I quickly rushed through the hall. My toenail snagged the carpet, and I fell before reaching the stairs.

"You can't fend for yourself, can you, princess?" Callum said as he lifted me up off the ground. When I said nothing, he looked at me and did a double take before taking off down the stairs. He laughed with darkness in his voice. "Sandi?"

I didn't want to hear it. I grabbed my jacket and headed down the stairs.

"Are you sure white is a good color to wear?" he asked.

Say no more, I thought. I rolled my eyes, stood on the balls of my feet and turned 180 degrees to face him. My orange hair was soft, silky, full of volume, and bouncy, and it did a dance as I turned and jolted to a stop. I tilted my head to the side and rubbed my front teeth with my tongue inside my tightly sealed glittery pink lip glossed mouth. I grabbed the slick wood railing and trailed up the stairs with my eyes fixated on Callum.

"How cute." He teased and winked at me.

After I changed into a blue pencil skirt and curled my hair, I walked back down the stairs. I went into the living room where I met Callum's aunts and uncles who were forlorn and drunk. I was about to sit next to Callum's aunt, Jeni...or something like that when he stopped me.

"Whoa! I'm not so sure I want you sitting on my couch! Do you need this on it first?" he said as he pulled a pad out of his jacket pocket. I stomped on his foot with my heel, and he put it away. I gave him a look of anger and distress. He laughed and ran his hand through my hair. "Don't worry. They're drunk or too sad to care. They won't remember a thing," he reassured me.

He sat me down and went back to the couch across from me and gave me a hard rivet. He looked at me as if he was a computer that had the capability of analyzing my DNA code. I looked back at him, but I couldn't be as focused on him as he was on me. His stare made me feel like I was looking into the eyes of my predator, and I knew all too well I was the prey. For a brief moment, I imagined what it would sound like to make his lips speak my name with a voluptuous tone. I'd had fantasies before, as shameful as I was to admit them but none with Callum. I pushed that thought aside, shivered, and looked away.

"Let's go upstairs," Callum whispered in my ear.

Jaycelyn stared at me with a scrutinizing look on her face, but twin number one took care of her curiosity. I looked at Callum, bit my lip, and nodded. My hormones must have been out of control because, before I knew it, I was leaning on a closed door in Callum's bedroom with racy fantasies flooding my mind. Keep up with the time, or you'll be left behind, I thought.

I bit down on my lip and looked to my right at a mirror posted up on Callum's wall. It stretched down to the floor. I looked good, but my positioning was way out of my league. I was seductively arched in the all right places, head slightly off my shoulders, one foot on the door and an inviting smile across my face.

Callum put one hand on the door and his forehead next to mine. I tilted my head down and looked at my shoes. He put a finger to my chin and tilted my head upward to look at his beautiful hazel eyes. How could scientists say there was no such thing as hazel eyes? I wondered. As he came closer and closer, I could tell they were real. Making an effort for our bodies not to touch, I pressed myself to the door so much that I was practically a part of it. I turned my head to the left so quickly that I got a quick waft of the air. It smelled of womanly perfume from Callum's mom's makeup bag and deep un-impenetrable lust.

Chapter 13

I WALKED INTO MY BEDROOM late that night, thinking about my encounter with Callum earlier. God, I needed him but only as a friend, *only* a friend. Then, there was a knock on the door. Jaycelyn walked into the room and sat down on my bed. She felt my forehead and then my cheek and my neck. "You okay?" she asked.

I looked at her with utter confusion. What could she possibly be talking about?

"Jaycelyn, I am completely fine," I said.

She looked at me strangely and gave me a warning look.

"God, Jaycelyn! I've done nothing wrong! *Nothing!* I swear!" I exclaimed embarrassingly.

She gathered herself and walked out of the room. As if on cue, Callum walked into the room. "Hey, cutie." He walked in and tackled me on my bed and pinned me down to my pillow. "You missed out on all the fun today!" he said as he lifted me onto his back and spun me around.

"God! Gosh, Callum." I was running out of words to say lately. "Put me down!" I said through my constant giggling.

He stood me on my feet and looked at me. I lay back down and looked at him. He gawked at me as if I was a piece of art. I wasn't going to lie. It made me feel special, real special. He looked away, his eyes fixed on the door.

"Jaycelyn came in here and checked up on you?" he asked.

"Yeah, I dunno why she…"

He looked at me with something different in his eyes.

"Oh, like you care!" I yelled.

The lasciviousness in his eyes made my skin crawl. He walked toward me. His body gestures were different. He got down on his knees as I rolled over, so I could lie on my stomach. He stroked my face with the back of his hand and looked at me. I leaned forward and put my forehead on his, so I could feel his hunger for me. He tilted my head up to look at the ceiling and brushed his lips against my neck. I could feel him breathing heavily. I *want* him. I *need* him; I've always longed for him. I tilted my head and looked down at him. My cheek met his temple and his hair as he grabbed my shoulder and kissed my neck softly. My left arm quickly reacted without thinking, and my hand ran through his hair. I breathed in sharply as he kissed harder and harder and wrapped my arm around his shoulders. Then, in a split second, I was on my back with Callum hovering over me. He looked phenomenal topless, and I wanted him. He leaned down and then went back up and looked at me with a crooked smile. I spread my arms and fingers wide open and made a grabbing motion, like when a baby asks to be picked up, and threw my head back and giggled. He smiled and plunged into me, grabbing my A-cup breasts and squeezing repeatedly until I moaned uncontrollably. I buried my face into his neck as he kissed mine. My pelvis was digging a rut into the bed from his strong, rapid motion. When I went up, he strongly thrust his pelvis into mine in a downward motion. I threw my head back and moaned. He glanced at me, and I could feel his lips form a smile against my neck. He unbuttoned my pants and slid his hand down. I grabbed his wrists to ward him off, but he didn't seem to care. Nasty, I thought and giggled. With his other hand, he gently tugged and rubbed my nipples. I tried to hold back any noise that I would make, but then he rubbed in that sensitive spot and moans came out like a symphony. He was a pro at what he did, my best friend…I thought we had *no* secrets. Then again, this was a good one to keep as a surprise later on.

* * *

I lifted my sunken body from underneath the water and rubbed my eyes. The stain red water dripped off my face. I stood up and washed myself with the aromatic soap and drained the tub. I wrapped a towel around myself and told Jaycelyn what happened. She looked at me, shocked to see that I was still bleeding. She rushed me to the bathroom and quickly grabbed out a teal wrapped pad and showed me how it worked and how to put it on. Once I was dressed, she checked to make sure it was on right so that nothing would seep from behind or underneath the pad. I walked down the stairs and into the kitchen for a snack. I wore feet-in Mickey Mouse pajamas and had slid my way across the floor. My wet hair was soaking my pajamas, but I didn't care. I went into a jar and grabbed a cookie. Suddenly, I felt Callum grab me out of nowhere. I screamed and thought I'd peed, but then I remember I was on my *period*. Callum led me to his room which I had yet to see. After a time of sitting on his bed watching movies and eating junk food, I fell asleep.

Alarmed, I woke up to some noise that the others in the house didn't seem to hear. I got out of Callum's bed and walked down the hall to the staircase. I leaned over and saw two shadows. One was smaller than the other, so I figured it was Callum's parents. "Lidianna, you can't just bring people here, especially if you don't know them!" a male voice shouted.

"Rohan-Kyle, don't shout at me! I brought them here because Callum knows them from the hospital," Lidianna exclaimed.

I walked down the stairs with Callum, and he hugged the man. *Rohan-Kyle.* He turned to look at me and just glared. I felt a bit uncomfortable, but I wasn't going to show him that. I simply walked up to him with a cheery smile and held out my hand. He firmly grasped my hand and shook it. "I'm Sandi Jacobs!" I said in a light voice, but he just continued to stare at me.

"Rohan-Kyle, Miss Jacobs," he said in a dark voice. He was a tall Filipino man with dark hair and dark eyes. Tanned skin and his hair covered one eye that seemed to have a scar just below it on his cheekbone. Lidianna looked at me worriedly, as if she knew her husband wouldn't make me feel very welcome. Then, he released my hand and went into his trench coat and pulled out a book. "I believe then, Miss Jacobs," he started, trying to use the dim light to search his pockets, "this belongs to you." He handed me my book.

"Oh! Thank you!" I said as I ran to hug him.

He clenched his teeth at first, then grinned and hugged me. "You're quite welcome," he said as he looked down at me.

I grabbed Callum's hand and rushed up the stairs.

We sat on Callum's bed and began to read the book. I told him about all that had happened and even read things over with him. "This is the part I last left off on!" I said as we turned the page. As eager as I was to get to the end, I would never miss a chance to read the beginning all over again. Callum looked at me curiously. "What is it?" I asked as I looked up at him.

"Are you sure this isn't for just your eyes only?" he asked.

"Callum, someday, a long time from now, someone else will have this book, and I want them to know as much about me and you as I do about this book. You're my best friend," I said as I put one hand on his shoulder. "No secrets," I said with a smile.

He agreed, and we continued to flip through pages of the book.

* * *

Ha! Ha! What a fool he could make of me, I thought as I looked at myself in the bathroom mirror. Callum has his name written all over me. I hadn't showered yet, and I still felt sticky from Callum's saliva being spread out across my torso. I unlocked the bathroom door and walked downstairs into the kitchen and sat on one of the stools at the counter. Lidianna and Rohan-Kyle were at work, and Jaycelyn had taken the twins to the theater to see *Cats*. Dustin only visited during the weekends when he'd come up from Tennessee to see the twins. His station of work moved him down there, so whenever he could, he would come see Jaycelyn, but it had been less and less ever since the twins were born. Callum was at school like I should be, but he told Lidianna the reason we went upstairs was because I wasn't feeling well. No wonder why Jaycelyn came to...*check up on me.* I ran my fingers through my hair and tried to clear my mind. Callum is the only thing I could think about. The only thing I wanted to think about...

* * *

We were just about to focus and settle down to read when I realized I forgot to change my pad. I rushed to the downstairs bathroom and closed the door. Surprisingly, there was nothing in the pad. I changed it anyway and went back up the stairs.

"Are you ready now?" Callum asked anxiously.

"Yes," I replied with a smile.

* * *

Being seventeen wasn't so hard when you and your best friend had every single class together. However, me and Veronica were going to waste the night away watching movies and talking about guys we liked in the ninth grade. She painted my nails and toenails and just sat quietly as I painted hers. Something was bothering her, and I wanted to know what it was.

"Veronica, what is the matter with you?" I asked.

"Serenity, I...umm... I slept with J—"

She was interrupted by her walkie talkie ringing.

"Ver-Bear, you there?" Macy-Antonia said with urgency in her voice.

Veronica ripped away from me to answer the walkie talkie. "Yeah, I'm here. Something wrong?" she replied.

I tried to listen, but the loud static kept serving as a big distraction. Then, there were loud beeping noises coming from the walkie talkie. Veronica turned to look at me, and with bewilderment in her eyes, she calmly excused herself from the room and went to the front door. I followed her to the front door of the house.

"Where are you going?!" I asked.

But Veronica only said "I gotta go!" as she ran down the street.

So much for wasting the night away, huh? I thought as I closed the door and walked into my room.

Veronica had been acting super strange ever since Josh Hinkle and I started dating.

"Serenity, come down here now please!" Nana shouted.

We were having dinner late that evening, and I wasn't going to keep starving company waiting any longer than they already had. We all sat in the dining room at the great table. I still had no clue why it was called that, but it was. We said grace and then prepared to eat.

"Where is the little darling you hang with, Ser?" Carmen asked. The table fell quiet as everyone awaited my reply. My face felt hot and red. *Serenity, I…umm… I slept with J—.*

The air was still with the dreaded silence that stung my face. "She… uh…ran out. Some kind of emergency," I replied.

After that, it seemed like time couldn't go any faster.

It was nine o'clock, and I was supposed to be showering and getting ready for bed, but I couldn't stop thinking. *Serenity, I…umm…I slept with…* I took the J I heard out of the sentence because it disturbed me *way* too much. I looked at myself in the mirror. I knew what she was going to say…I just wish she wouldn't. I pulled my long chestnut-brown hair into a bun. I rubbed lotion onto my hairless legs. Thankfully, I didn't need to shave, and I wasn't planning on it. I put on a sports bra and black panties and slipped into my bed. I didn't feel like wrapping my hair tonight. Even though my dad was Caucasian, my mom was African-American, and I had inherited her thick hair, and my hair got nappy. Along with that, I had my dad's soft-to-the-touch, flowing, silky hair. At least, when the nappy part was done and over with. My hair color changed from the medium-brown to an ash blond tinted color. I looked at the ceiling and thought hard for a moment. Tears stung my eyes and rolled down my face like a waterfall. Just then, my bedroom telephone rang. I answered it before anyone else could hear its aggressive ringing. I was silent listening to the breathing on the phone.

"Serenity?" Josh asked solicitously.

Warily, I answered him. "This is she," I sighed. I didn't know what to do now.

"Serenity, are you okay?" he asked more worried than the first time.

Tears streamed down my face, and I had no words to speak. At least, not any that would be translated through heavy sobs. He knew I wasn't okay and still preceded to play the innocent card. I had nothing more to say to him…or to *her. Serenity, I…umm…I slept with Josh.* This time, I finished the sentence myself. Without saying a word, I hung up the phone and unplugged it, so I wouldn't hear hell's bells for the rest of the night.

I woke up the next morning with swollen eyelids from crying so much. I got dressed in whatever I could pull together at the time. Floral print white pants and a peach off-the-shoulder shirt with golden mid-sized circles for a strap was what I pulled together. I didn't mean to look better than I felt.

I walked into the school building and to the west wing where my purple locker and my "best friend" were waiting for me. I clenched my teeth and held onto my over-the-shoulder bag and stopped in my tracks. I took a sharp breath and walked forward. You're strong. You can do this, I repeated to myself over and over, but when I got there, the complete opposite happened. Josh started to walk my way, and I tried to get away so quick that I smashed my knuckles in the locker door. God! What happened? How could you do this, Serenity?! I wondered. Sanguine fluid oozed down the locker and onto the floor. I groaned and looked up at Josh and let out a pain-filled smile.

"What happened to you last night?" he asked as he reached his hand out to caress my face.

I moved my face away and looked down at the blood staining the bottom of the locker and seeping onto the floor.

"Nothing, Josh," I replied through a deep sigh.

Damn. These lockers need to be a part of the no-weapon policy.

Veronica stood back with a saturated look of regret on her face. Josh gave her a look full of repugnance as she backed away. I could see his words written all across his face: "If you ruin this, I'll do way worse to you."

I shuddered and put that thought out of my mind. I would have pushed it to the back, but I didn't want that statement anywhere in my mind.

He looked at my hand hidden in the locker and slowly but swiftly reached for my arm and pulled it out. The damage was worse than I thought, but the pain was better when I didn't see it. Of course, Veronica already ran away… or *disintegrated* from Josh's death ray, which one I wasn't sure, but the air felt lighter without her around. Josh looked at me shockingly and then took off his jacket and cut the sleeves with a pair of scissors out of my pencil bag. He dabbed the blood away with one sleeve and then firmly wrapped it with the other one. I didn't know if he was with me or against me. Impetuously, I kissed his cheek and wrapped my arms around him. It hurt to move my hand, but luckily, it wasn't broken…my hand wasn't broken, but the knuckles might've been. He looked at me with deep repentance in his eyes.

"Josh," I said as I caressed his face.

He looked away from me. I could see tears forming in his eyes.

"I forgive you, babe. Everything is okay. Don't even think about it. It's me and you against the world, yeah?"

Even though I sounded strong and reassuring, inside I was weak and bone-tired. So tired. Too tired.

* * *

Callum walked through the door later in the evening, and no one was home. God, I hated being home alone, but with Callum, it's no better, I thought. I was still at the counter, writing away. I was so quiet that I startled him with my silence.

"Whatcha working on, Sandi?" he asked as he dropped his backpack onto a bench in the far-left side of the kitchen.

I tossed a glance over my shoulder and continued to work. "Nothing. Just a little at-home project," I said with slight anger in my voice. I hated being sick, and he knew it. Pretending to be sick, I hated just as much because it meant I couldn't do *anything*. He waltzed across the room, slowly making his way to me. Instead of sitting there waiting, I moved and went into the living room. *Mistake.* He pushed me down onto the couch and hugged me so tight I couldn't breathe. "My god, Callum. I just heard my lung pop," I said sarcastically. He laughed and loosened up a bit before returning to his firm grasp. I gasped when he kissed along my collarbone.

"Tough love, Miss Jacobs," he said. For whatever reason, his father never called me Sandi, but he never hesitated to refer to Jaycelyn by her first name. Miss Jacobs was all I was, a stranger in a house I'd been living in for eight years.

"Callum, get up! Someone's coming!" I yelled while trying to push him off me.

"Shut up, little girl. It's just the dog," Callum said as the dog scratched at the door. He kissed my neck and moved up to my jawline.

"Wh-wh-when did we get a dog?" I stuttered.

He looked up at me as he tugged at the collar of my shirt. "Are you actually including yourself as a part of the family?" he said. Then, he licked my neck and kissed it repeatedly. I grabbed the back of his shirt and slid down on the couch. He kissed my eyelid and put his mouth to my ear. He slid his hand up my shirt. "You never answered my question, Sandi," he said smoothly as he began to slide my shirt up.

"Callum," I whispered.

He looked at me with satisfaction in his eyes, satisfaction and *amusement*. Then, his mouth was greedily upon me, moving so fast I barely had time to respond.

"God!" I yelled in frustration as I arched my back and ran my fingers through his hair.

He unsnapped my bra from the front and suckled. Then, he nibbled a bit and licked my nipples.

"Callum…God. Please stop," I said as I moaned.

Ignoring me, he kissed my ribcage and then down my stomach to my waistline. He unzipped my pants and slid them off. He licked my waistline and rubbed. I ran my hand down my face, and I pulled at my hair. He rubbed harder and harder as he watched my reaction.

"You look like you want me to pull your hair," he said as he tugged at it.

I bit my lip and laughed voluptuously. He kissed me and fondled my breasts with his other hand.

I moaned louder, and the louder I moaned, the harder he pulled my hair and rubbed me. I arched my back over the arm of the couch and moaned so loud I pretty much shook the walls in the living room.

"Come here, Sandi. I'm not done with you just yet," he said, and he lifted me up off the couch. Suddenly, I felt the wall, hard and cold behind me. I would have shivered, but Callum's body was warm, too warm.

"Wait!" I shouted and pushed him away from me.

Startled by my sudden outburst, he grabbed my waist. "What?!" he shouted back with frustration. I could feel his sexual tension take over the room. It made it hard to breathe and made me anxious.

"There's a problem," I started as I walked along the wall and then trailed off through the doors and into the kitchen.

"God, Sandi, what? What is it?" he said in a low snarl.

I sexily leaned against the kitchen counter and looked at him. I could feel the greed in my eyes as I stared at him, plotting what I'd do to that masculine body of his. "You're still fully clothed," I said as I toiled with my hair. With a quick motion of my finger, I urged him to come over.

"Well, we can always change that," he said as he undid his belt and took off his socks and shoes. He hurried over and took off his shirt.

Then, he attacked my neck and lips with a thousand tiny kisses.

"Hey, tiger, save some fun for me!" I said.

Callum laughed and I could feel his smile turn into a kiss as he pressed his lips against my skin.

He propped me up onto the counter as he kissed me. I slid my hand down to slide off his pants. He shivered a bit and looked at me. "Why are your hands so cold, woman?!" he said as he grabbed my hands.

"I don't know. Maybe because I've been leaning against the cold counter and the cold wall," I said sarcastically.

He grabbed me, threw me over his shoulder, and spun me around. Then, he quickly pressed me down to the cold floor and shot me a devilish grin. "The floor's colder, isn't it?" he asked.

"How about you feel it, huh?" I replied as I rolled him over and pressed him to the floor. I kissed his neck and made my way down to his abs as I tugged at his underwear. He lost his pants somewhere between the counter and the floor. I kissed and licked at his waistline and then slightly below that. I could feel him pulling and tugging at my hair.

"Babe, move your hair out your face," he said while trying to hold back a moan.

I looked up at him playfully. "Don't you mean out *of* my face?" I said as I slid my hand up and down his underwear.

He roughly grabbed me and pulled me close to him and kissed me.

"Sandi, I brought some soup!" Jaycelyn said.

I could hear her footsteps go up the stairs as I ran to the living room to grab my clothes. When I came back into the kitchen, Callum was still laying on the floor. "Callum, get up! What are you doing, you idiot? My sister will see you!" I said as I threw his clothes at him.

"*Stop*! I'm frustrated and I can't focus!" he yelled as he rolled to his side.

I ran over to him and sat him up against the counter. I caressed his face and kissed him. "Callum, please?" I said as I handed him his shirt.

He snatched it and put it around his neck. He grumbled under his breath as he fastened his belt.

"I'm sorry, *bestie*. What was that?" I said, putting as much emphasis as I could on "bestie."

"F you, Sandi," he murmured. I walked over to him and pushed him into the counter.

"When?" I asked.

He didn't seem amused at all, just frustrated. He clenched my arm and pressed my pelvis into his. "Do you feel that, Sandi? I'm not in the mood to be playing around," he said between clenched teeth and then stormed off.

"Sandi, are you okay?" Jaycelyn said as she walked through the door.

"Yeah, I am. Sorry I didn't answer before. I was focusing on something and didn't want to be distracted," I lied. Technically, it wasn't a lie, was it? After all, Callum needed my attention…bad, I thought quietly.

It was the middle of the night, and I could hear Callum shifting around in my room. I turned over to the left, toward the door, and put my face inside my pillow. "What are you doing?!" I grumbled angrily. I picked up my decorative pillows and threw one at him. He collapsed onto my bed. "Ouch! Idiot! Get up!"

But he didn't. He didn't even respond. I smelt copper in the air. "Oh, my God! Callum! Help! Somebody help!" I yelled frantically as he grabbed on to me. Even after all these years, his childhood disease still fazed him. Even after all these years, the doctors still had no iota of an idea of what they were supposed to do. Nobody could help him…not even me. His father burst into the room, and Callum pulled me close. He wasn't afraid of death, but I surely was. Not for myself but for the people that I *loved*. Callum's grip loosened, and the room fell silent. The smell of death was in the air…today, it decided to play its sick game. A shadow fell over the room creepily close to Callum's body.

I violently shook myself awake and ran into Callum's room as fast as my feet could take me. "Callum! Oh, God! Somebody help!" I shouted.

His father's footsteps were growing closer. I threw myself over the bed that had been stained red and opened the door. "Mom, Mom, Mom!" I yelled. I never called her "Mom" unless there was an emergency. When she ran up the stairs, I was locked out of the room…waiting for news. Dustin had stayed over. Thank God, and he comforted me like only he could.

"If I don't have Callum, I don't know what I'll do!" I shouted through my hysterical sobs.

Then, Dustin cradled and rocked me, and I thought back into my childhood. All the things I couldn't have done without Callum there. What I would give to make him feel better. Not just for a few years but for a century…many centuries. That was when it hit me… I am in love with my best friend… just like Dustin and Jaycelyn.

* * *

For a while, I was afraid to move. I didn't want to break anything. In my own home, I was also afraid to move, but that was because of Lee, always because of Lee. Callum's mom said I didn't have to worry about that there. I felt Callum plop down on the couch cushion beside me.

"Whatcha doing, Sandi?" Callum asked with excitement in his voice.

"Nothing. Just writing," I said in a boring voice.

He studied the book and glanced at me every few seconds. When he was finished, he stared at me.

"What is it, Callum?" I asked as he furrowed his brow, trying to imitate his father.

"Miss Jacobs…you seem to be holding a very interesting piece of literature," he said, trying to make his voice sound manlier.

"Callum, why are you in such a hurry to grow up?" his father said as he strode in through the front door. He smiled at Callum and turned to me. "Miss Jacobs," he said as he did a slight nod, straightened out his coat, and hung it on the black coat hanger.

"Honey, you're home!" Callum's mother cheerfully said with arms wide open as she walked toward her husband. Jaycelyn wobbled through the room and sat on the couch. "My gosh! You look like you're going to burst!" Callum's mother said.

"I know! I feel like it, too!" Jaycelyn replied.

They all engaged in conversation, except me. I would glance up and see Callum's father looking down on me. What was it that I'd done to him? Maybe it was because I looked strange. I'd been in the mental institution for some time. That may be why. Did he see me as a bad influence on Callum?

"Sandi…" a voice said.

My name was repeated in a crescendo, but I couldn't look because I had locked eyes with Callum's father. For the first time, he actually looked at me. Not through me, or past me, or down at me, but at me.

Callum shoved me into the arm of the couch, breaking my concentration. "What's the matter with you?" Callum said as he felt my forehead.

"Sandi," Jaycelyn said as she walked over to me. "You feeling all right?"

"Yeah. Sorry." I glanced at Callum's father. He caught me looking and furrowed his brow with confusion. "I just zoned out for a bit. That's all," I said with a slight smile. I could feel Callum's father's eyes on me, and my face felt hot.

"Miss Jacobs, if you aren't feeling well…" He shot me a glare and gave his son a soft look. "Maybe we should take you to see the *doctor*," he said with a dark tone in his voice.

"I-I…" I looked down at the floor, to where my book had fallen. I picked it up and continued writing. "I'm fine," I said in a cool voice.

His father threatened me in a way that only he could get away with. He knew everyone else wouldn't get the clue he had given me. The room filled with lively conversation from everyone, ***except me***. *Take me to the doctor he said… but I knew what kind of doctor he was talking about. Not the kind of doctor I wanted to see… I lost myself in that place… and they knew that… that's why they kept me there. Yet Callum's father was willing to send me back…* for that, I resented him.

Callum and I lay on the floor in his room, ignoring his bed that was right next to us. "Hey, Sandi?" Callum asked with a blank expression on his face. He pulled me close to him and held me there. I hugged him tightly and looked at him. His eyes seemed to roll back and he made jerky movements. He started coughing violently. Putting my hand on his face, I caressed it and stared at him. "C'mon, Callum. You can do it. You're stronger than this." He pulled me closer and put my head to his chest. His grip hurt, but I wanted him to be better. When he loosened his grip, I put my mouth to his and tried to give him as much air as he could take. He took a lot. He began coughing up blood, and he held my forearm. So he wouldn't choke, I drank the blood or spit it out quickly enough, so I could give him air before he choked again. I did this about five or six times. When he finally recovered, I slowly stood him up.

"Sandi," he whispered. He was struggling to catch his breath. I rubbed his back and stood quiet. He looked at my shirt. I had stains from blood soaking my shirt and making my skin feel moist. There was dried blood on my hands and in the corners of my mouth. He whispered, "Don't tell my parents about this… I don't want to be in the hospital forever" while he wiped blood from the corners of my mouth. His eyes were dancing with life and gratitude. I grabbed his hand and squeezed, I can't lose him, and I will do ***anything*** to help him. If this isn't a best friend for life, I don't know what is.

Later that night, Callum's mom had figured out what happened. I was worried and frightened. I didn't know what was going to happen. I turned over and looked at the clock. It was five in the morning, and I was afraid that I would have school today. Even though it was Friday and there was no point in going at the end of the week, Callum's father was more than ready to get rid of me. Not Jaycelyn. No, never her. She was a precious jewel here…his father loved Jaycelyn, always had no bother with calling her by her first name. I turned over and looked at the door. I could hear Callum's mother and father talking about us outside.

"Rohan-Kyle, please be nice. She was only helping him!" Lidianna yelled as he practically broke down my door. Then again, it was his house…so his door. I shut my eyes tightly and balled up under my comforter. Lidianna had her hand over her mouth as Rohan-Kyle walked in and glared at me. Before she could walk to the door, he slammed it shut and pulled a chair up to my bedside. I had only been here about a week and a half so far, and Callum's father seemed to be more than ready to send me back. I'd been released on May fifth, twelve days before Jaycelyn's birthday. Thank God, too. I was missing so much with the twins, missing so much with my family…he was not going to send me back. No one was ever going to send me back.

"Miss Jacobs," Rohan-Kyle said as he cleared his throat and also broke my concentration.

I put my petite hands over my eyes and turned my head to the left.

"Miss Jacobs, I hear you helped my boy today," he said as he glared at me.

I didn't move my hand from over my eyes, and I stayed completely still.

He patted the top of my head. "Good job, Miss Jacobs. Much appreciation," he said as he put the chair back and walked away.

I slid my fingers open to watch him exit the room. He gently closed the door behind him and walked briskly down the stairs.

Startled, I sat fully up on my bed at the sound of my door opening again. This time, it was Callum. I let out a sigh of relief and sunk back down into the bed. "Yes, Callum?" I asked.

"Sandi, there is a phone call for you…some woman on the phone," he replied worriedly.

"Oh?" I said as I slid out of bed and walked down the stairs.

"Sandi…a woman has called asking for you. She won't give me a name…just that it's urgent she spoke to you," Lidianna said as she held the phone out for me.

It wasn't cordless, so I had to stand at the coffee table and talk to her. I sat down on the bright orange couch and held my hand over the bottom part of the phone. My voice wasn't as loud at night, so I had to project my voice. "Hello?" I said in a raspy voice.

"Sandi?" the woman asked cautiously so as not to start speaking.

"Yes, this is she," I said unsurely. I never understood why adults said that, but it was the right thing to say. At first, I listened to her breathing and looked around the room at everyone watching me.

"You aren't alone, are you?" the woman stated.

"No," I answered dryly.

"Well, can you fix that?" the woman asked.

"Hmm… state your business please. It really is late, and I am exhausted," I answered dryer than before.

"Sandi. *È Sua madre… dell› Italia*," the woman said.

I was fully awake now and looked at Jaycelyn. My heart raced, and my face turned pale. I ran her sentence back over in my mind. *Sandi, it's your mother… from Italy.*

"Excuse me?!" I shouted into the phone. I had no problem projecting my voice now.

"Please calm down. I had to wait until you got away to explain to you!" the woman exclaimed.

"Please! Got away?! What do you mean 'got away'?!" I yelled.

Jaycelyn trotted over with a worried look. I put my hand up to stop her and walked around the table, so she couldn't hear the woman speaking on the phone.

"Sandi, please! Allow me to explain! All I need is an hour or two of your time," the woman exclaimed.

"I have no time for games, ma'am… I've been through enough already!" I yelled.

All I could do was yell and yell. Life was already confusing, and this was just absurd. "Is Jaycelyn with you?" the woman asked.

I glanced over at Jaycelyn with a worried look. She grabbed me by the shoulders.

"Sandi?" the woman said worryingly. *If she says Jaycelyn isn't my sister… if she says that this isn't my family…* Jaycelyn and I looked deeply into each other's eyes. It was as if I could see nothing of resemblance in her. "Jaycelyn is as related to you as I am… dear, please listen to me," the woman said.

"No, as long as Jaycelyn is to me who she should be… I don't need any other family," I replied.

"Please, Sandi… I don't know when I will see you again," she replied through slight sobs.

Ignoring her last comment, I answered dryly, "No. That is all I need to hear." and hung up the phone.

"Are you all right, Sandi? What happened?!" Jaycelyn asked.

I looked at her and smiled as I caressed her face. "I'm fine. It's nothing," I said with a blank expression on my face. I walked up the stairs and silently lay in bed. *Sandi, it's your mother… from Italy. What did she mean? I know for a fact that my parents are my actual parents… so what did she mean? And the fact that she said I had to get away before she could contact me… away from the mental institution or worse… away from my parents…?*

Chapter 14

ALL MY THINKING TIRED ME out more, and I felt myself drifting into a deep sleepless sleep. My ominous chimeras began to keep me sleep deprived all night. I kept dreaming of a lady. She had piercingly beautiful green eyes and thick, voluminous, deep cherry brown hair. She had a slightly bigger than thin figure with curves in all the right places. Her hair was naturally wavy, and her lips were petite and were perfectly aligned with her slim nose that stuck out to a very tiny round point. Her eyebrows were thick, arched, gorgeous, and slightly darker than her cherry brown hair. Short, black eyelashes, full of volume and complemented the eyes of a goddess. When she walked, people moved out of the way in awe and watched her every move. Women wanted to be her, and men wanted to be with her. She never failed to catch someone's eye. She never failed to impress from aura to toe and had an air to her that you just found yourself attracted to like moths to lights. When you would go home, even from interacting with her for five minutes, you would ring her personality out of your clothing. A gift from the gods indeed...if you believe in that kind of stuff. As for me, I don't know what I believe, except the feeling that I knew I needed to find her.

Abruptly, I woke up to what seemed to be the ethereal being of the woman standing beside my desk, touching my book, and caressing my book with her fingers. *What is she doing touching my book...better yet how did she get here? Maybe it was hers?* As if she could read my thoughts, she answered me. "I, too, once held this, my friend," she started as she strolled over with that elegant stride of hers. She sat down on the edge of my bed and wrapped her right arm around my shoulder. "It used to be of good value, but we always pass it down to the children." She paused and looked away from me with a somber look. "But I could never bear any children of my own…so I passed it down to you," she said as her face brightened up with cheer, and she shook my chin. Just like in my dream, I sat there in awe. She moved my hair out of my face and behind my ear. "From the moment, I saw you. I knew you'd been something special, Sandi. Oh, promise me you'll never give up hope," she said as she pressed her hands to her cheeks. She got up and twirled around in a straight line toward the door. Her white lace wedding dress flew in the wind and twirled with her. When she got to the door, she made a thump as her back hit the door. She looked at me and giggled. She had a beautiful, pearly white smile, with perfectly straight teeth.

I managed to scrape up a few words. "What's your name?" I asked.

She strode over, touching the floor so softly that she seemed to be hovering above it. She sits my chin lightly upon the knuckle of her first finger and tilted my head up to look at her gorgeous features of a face. "Why, it's Emiliana, young child," she started. She smiled at me and caressed each side of my jawline with two fingers from each hand until they met at the tip of my chin. "You look just like your mother… yes, yes, just like her." She paused and looked back at the door and then looked at me frantically. "Oh! I missed you all so much! Sandi… promise me you and Jaycelyn will come for a visit? It's been so long since I've seen you both," she said as she squeezed my cheeks lightly. She briskly walked toward the corner of the wall behind the door and near my desk. "WAIT!" I yelled frantically as I remembered a question I wanted to ask. She slowly turned around with a smirk on her face as if she'd been waiting on this the entire time.

"Yes?" she asked as she lightly performed a curtsey, waiting for her time of departure.

"Who are you?" I asked as I nervously was waiting for an answer. She knew how I meant to phrase the question and exactly what answer I wanted.

Slyly, she replied, "Emiliana Abbaticchio." She pointed at the book and caressed it one last time. "If you have any more questions, in here, you will find me." She twirled around happily and disappeared. "Good night and good morning," the air whispered quietly.

In complete awe, I looked at my book. I ran for the desk and grabbed the book and looked at it carefully. The book was so huge that it could take years to read. *She said I would find her in here… but where in here… where?* Before I opened the cover of the book, Jaycelyn and Dustin walked in.

"Sandi?" Jaycelyn said with a troubled tone.

"I'm here," I said, wondering why they had come.

"We heard a voice in here… it didn't sound like Lidianna," Dustin started. He looked around the room puzzled and then proceeded to stroll into the room and slightly drug Jaycelyn into the room by her wrist.

"She spoke very properly, had a melodic voice," Jaycelyn said as she turned to me. She tilted her head a bit and looked at me. "Hey, Sandi… how much of that book have you read?" she asked.

"Oh, I barely put a dent in it!" I said.

Jaycelyn giggled and hugged me. "Guess you want to start now huh?" she asked with a smile.

"Yes, please!" I said anxiously as I nodded.

"Come on, Dustin," Jaycelyn said as she exited the room.

He stood there looking at me before following her footsteps. When he finally made his feet move toward the door, I looked at him over my shoulder.

"Who is she, Dustin?"

He stopped and put his hand on the doorknob. He sighed and looked at me, hiding more than half of his face with the door. "Emiliana Abbaticchio… is your aunt. She's your godmother… from Italy," he said, as if he knew the expression on my face he said, "Yes. You have met her, and no, she is not dead." With those words, he walked out the door, closing it shut behind him.

My aunt? I never knew we had any other family! No one ever talks about them! How then did Dustin know?! Out of everybody, Dustin was the one who knew... how did he? I shook my head to scramble my thoughts. I sat down on my desk chair and turned on the lamp. I opened the book and slid my hands through the delicate pages. *I last left off with Serenity slamming her hand in the locker and then forgiving her boyfriend... ah ha! Found it. Today wouldn't just be a day of reading, it would be a day of searching... searching for answers I've wanted to know for so long...* I skimmed through the part I already read and flipped the page. I looked up at the ceiling and then closed my eyes, tilted my head back down to face the book, and put my finger on the paragraph I was about to read. *All right, Sandi, brace yourself.* With my eyes shut tight and spirit held high, I opened my eyes and began my adventure.

* * *

After that encounter with Josh, I spoke to no one for the rest of the day. When I got home, I was greeted by all my aunts and uncles and my grandparents. I was used to the house being filled with so many people, but today I felt claustrophobic.

"Carmen, can you do me a favor?" Nana asked.

"Okay. What is it, Ma?" she asked.

"Can you take the kids out? The house does get a bit cramped every once in a while, don't you think?" Nana asked.

"Why don't we all go out?!" my dad said as he walked through the door.

"Paulo, fifteen people going out?" Nana asked.

"That does seem a little absurd," my uncle Caddis said.

"Oh, Caddis! Come on. Why do you always have to be the party pooper?" my uncle Colt said.

I giggled. It was funny to hear them all talking at once. As if I interrupted their conversation, they looked at me. Nana smiled at me. "What are you laughing about, little girl?" she said sweetly as she looked at me over her shoulder.

I didn't realize she was doing the dishes by herself. "Oh, nothing. You all are just too funny!" I said as I walked over to help her out with the dishes.

My aunt Sherry walked over to help, and she smiled at me. It was so weird having to call someone who was younger than me aunt or uncle. Of course, I had respect for her, but I had to have a high level of respect since she was "the boss."

Nana removed herself from the kitchen and into the dining room with everyone else to plan out what we were going to do today. Aunt Sherry looked at me with a smile and slowly washed her dish. "What are you looking at me like that for?" I asked curiously as I laughed nervously.

"Nothing, kid." She winked at me with that statement and grinned.

"I was just wondering if you…" her voice trailed off, so I couldn't hear her sentence.

Then my uncle Collin, who was the same age as me, walked over and joined in on the fun. "Come on. Did you ask her already?!" he shouted.

"Shhh! Or they'll hear you!" she scolded. She had the right to do that since he was her brother. If she scolded me, however, I think I'd have a problem… I mean, I know she was my aunt and all, but still, she was younger than me.

"Okay. So what is it that you wanted to say?" I asked. I would've ended my sentence with Aunt Sherry, but heaven knew we both hated that.

"Well…" She looked back to see if anyone was listening. "There's this house party near the outskirts of tow—"

"WHAT?!" I exclaimed in shock.

"Shhhhh!" she scolded.

I rolled my eyes and looked at her. I brought my voice to a whisper, "You know we aren't supposed to go outside of town, *AUNT* Sherry." I put as much emphasis on "aunt" as I could. She knew she was supposed to be a good influence, and by saying Aunt, I hoped I was reminding her of that.

"Well, *niece*," she started as she titled her head down and hissed, "you'll be happy to know that it is NEAR the outskirts, not ON but NEAR."

"Well, what's an sophmore doing at a house party anyway?" I asked.

"I'd say the same for you!"

"Aha! But I'm almost done with high school," I replied slyly.

"Which is exactly why you're going, smart ass," she whispered as she pinched my arm.

I laughed a bit at the thought of me going out. Then again, I do need to get out. I've had a lot on my mind lately. "Fine. We'll go," I said with a slight grin.

Aunt Sherry and Uncle Collin high fived each other and ran toward the stairs.

"Oh, Serenity," Aunt Sherry whispered.

"Yes?" I replied.

"Be ready to leave at…" She paused and looked around with a devilish grin. "Ten." She hissed in a whisper.

"What?!" I said and looked toward the stairs, but by the time I turned my head, they were both gone.

My family had such a hard time figuring out what to do that we ended up doing nothing all day. It was nine o'clock, and Aunt Sherry and I were in the bathroom getting ready. "Should I wear a red dress?" she asked.

I looked at her as she held the dress up to her body and smiled. "Hmm… I don't think so. Unlike me, you've got the red hair from Nana. You should spice it up," I replied.

"Sooo black?" she asked.

"No… that's not what I meant," I said as I laughed. I went over to the armoire in the bathroom and opened the doors wide. "Look at all these selections. I'm sure you can find something!"

"Sooo help me niece!" she said as she giggled. I looked to the back of the armoire to find a beautiful green dress.

"Oh, my gosh! This would look extravagant on you!" I said as I pulled the dress from the hanger and showed it to her.

She gasped and held it up to her in the mirror. The dress was strapless with a heart shape at the top for the top of breasts. Right where the underwire of a woman's bra would be, the shape ended and a shiny, silky, lime green ribbon covered the ending of the shape and around the back. It didn't tie in the back in a pretty bow; instead, it overlapped until there was no more ribbon left. The shape was covered in a first layer of lime green sparkles that were a tint darker than the ribbon. Then a small layer of hunter green and a color two shades darker than lime green were mixed together and sprinkled neatly across the first layer.

Then, the dress itself went past the knee and fell to a quarter of the calves. The first layer of the dress was a light lime-green silk that stopped about two inches below the knees. Then, sheer silk overlapped the first layer of the dress and took on its color and blended in with the dress. Except the silk had a diagonal pattern of leaves that got thicker and looked like feathers as they started from the left-most center of the dress and then spread out horizontally across it. They were a beautiful hunter green and spread out all the way down and stopped a quarter of the way before the silk ended. At this quarter of the dress, the shape looked like a tad deeper aqua blue and looked like small misshapen cylinders and started at the middle of the last quarter of the silk and did the same pattern. Except they went the opposite direction. They went from the left and proceeded to move out horizontally to the right. She shot me a strange look, I always found myself lost in small details.

She admired the dress and put it on. It fit perfectly and fell beautifully. It complemented her skin and her hair, gave it a little splash of color and spice. I helped her brush her hair out to a spider silk feel. Her hair ended at the back of her bra, the part you hook together. She put it up in a ponytail and slightly pulled the hair. It looked thick and healthy and voluminous, the way hair should look for an African-American woman. She pushed her bang behind her ear to perform her trick. She wet her hairbrush slightly and handed it to me. I brushed her hair with it not enough to soak it but to make it look like dew on grass early in the morning. Then gently, I slid the hair out of the ponytail that went to the nape of her neck, so I could brush most of the hair, except the top. Within seconds, the hair turned into wavy silk. She took her bang to the brush and brushed it back. I put a pin in it and pulled it out, so it would look like a bump. It was a very long bang, and the ends of it stopped at the middle of her head and blended in with that same wavy silk look. *She looks amazing, and I still haven't gotten dressed yet!* I giggled at the thought. "You look amazing, Aunt Sherry," I said caringly, wishing I looked half as good as her.

"Thank you, niece." She clasped her hands together and turned to the right to look at me. She smiled as the dress twirled in the wind. I knew she felt like a princess. "Now you," she said as she eyed me up and down and smiled.

My dress was a pale pink silk that fell a tad bit after my mid-thigh and was covered in one more layer of silk. Then, two layers of light-pale pink lace with a diverse design of flowers on it. The first layer was long and came to the length of the silk, and the second layer came to the bikini line. The dress was strapless and had a normal shape, instead of something fancy. Black lace covered a little past where the middle of a woman's bra would go and had a rose and leaf-vine pattern and ended where the hip bone actually started. Around it was a beautiful, thick, black, ribbon tied into a bow on the right side of the dress. The different layers gave it a thick, full, beautiful, choppy, layered look.

"Yes, yes, yes!" Aunt Sherry said in awe.

"I hate pink…are you sure?" I replied.

"Of course, I am! Now come here!" she said as she yanked me over to the sink. She put a robe over my dress and tied it tight so none of the dress was exposed. She leaned my hair into the sink and ran the water. "Okay! I think that's enough water!" I yelled over the noisy faucet. She squeezed my hair out and damped it dry with a towel. It ended up getting nappy, so she brushed it to a thick silk. Mine would have taken too long to be spider silk. It curled up and luckily fell to nice, bouncy, separate curls. She grabbed a pink ribbon and tied it at the middle of my hair into a beautiful bow. She pulled my hair and then fixed my bang to swipe sexily over my left eye and tucked behind my ear.

"Perfect!" she said as she glossed my lips. There was a knock on the door right before she took off my robe. "Who is it?" Aunt Sherry said anxiously.

"Girls, are you ready to go?" Collin asked.

We slowly opened the door, and Collin looked at us.

"Okay. So you're wearing a robe?" he joked.

Sherry with one quick swipe ripped the robed off me and made sure my hair still looked nice. I glossed her lips and then put my arm through hers and Collin's as we walked down the old, narrow stairs together and out the door. Sherry hopped in Nana's van, and away we drove for what seemed to be an hour, to the outskirts of Little Compton, Rhode Island. We drove for about thirty minutes to a big cabin. When we entered, we were invited on a tour by two Caucasian women. They were twins. Both had blond, naturally tight curly hair, green eyes, and stood about 5'2". They both wore long black ballroom dresses that were strapless but had a long sleeve crop top of lace over it. Their lips were stained a deep red from the wine they were drinking, which they held in hand, giving the illusion of makeup. We stopped back at the main room, and *somewhat* to my surprise, there was Veronica and Josh, making out in front of everybody.

"Seren—" Sherry and Collin both said at the same time.

I put up my hand and replied, "It's fine. Let's stay." Then, I put on a smile and locked arms with Sherry and Collin as we proceed to admire the house. That, for sure, was the last time I speak to either one of them.

We walked down the stairs and into the center of the floor when a young man three years older than me and five years older than Sherry stopped us. "May I have this dance, beautiful?" he asked Sherry.

"Why certainly you may," she replied elegantly.

He was African American and Indian. He had black hair and brown eyes. His eyes were slightly wide and opened up beautifully. He had a chiseled jaw and slightly bigger than average lips. His hair was smooth and laid out on top of his head. His hands were huge and muscular like his body, and his mustache was black and slightly thick but not too thick. He was a handsome young man. He looked at me as I admired him. *I want him. I need him... I've never wanted a man like this before. Oh, no... what about Josh? NO. Forget Josh. You're a single woman. I've got all of my time to myself.* He bowed to Sherry and then held his hand out to me. I curtseyed gracefully and glided across the floor, one hand over his neck, the other slightly in the air, hand and hand with him. We performed a mid-twirl to the right and then to the left and then step back and forth and twirl to the left. Our foreheads touched the entire time, and we were both grinning from ear to ear. *His smile is amazing. His teeth were so clean and white, even though his breath smelled a tad of wine.*

"You must be the older sister," he said in a melodic tone. His voice made me melt, and I could feel our bodies inching closer and closer together. "Oh, no! That fair maiden there is my aunt Sherry and that devilish fellow with her now is my uncle Collin!" I said in a cheery voice.

"And who might this beautiful maiden that I've found myself holding close be?" he said as he used his left arm wrapped around my waist to squeeze me closer.

"I'm Serenity Arredono. Glad you could meet some of my crazy family," I said with a smile.

"I'd love to get to know them more." He touched my chin and rested it on his first finger and caressed it with his thumb. He slightly brushed his thumb down my bottom lip and moved in to kiss me. *My God! He's so intimate... but he moves so slow... just kiss me already!* Unfortunately, to interrupt my moment, Josh spotted me and ended up making a huge scene with Veronica. I didn't care, as if nothing had gone on he continued to inch closer and closer. Then, I felt someone yank my arm and pull me away, but the new guy grabbed my hand.

"What are you doing?!" Josh exclaimed.

The whole party stopped and watched the scene.

"We don't go out anymore!" I said as I pulled away from him. "I gave you the best years of my life. You can't leave me!" he exclaimed.

"Oh, please, I don't have time for you! One, we're seventeen, you've got way more life! Why waste my time with a guy who cheats on me with my supposed to be best friend?! Yeah, sorry, I don't need the stress!" I yelled as I turned away.

"I wasn't cheating. I was exploring my options!" he yelled.

"Come on, you guys. Let's go somewhere else," the new guy said. He had Sherry on his right arm and me on his left, hooking arms with Collin.

"Yeah! I don't need you! You were so five minutes ago!" he yelled with tears stinging his eyes.

"Oh! You're so five hours ago, babe! Have a nice life!" I said as we walked toward the door. The twins we met from before dumped two whole bottles of wine on Josh and kicked him in the you-know-what. As we got into the car, I sat in the back with Sherry and the new guy. He began flirting with her, and it made me nervous and a bit jealous.

"Hey! What's your name?" I said to break their flirty behavior.

Instead of him answering, he kissed Sherry and laughed.

"Monte Hawthorne," Sherry said as she bit her whole bottom lip and laughed.

Despite the behavior being displayed, I knew that Serenity Hawthorne was the name I was bound to have. *I just know it...*

Once Aunt Sherry turned eighteen, even though I was still older than her, she had the authority, and I had no choice but to call her Aunt Sherry. She got together with Monte for a night, and when Sherry ended up finding out she was pregnant with a baby girl named Chloe, he disappeared for the whole nine months and then some. He and I kept in contact a bit but not enough to really exchange much information. It was always when he ran into me on the street as I was walking home. He'd offer me a ride, but I always refused. During the time that Aunt Sherry was pregnant, he had gone and slept with my Aunt Caddy and another woman. The woman he was messing around with was Brook Stark, who was married, and she had a daughter named Margaret. She had Margaret after Monte promised to stop sleeping around and Aunt Sherry had her second kid. This time, she had a boy named Ethan. After Ethan grew up to be a young adult, Margaret was a teenager. He had broken his promise to her once again, but he still wasn't finished. His eyes were set on one thing only. *Me.* What a pig, I thought, trying to convince myself I was above his charm.

He showed up at my parents' doorstep, asking for me. He slowly strolled inside and took me upstairs into my room to talk. He kissed me deeply, and I kissed him back. *Oh, how tender he is with every kiss.* It made my heart melt, and my body loosened up in his arms. I finally pulled away abruptly, ruining the moment, and looked at him. "Monte, this isn't right. I'm sorry, but I just can't do this," I said with a sigh.

"I've got commitment issues. It's not because I like sleeping with different women," he replied.

"Yes, Monte, it is. You just use that one as an excuse."

"I'd be faithful to you… I will change my ways."

"Monte," I sighed as I looked at myself in the mirror. "You're my auntie's boyfriend… I can't do tha—"

He briskly walked over to me and moved my hair aside as he kissed my neck. "Who told you that?"

"She did Monte!" I said as I banged my hand on the dresser I had been latched to.

"No, I'm not. I'm not committed to her at all," he said as he wrapped his arms around my waist from behind. "Having kids with someone doesn't mean you're married."

"No, Monte, this is w-wrong," I said as I turned to face him.

He pushed me back onto the dresser with his body pressing against mine.

"Fine," he said and kissed me. He smiled slightly and then gave me a locket. "I knew, from the first time I saw you, that you are the one I'm destined to marry." He kissed me again, deep and rough. "So I'll wait."

"Oh, yeah? What's your definition of *waiting*?" I asked warily from thinking so much.

"I'll go back to your Aunt Sherry's house and stay there. You come and get me when you're ready."

"Monte… that's not waiting. That's wrong."

"So is keeping your future husband unhappy."

"I don't even go over there anymore! That'd look weird!" I exclaimed in shock.

"Oh, but you don't deny that I'd be your future husband, did you?" he asked slyly.

I couldn't help myself at all. I wanted him so bad, and he knew it. I moved in and kissed him, but this time, it was slow and passionate. He returned the favor, and within minutes, I found myself sprawled across the bed on my back. I got up and moved away as quickly as I could, but he and my body wouldn't let me move as fast as I wanted to. He got up and walked to the door. I walked him downstairs and outside.

"I'll be waiting," he said as he stood on the porch.

"You do that," I said as I slammed the door shut behind me.

Three weeks passed, and I haven't heard or seen any sign of Monte around. *What the hell are you thinking, Serenity? Aunt Sherry will never forgive you. Wait… like he said, he isn't in a commitment with her. I mean, it's pretty obvious he isn't. No. Shut up, Serenity, and stop thinking like this, why am I thinking like this anyway? He's a man with commitment issues, remember? He can't stick to one person… then again, he said he was waiting on me… hmm.* Just then, in the middle of my thinking, the house phone rang.

"Hello?" I said, waiting for a response.

"Hi, love! It's Aunt Sherry," she said. I could feel the cheer in her voice all the way over here, which was pretty far considering that she lived near the outskirts of the city.

"Hi! Is there something I can do for you?" I said with as much cheer as I could bring to the conversation, which wasn't much.

"I need to come see you, so I can interview you and give a report for the police department. It's a new segment we're doing about journaling. If you don't mind, can I come today?" she said.

"Yes, of cour— NO!" I said, tripping over my words.

"Huh?" I could feel her confusion over the phone.

"What I mean is I'll come to you! It's been a long time, and I haven't seen the kids in a while, too!" I lied. I knew then that I'd made up my mind. I was going over there to become Serenity Hawthorne… the *only* Hawthorne in town.

When I arrived, everyone greeted me with warmth and love. Everyone except Monte, who was in the kitchen, hiding behind his newspaper, drinking his coffee. Aunt Sherry sat me down in a chair, and I had a view into the kitchen of Monte sitting at the table, eyeing me every now and then. Once my interview was done, we talked while she typed. "Monte and I are thinking of having another child," she said with a wide smile on her face.

"Oh! Is that so?"

"Yup!" she said with excitement. Is she stupid? I thought.

Monte slid down his newspaper, so I could see his eyes, and he watched the expression on my face.

"Umm… so you both are thinking about this?" I asked.

"Well, I'm still trying to get Monte in on it," she said as she rested her chin on her folded fist and concentrated on the computer screen. She is stupid, I confirmed.

He looked at me and nodded. "Umm… can I have a drink?" I asked, trying to excuse myself from the uncomfortable conversation.

"Yes, of course," she looked at me and smiled slightly. "Do you still remember where everything is, or do I need to help you?" she joked.

"Very funny, Aunt Sherry. I can get it myself," I said as I walked toward the kitchen.

"If you need anything else, ask your uncle Monte to help you," she said.

I stopped in my tracks, and Monte looked at me. I eyed him sharply, as if I was making incisions in his skin and mumbled, "Don't call him that."

He looked at me and smiled. "Looks like you've made up your mind." He shot me a devilish grin.

"Looks like I have," I replied as I leaned against the counter and sipped on my water.

Chapter 15

He ushered me away from the sight of the door to sit down. "I want to hear you say it, Serenity," he said as he looked into my eyes.

"Say what, Monte?" I asked.

"No, no, no! Show your uncle some respect, little girl!" he said as he moved closer.

"Shut up! You're not my uncle. You're my *husband*," I replied angrily.

"Atta, girl." He came in closer. "Why don't you say we get outta here?" he asked.

"That'll look weird… we can't both leave at the same time," I said nervously.

"Sure, we can. Watch this," he said as he got up and walked to the doorway. "Babe?" he said.

"Yes, honey?" Aunt Sherry replied. "Serenity and I are going to catch a movie. You wanna come join us?"

"No, that's okay. I've got a lot of work to do here. Can the kids go?" she asked.

"Sure they can!" he said as we all hurried for the door.

When we got there, cousin Chloe and Ethan went to see a different movie and later hung out with their friends. Monte and I went back to my place. Luckily, no one was home. We got straight down to what we seemed to be waiting for ever since that party about twenty-two years ago. We lay in bed all night looking at each other. He caressed my face and kissed me deeply. I hugged him and buried my face inside his neck. "No… don't hide from me… look at me," he said sweetly. He held my chin on his finger and tears stung my eyes. "What's wrong?" he asked sympathetically.

"You better not leave me… please don't, Monte."

He wrapped his arms around me and held me close. "I would never leave you." That was the last thing I heard him say because I fell asleep shortly after that, feeling warm and safe in his arms. As close as I was, excuse me as close as I should have been to menopause, I didn't think I would get pregnant, but there I was three weeks later with my Aunt Sherry holding her breath waiting for the results.

"Was it a fluke? If it's a bad test, I can go buy another one," she said anxiously.

I'd already sent her back out six times to get different brands. They all came out the same, *positive.* Aunt Sherry could hear me in the bathroom banging my head on the counter. She slowly walked in the bathroom and looked at me. "Serenity… it's okay." She said as she put her hand on my forehead. As if on time, Monte walked in unlocking the door with his key. *Shit.*

"Babe? Are you in here?" he called out as he walked up the stairs.

"In here!" Aunt Sherry called out. *Be careful, Monte.*

"Hey! I need to ta—" Aunt Sherry's presence interrupted his sentence. She hugged him and kissed him on the cheek. She strung herself on his arm and watched as Monte studied me and then the six different tests. He chuckled. "Who's the lucky guy?" he joked.

"That's not funny, honey!" Aunt Sherry said as she hit his chest.

"Ouch, someone is packing some muscle now!" he said.

"Exactly so you better be home in time for dinner or you're getting it," she said as she looked at her watch. She came over hugged and then kissed me on the forehead. "Sorry, Serenity. I've gotta run! Catch you later!" she said as she ran out the door.

I gave Monte an evil look as he walked away from the doorframe and into the bathroom. "Babe, what did I do?" he asked as he hugged me.

"I don't ever want to see that again… it makes me sick," I replied.

"Mmm…you're so demanding. How do you suppose I fix that problem?" he asked sarcastically.

"Monte, that isn't funny."

"Babe," he replied.

"Huh?" I asked, confused.

"From now on, I want you to call me 'babe' or 'honey' or 'darling.' Something sweet and loving, like a married couple would do," he said as he walked around in a circle, making fancy hand motions in the air.

"I don't do that because we aren't in any kind of relationship together. I'm not like the rest of them."

"Yesss," he hissed, "I know that for a fact, which is why I'm going to make you," he said cheerfully. "But just a slight," he cleared his throat and stopped walking around. He stood me up and held my hands. "Major difference." He got down on one knee and pulled out an emerald ring from his pocket. It was beautiful. There was a small emerald inside surrounded by the shape of a knight's shield except the sides curved at the top and slightly underneath to come out to a point on all four corners. The middle and the top and bottom was a misshapen square that curved upward from the bottom and to a dull point on each corner and a rounded top shape. Inside the shape were diamonds, enough to fill the shape. Then, the band that connected to the center of the shape where the emerald was had a skinny ring part first. It had diamonds placed neatly next to each other, covering every inch of the circle. Then leaving a small misshapen rhombus shape slit a thicker sliver ring was at the top and one identical at the bottom with slits on the left and right sides. They both connected behind the corners of the misshaped shield.

"Marry me, Serenity," he stated.

I laughed and threw my head back. "Are you asking me or telling me?" I said as he put the ring on my finger.

"Neither. I'm making you," he said as he laughed and hugged me.

"In that case, if I had a choice, I'd say, 'Hell yes.'"

He kissed me and then felt my stomach. "We've got quite the future ahead of us," he said as he touched his forehead with mine.

"Yes, we do," I replied cheerfully. *Finally, after twenty-two years of waiting, Monte Hawthorne is finally mine.*

As if he read my thoughts, he said, "I was yours from the moment our eyes met."

I giggled and we walked downstairs to start making wedding arrangements.

We got married a month later, and everyone was invited including my aunt Caddy, but we all kept Aunt Sherry out of the loop. Until she showed up at the reception. We were about to leave the house and into the limousine to go on our honeymoon. Aunt Sherry busted through the crowd to make a scene. "I CAN'T BELIEVE YOU!" she yelled through the window at me. "I trusted you with my life, Serenity, and this is the thanks I get?!" she scolded.

"Aunt Sherry, I—"

"She has nothing to apologize for, and you have nothing to be upset about. I have nor have I any commitment to you, Sherry. You know that," he said, interrupting my sentence. He ushered for the driver to drive off, and that was the last I ever heard from Aunt Sherry. Our family tried to explain to her that he was never hers to begin with if he was sleeping around with other people, even though I was in the wrong. Nevertheless, she still resented him… but mostly *me.*

A couple of days after baby Phoebe was born, my uncle Coyle, his son Vivek, and his wife Yee, who was from China, asked to see the baby. We drove near the outskirts of town to their house, and to our surprise, Aunt Sherry was there. Not only her but her two kids as well, the entire family seemed to hate me. When she came over to speak, she only spoke to Monte and clung to his arm, believing that he was still one to stray. She was pissed when she found out me and Monte were expecting another little girl named Cambree five years later. Still she attempted to try to break us up, even though we still stuck together. When I was pregnant with triplets five years later at forty-six, the most stressful time of my life, she convinced my daughter that her father was cheating. She told me that she saw him and the whole shebang. I believed it for eight months until I finally broke down and told Monte. He denied all accusations, and seeing that she was breaking her mother's heart, Phoebe told me what Aunt Sherry had done. Monte and I lived happily together from there on out.

My mother and father are an adorable couple… I hope I have someone like that. "Cambree, Cambree, Cambree!" my younger sister Chantelle yelled.

"What is it, Chantelle?!" I said with worry.

Then, my younger brothers Victor and Jericho came rushing up the stairs. I was already twenty-five and still had no one interested in me. My younger brother got engaged to a horse racing champion named Star and had a little boy named Rodney McCauley. He took his mother's last name since they weren't married yet. My brother was younger than me and already had a love life. I closed my diary my mother gave me for a hot second to look at the sun. It was already setting, and I had only been out for thirty minutes. My older cousins, Colt and Catrina, had me waiting outside the supermarket. They were my Aunt Caddy's children, and they stuck together like a pack of wolves. Then as if God had answered prayers that I never prayed, there was Eben Canales. My old childhood friend and next-door neighbor. We talked, we walked a bit, and when I finally made my way back around to the supermarket, the twins wanted to know everything that happened.

My love story is short and brief. I am not one for many details about the past. I lived a good and spoiled childhood with my cousins and my immediate family. Soon enough, it was my turn to start a family and, boy, was I glad. My older sister already had two twin boys named William and Logan Smith. She was already done having children, even though my parents begged for more grandchildren. Our first year Eben and I had Vicita Canales. Then, we waited a good twelve years and then had a child every year. There was Joey, Casandra, who died as a toddler, Rob, Lisa, Cassie. Once Eben died, I went on a mad craze and adopted Eben, Thoron and Catrina Hawthorne when their parents passed.

Like my mother said, her story was quick and brief. She didn't really have time for a diary. She was highly appreciative but handed it down to me to keep watch. I learned at an early age that we are a huge family with many intertwined problems. My aunt-cousin Catrina was taken away for five years and grotesquely abused. It took a mighty huge toll on her, and I don't blame her. She never stayed at home though. Sometimes people heckled her and said she wanted it to happen, but we all banded together as a family to help each other out. My aunt Sherry and my grandma Serenity made up with joyful tears, but she still resented my grandma. Unfortunately, all this making up had been done after Aunt Sherry woke from her coma, so maybe they both were feeling sorry for each other. Either way, it was to bring family back together again, and it worked most of the time.

"Vicita Hawthorne, you're going to be late to school!" Mother shouted up the stairs. We all still lived in that white Victorian home with three stories and a black roof. I always went to stay in the guest house that was built when Aunt Phoebe and her husband used to stay here.

Everyone lived in this same house with their aunts and uncles and sisters and nieces and nephews. Except those few that moved out to start an adventure. I was going to be that one to start an adventure and move out. I just hadn't mentioned it to my parents yet or my grandma. Right now, I just had to focus on the seventh grade, and it was pretty easy.

"Vicita, let's go, or you'll be late!" Mother shouted angrily. She was a very kind and loving woman, but no one should make her angry. I slumped down the stairs and ran down when I saw Grandpa.

"Grandpa!" I screamed as I flew down the stairs.

"Hey, kiddo!" he said as he caught me and patted me on the head.

My mother eyed me angrily.

"You better get to going now. Mommy looks kind of angry," he said as he kissed me on the forehead.

I headed out the door with my mother and sat quietly in the car.

"You're awfully quiet today, Vicita," Mother said as she looked at me, using the rearview mirror.

"Why is that?" she asked.

"Because," I started but hesitated to finish my sentence. "Because I'm going to move out, Mom. For sure." I finished.

She stopped the car and looked at me in shock.

Chapter 16

When I was twenty-five, that's exactly what I did. Right after my fifth trip to France, I ran into a guy who was twenty-nine outside of the movie theater. His name he was christened with at birth was Cody McCauley. We had a small wedding at a courthouse, and to our surprise found out that he and his sister Star McCauley were in a way related to us. My uncle William Smith had gotten with their mother while they were teenagers and she had a bunch of children. They stayed together but never got married and he wasn't their father, so it was okay. He laid me down and caressed my body with his hands, softly and slowly. Nine months later, we were blessed with our first baby boy, and we named him Ezra. It really was a miracle since I wasn't supposed to be able to have children. The year after that, I had Evangelista. Then the next year, I had Sereniva. They were all so smart and were a tight pack. They made plans for the future and always sat around talking about what their lives would be like once they grew up.

Five years later, I had Minerva, and she was one of the few single kids I had. The next year I had Oliver and Audrey who were both twins. Oliver, Minerva, and Evangelista had red hair like my mother, and Ezra, Sereniva, and Audrey had black hair like mine. I had a child every year after that, and my son Lee McCauley died after childbirth, and for the nine months that I was pregnant with Shon, I mourned over Lee, the son I barely had. After having Shon, things got better. I had another pair of red-headed twins, two boys named Kasey and Cecil. Then I had Cody Jr, Cody the III, and then two twins with black hair, Gus and

Doyle McCauley.

During my pregnancy with Cody the III, Cody cheated on me with another woman and had a girl named Tonite Sowers, born the same day as him. The woman was his daughter-in-law since Shon married Beverly who was this floozy's her sister. After I had found out, we divorced, but we all continued to sleep under the same roof, and it got crowded. I wanted her out, but he wouldn't let her leave. We got remarried, and he neglected her for the longest time, and it made me extremely happy. When my two boys Gus and Doyle turned five, it was the happiest moment of my life. On Halloween, the kids and I carved pumpkins and set them up neatly outside the house and lit them. The kids went trick or treating like a swarm of flies and came back to the house to sit in front of the fire and roast marshmallows. That night, I died at 10:45 p.m., and that same night Cody married his other woman and enjoyed their night together. My diary was sent to go to my oldest children and Minerva, who had moved out like her brother and sisters years ago, came to my house and received the journal.

When my mom died, the neighborhood mourned for two days. I finished her last few sentences of her journal entry to reflect the audacity my father had.There was no funeral to say goodbye. I, along with my brother Ezra, who married a red-headed woman named Safari, and my two sisters Evangelista and Sereniva moved out to start our own lives. We all lived in the same house for a while. I married a black man with gorgeous, soft, brown hair. Sereniva married a dirty blond-headed white man named Moran Mees, and Evangelista married a slender, sleek, black-haired white man named Allen Rockwell. Evangelista and I hadn't had children yet, but Sereniva had gotten pregnant first and like our contest said we had to move out. She forcibly pushed us out without knowing if we'd find somewhere or not, but we did, and we settled down and never really talked after that. She had Darlene, Logan, and Owen Mees by birth and adopted an African American girl named Maute and a boy named Ronald.

Evangelista being married four years still didn't have any children, but they were planning on it. As for me, I wasn't planning on it at all. I had been married for one year and living in this huge house made me and Benito Pesano, my husband, feel lonely. We didn't really talk much, and the only time we really made contact was when we'd sleep in the same bed, and sometimes that wasn't even the case. Until one night after Benito and I went out and got hired for the jobs we wanted. I was reading a book to try to better my speaking skills since I moved into the political career. After my first miscarriage, things got pretty lonely. I lost my baby boy Warren Pesano, and I wouldn't feel the same after that. My little brother Oliver had a boy named Scott McCauley, and although I was happy for him, it did make me sad. That night, Benito came to me and told me he felt lonely. It was a mutual feeling, and that was the first time we had sex in a whole year.

Now I'm pregnant and excited. Although I didn't want to, I had to take maternity leave from my job the first few weeks after I had my baby. I planned to throw a Thanksgiving party and get the family back together again or as much of the family as I could fit into the house, which was quite a lot.

"Honey?" Benito said curiously.

"Yes, Benito?" I replied.

"What are you doing exactly?" he asked.

"Oh, well, I'm going to throw a Thanksgiving party and invite the family."

"Did you make a list yet?"

"Yes, I couldn't possibly keep up with everyone if I didn't make a list," I said with a sour expression on my face.

"Hmm… something wrong, dear?"

* * *

"Sandi!" someone shouted from downstairs. I had fallen asleep in front of my desk. I woke up with alarm; I knew we rarely had those days where an unfamiliar voice would actually enter the house, let alone even show up to our doorstep. I slowly got up, holding my book close to my heart and guarding it with both my arms. I sat it in the middle of my desk and pushed in the chair all the way, so if it fell, the chair would catch it. I slowly walked into the hallway and was about to reach the stairs when I felt an eerie breeze. The hair on the back of my neck stood up, I slowly turned around and gazed into the room. I was transfixed by the tall, brooding figure of a man, a shadow of a man. It whisked its way past my bed and toward the closet. I ran back to the room and turned on my table lamp. No one was there. I searched the closet, underneath my bed and desk, no human life except me. I felt daft and took a minute to breathe. For some reason, I felt a sense of foreboding engulf the room as I sat in it. *Breathe, Sandi, breathe... you're all right.* I slowly walked out of the room, leaving my lamp on, hoping it would give me some peace of mind.

I slowly walked downstairs, letting my hand glide gently down the railing.

"Yes?" I answered softly. I saw a woman with an hour-glass figure, with long, wavy, honey blonde hair. She put her hands on her hips as she turned around slowly, like a carousel, to face me. Her lips were a voluptuous rosy pink, and her eyes the deepest, emerald green ever. As if God handpicked crystals of the finest quality to be her eyes. She was a light-skinned African American goddess; the angels from heaven would come to her funeral personally. She stretched her arm out to me. I went for a handshake, but she pulled me in for a hug. Her breasts were like two beautiful cumulus clouds... and they were killing me.

"Oh, come on now, Sandra. You are going to suffocate her," Lidianna said as she chuckled. She was right. I couldn't breathe! I put my hand firmly on her stomach. I felt life, so I softened and moved away. She only had a small baby bump in the tight, skimpy, black outfit she was wearing. It was a one piece, leather like shirt that oddly enough reminded me of a bathing suit... *maybe that was the point. Was the baby suffocating, too? Ha!* I chuckled at myself. "Nice to meet you, miss. I'm Sandi," I said. "Oh, I know who you are... *I just had* to meet you," she said with a smile. "Is Sandi short for something? Like Sandra… is your name Sandra, too?" she said cheerfully.

I giggled. "No, ma'am. It's ju—"

"Call me Sandra, dear. Go on."

"No… Sa… Miss Sandra… it's just Sandi," I replied.

"Well, you've got a nickname Sandi?"

I could hear that southern drawl. It was attractive yet annoying… ah. *Eureka*, it's *annoyingly* attractive. "Umm… no? You could give me one, though?" I replied. I found her odd. Just odd.

Then, her husband walked downstairs. "Rok."

Rok? Who is that?

"Yeah, having trouble?" Rohan-Kyle answered. "Yes, the house is so big I can't find the bathroom!" he replied in distress. "Sandi, would you show him the way please?" Rohan-Kyle asked.

I nodded. *Great, another man in the house.*

"So you will be staying with us then, won't you?" Lidianna asked.

"Yes, we're scaring the kids a little. They think we are just driving into the middle of the wilderness," she said as she chuckled.

Then, their conversation became a distant buzzing noise.

"So… how old are you, Sandi?" the man asked.

"Eight," I said cheerfully as I exited the staircase.

"Oh, God…" I turned sharply to face the man.

"What?" I said fearfully.

"Our son is going to have you runnin' 'round the house like a chicken with yer head cut off!" he said joyfully.

We laughed.

"The bathroom is that way," I said as I pointed.

He stood in the doorway and shot me a smile. "Thanks, pumpkin."

I turned on the balls of my feet. *Pumpkin…* I thought to myself. I felt like family… I've never had a family.

Lidianna sent us upstairs to bed while the guests got situated. I lay down, peacefully.

"Sandi… are you asleep yet?" Callum asked.

I sighed. "Nope, just relaxing as always. Need something?"

"Yes."

Before I knew it, he was on my bed lying next to me. We looked up at the glow stars on the ceiling. "Kennith says he a crush on you… and that you are gonna get married… and move far away… I hate him," he said bitterly.

I turned over, onto my right side, and looked at him. "Callum. That's your favorite cousin. Don't say that. Just calm down," I replied as I patted his shoulder.

"Not if he's going to take my best friend away… he can't have you… no one can."

"But…"

"No. No. No."

"Callum!"

"Sandi!"

"But, Callu—"

"No, Sandi! No ifs, ands, or buts about it," he said sternly.

It scared me, how much he could be like his father. We sat in silence for a moment. Then, I sighed loudly. "Callum, if no one can have me… I'll be lonely… and lonely don't feel so good."

He *clasped* my hand. I could feel him gazing into my soul. He made my soul feel beautiful. "No, you won't, Sandi. You've got me. I'll be there with you… actually here with you." Then, he moved in close and put his forehead to mine. I could practically taste his breath. I hugged him tight. *I'm too young to love… I'm too young.* Therefore, I've been pushing it away. *Ever since.*

The next time I looked up at the clock, it was five in the morning, and I was in a daze. Why? Simply for no reason, I guess. I should have been wondering why I was up so early, or where Callum was. I slowly sat up, everything was spinning. Just when I thought nothing could get worse, I looked at my desk and my book, *my book* was gone. "NO!" I screamed as I snapped out of my daze and scrambled out of bed. "Where is it? Where is it?!" I said, progressively rising in volume.

Callum came bursting through the door. "Sandi?" he asked worriedly.

"I can't find the book… I can't find it!" I shouted frantically.

Jaycelyn quickly ran into the room. Callum had left the door wide open. "Sandi, calm down! You're going to wake everyone," she said as she handed me a glittery diary with stickers all over it. She picked me up and sat me on my bed. They continued looking for it as I hyperventilated. I ended up putting myself to sleep, and Callum stayed with me. I just rolled over and lay on his lap. I could hear him sigh. "What's wrong, Callum?" I asked with my eyes closed.

He sighed again. "Does she still visit you?" he asked.

"Who?" I replied.

"Schiz."

My eyes opened wide. I shuffled around on his lap. I looked up at him guilty and worryingly.

"You're going to make my dad send you back… and this time, they are going to wonder where your parents are… and I'll never see you again… never." He sighed, and a teardrop fell from his cheek.

I sat up and hugged his head as it rested on my chest. "Wha—"

"I heard them… talking. My dad said… you stay… effed up in the head… and that he doesn't want you around me. Can't you make her… can't you make… your disease go away?" he asked as he sobbed.

"I think it's stuck with me… like you're stuck with." I stopped my sentence. No one knows what he's stuck with.

"You think they would send me with you? We both have a disease."

"Oh, Callum… you don't want to go there. The people are mean… and you'd have no friends. Plus, our diseases are completely different. And plus we woul—"

"Sandi." he said as he tightened his grip around me.

"Yeah?" I answered.

"I love you."

I sat there back in a daze. I knew this day would come but not now. "C-Callum," I stuttered, slowly processing the words I was going to say.

He sat up, face fully dry, and put his forehead to mine. "I love you too." He with two hands on my face and I with one on his, leaned in, following his steps. Then, I saw it again. The black shadow walking away and going into the backlit blue darkness… how long had it… whoever it was, been standing there?

Callum could tell I was distracted and looked back. I could still see the figure standing there. "What, Sandi?" he said, sounding like his father when slightly irritated.

"Come with me," I said as I crawled across the bed and into the darkness. I saw the shadow fly back into the darkness… into the wall? I knew it was a human figure. I knew it was. Callum turned the hallway light on, and I was staring at a yellow wall.

"What?" he asked.

I turned around and smiled. "Umm… nothing. I don't remember," I lied as I walked back at him. I lied… I never lied to Callum. *Never.*

* * *

"Sandi?" I couldn't answer. I was hyperventilating myself into shock. My heart was racing, and I couldn't breathe. I was literally now sitting in a puddle of tears. My shirt sleeve was soaked with snot and my chest and face with my own precipitation. The way of cleansing the cloud we call the human body. I hadn't ever sweated so much in my life. I'm a really dark cloud then… **really dark.** My head was pounding, and I had a sharp pain in my head. I was already on my knees with Dustin trying to hold me, but it wasn't helping. I put my forehead to the floor. I couldn't see. My vision was going blurry. My face felt two times bigger than normal. My eyelids were swollen and so was my waterline. My nose was flared and red. My cheeks were fire-truck red. I lay flat out on my stomach. The ambulance arrived. I could see the panicked footsteps from underneath the door. Then, it got dark, and I heard the stretcher rushing up the stairs.

"Move, sir! Move sir!" I heard a man say. I heard crying and his room door opening for the first time in a whole thirty minutes. Then, they took the stretcher downstairs… with *me* on it. I couldn't open my eyes. I pointed in a bunch of directions, hoping to point the right way.

"Please… my friend," I said with the little breath I had left. I felt an oxygen mask fall over my face.

"He's coming, honey. He's coming," Lidianna said as she clasped my hand with hers and kissed it. She held it to her forehead. "He'll be okay, Sandi. He'll be okay." Then, I heard the stretcher and Callum groan to the right of me. I sighed and fell into a deep black sleep.

* * *

"Pumpkin?" I heard a voice say. "Tehran, she doesn't wake easily," Rohan-Kyle said.

I rolled over and opened my eyes. "I'm awake, mister," I said sweetly.

"Call me Tehran. No need to be so formal," he said politely.

"Okay…" I hesitated. "Tehran. Do you need me for something?" I asked curiously.

"Yes, Sandra wants to see you."

"Oh!" I said as I perked up and got right out of bed.

Callum came with Kennith, who was eagerly waiting for me. I held tight to Callum's arm as he walked downstairs. Kennith's face was hot with furry. "Sandi," he said sternly, "do you like Callum?"

I paused and looked at Callum. He looked so proud. "Yes." I giggled and turned to face my interrogator.

"No," he paused and twisted his face a bit, "Sandi, I mean like him like him."

I trudged alongside them. Hesitatingly, I answered. "N-n-no." I said somberly. I lied… again. *Callum, please forgive me.*

"Come on, Kennith. let's go play a game," Callum said as we made it to Sandra's room door. He gave me a sour look. *Callum, I'm sorry…*

"Sandi! Come! Come!" she said excitingly as she quickly motioned with her hand for me to come in. I slowly entered, her daughter, Amina, was half-naked and getting dressed.

"Oh!" I screamed as I backed into the doorway.

"No, it's fine. She doesn't mind, child," Sandra said as she pulled me inside and closed the door behind me. She ushered me to the bed. "Close your eyes, hun." She said sweetly. I stood there for a minute. "Open!" the dress that was laid before me was absolutely beautiful. It was pink, not my first choice of color, and had lace wrapped at the stomach. It had a pretty rose pattern and was slightly puffed out at the bottom. The lace was a pale pink and the dress was a cartoon pig pink. It was quite the marvel. My shoes had a slight heel and were a creamy beige color that fit oddly enough with the dress. Sandra had me stand on the bed as she dressed me. "You're tall for your age!" she said with shock. Luckily, the dress fit. Amina, who had just turned twenty-one, took a strange liking to me. She put mousse in my hair and combed it.

"Yum." I mumbled as I sniffed my hair.

"Yeah, it smells like strawberries," she said as she giggled. She put so much in that it ***drenched*** my hair. She brushed the frizzy parts down and then braided my hair in one big braid.

"I look like Rapunzel!" I said with excitement.

"Yeah, you do!" she said with shock.

She took a flat iron to my hair and went over the braid until my hair was dry. I was a bit worried, considering that the heat was dangerous, but she told me the reason she put so much mousse in was so it would smell good after and it was a heat protectant. She went over it like five times, then let my hair cool off.

"What's your middle name, Sandi?"

I was puzzled. Did I even have one? "Oh, I don't know… I'm not sure?" I answered.

"What? What do you mean 'you're not sure'?" she asked, just as puzzled as I was. "Jaycelyn!" she yelled. "Jaycelyn!" she yelled again.

Jaycelyn came rushing down the stairs, one of her shoulders exposed, and it looked like her dark blue, V-neck shirt had been tugged on and stretched out a bit. She ran her fingers through her hair, leaned on the ledge of the doorway, and turned a bit pink in the face from the way Amina was looking at her. "Ahem," she cleared her throat slowly and sniffled.

"Yes, Amina?"

"You're her sister, correct, Jaycelyn?"

"Correct," she said as she wrinkled her face at the question.

"Then, you don't spend enough time with this poor girl! She doesn't know her own middle name! What kind of mother will you be if you can'—"

"Jessie!" Dustin said as he rushed to hug her. Amina stared at him lustfully.

"Amina," he said with a slight nod.

"Hello, Dustin!" she said with excitement and the sweetest voice she could find.

He just nodded again and kissed Jaycelyn on the head.

Amina rolled her eyes and cleared her throat. "Do you know it?" she said as she unbraided my hair.

Instead of Jaycelyn answering, Dustin did, "Well, little sister," he started, fixing his eyes from Amina to me.

"It's Sandi Ameliana Jacobs," he said as he smiled.

"You look beautiful, Sandi Ameliana Jacobs," Jaycelyn said.

I ran to them and hugged them. "You didn't let her finish, silly," Dustin said as he knelt to unbraid the rest. He combed through the posh waves with his fingers. "Smells good," he said.

"Thank you. Amina did it for me," I said as I twirled around.

Amina stared at us, green with envy. "Come back now," Sandra said as she dressed my hair.

"Why so fancy?" Jaycelyn asked curiously.

"Oh, we are going out for breakfast," she said quickly.

"Ah, sounds nice," Jaycelyn said.

Sandra tied a white bow loosely onto my hair, in a shape that was but wasn't a ponytail, and pulled a piece of my hair from the front, so it would sit by the side of my face. "You're welcome to join us," Sandra said with a sarcastic tone.

"Oh, no, you go. Have fun, Sandi," she said, making sure everyone knew she was *only* addressing me. Callum came running down the stairs with Kennith who was fully dressed. "Can I come, Aunt Sandra?" Callum asked.

"Oh, no, dear. I'm afraid not," she said as she shooed him away, while still attempting to make my hair look perfect.

"Oh, okay," he said with a somber tone.

"Miss Sandra, I'm sorry for wasting your time, but I don'—"

"Miss Sandra, about your earlier offer," Dustin started as he pulled Callum and Jaycelyn in close to him. "We would love to go." He smiled at her slyly.

I could hear Amina grumbling to herself. She really had a thing for Dustin.

* * *

I wanted the nonsense to stop. The chills I got when something bad was about to happen, especially to Callum. The sinking feeling in my stomach when I couldn't tell him my feelings for him, the longing to be with him, the way I had to watch my body language around him. How badly I *needed* him. That was when we woke up from this I had to tell him. I had to… he gasped, it was very violent. "Sandi?" he said worryingly.

Why was he so worried about me? I heard beeping on the monitor. *Callum! Is he okay?!* I looked up and sighed with relief. *Oh, it's only me. Thank God! …Oh… ouch.* I tried to take a deep breath.

"Sandi, breathe… breathe!" he yelled. He was working himself up too much. He started coughing again. "Callum." I couldn't breathe.

"Sandi?" he said worryingly.

"Callum, I'm all right. Don't worry." I could feel him clasp my hand tighter than the average person would. "You aren't going to leave me, are you? You aren't going to try again, are you?" he asked.

Again? What did he mean 'again'? Then, I remembered, as if it just happened today.

"Sandi?"

"Callum?"

"Sandi, don't play… get up."

"What?" I turned my head to face him. I started to slide my stretcher that way.

"Sandi." He gave me a dumbfounded look. "I can't believe you're trying that hard. GET UP."

I sighed slightly. I took off my mask and got up.

He held my hand as he guided me toward him. "Hey, best friend," he said and let out a soft chuckle.

I couldn't say anything. I walked over to a bin that housed a couple of water bottles and slid off my shirt.

"Sandi… w-what are you doing?" he asked nervously.

I dampened my shirt and walked over to him. I dabbed his face and chin clean.

"Sandi… you don't have to do this. This isn't why I made you get up."

He tried to move himself away, but we both knew he was too sore. He sighed reluctantly. This was all I could do to stop myself from kissing him. That and the annoying machine he had on his face. He took his breathing device off, or whatever it was called, the only thing helping me resist my temptation.

Damn! He's got that grateful look on his face.

"Sandi, look at me…" he said softly.

I wanted to, but I couldn't. I dabbed the blood off his lips and the creases of his mouth.

"Sandi Ameliana Jacobs."

I gasped slightly and looked down as he firmly squeezed my hand until I dropped my shirt out of it. He touched his forehead to mine. *God, why… why does he do this to me?* He put his lips to my neck.

"Sandi," he said with a breathy tone. I rested my right hand on his back. He kissed my neck. "Dammit! How long is this car ride?" He looked at me, shocked. "Did you speak?" he asked.

I just stared at him like a deer in the headlights. He caressed my face. *Come on, Callum. Kiss me already!*

"You know, you are so confusing."

"Well," I started. "Allow me to ease the confusion a bit." I moved in to kiss him. He grabbed my hips. Then, he moved me back. Ouch! Rejection stings… it stings a lot.

* * *

I decided to let my heart go, to rip it out and leave it on the table for spare parts since it was too beaten to be used as a whole. Slowly, one by one, so as not to startle anyone, my heartbeat dropped, and the monitor beeped. Louder and louder it got, but no one could hear it because I would come back to life for a minute and then die all over again. It was life, not death, that would kill me and death, not life, that would save me.

* * *

He smiled slightly at my disappointment. "See," he started as he stood up, grasping my waist to keep his balance. He pushed my lower back into the stretcher behind us. "You do like me, Sandi." I smiled softly, innocently. I looked at him. He had a gleam of happiness and hope in his eyes. He wants me just as bad, I thought, but still I want him more. He leaned in to kiss me and then came to a dramatic halt. "I wasn't rejecting you by the way," he said sweetly.

My cheeks turned red with embarrassment. "Callum I-I—"

He interrupted my sentence with a deep, rough kiss. I wrapped my arms around his neck, and I could feel his grip on my waist tighten. He sat me on the stretcher and stood between my legs. He wrapped his arms around my waist and squeezed tight. He slid off my bra strap and kissed my shoulder. Everything was moving so fast. He moved behind me and kissed the back of my neck, slow and soft.

"Callum!" I screamed with twenty-five percent pain, thirty-five percent pleasure, and forty percent shock.

"Hmph," he said with a devilish grin.

"Callum," I said as I grabbed the wrist he didn't have buried in my pants. He had his right hand holding the front of my neck as he kissed it.

I could feel his finger slide in and out, the sudden act made me scream like a school girl five minutes ago. Now it just made me moan. "Shh." He kissed my neck as he fondled my breasts. "You're getting too loud."

"Ha." I held his face close to mine. "Oops, it's your fault." He chuckled and kissed my cheek. He slid a second finger in and out and got progressively faster. He squeezed my left breast roughly. I could feel his vibe. He was getting excited, *super* excited. I leaned back into him and he pressed my back to his torso, restraining me with his arm covering my chest. I could only move my pelvis and, boy, was I doing a lot of it. I was practically humping his hand and moaning… *a lot.*

"Sandi… Sandi," he whispered.

Somehow, I managed to slide my hand into his pants, and apparently, I was good at what I was doing. "Ah!" I screamed. Everything was going so fast. *He* was going so fast. He undid my pants and… God, he's a miracle worker with his hands. Just as I was reaching the peak of my "excitement," the ambulance stopped.

"Callum! Ahh, God!"

"Mmm…" He kept making that noise continuously for about a good minute and a half.

I giggled, and I could feel him press his lips to my cheek. "Callum, you've got to stop." I tried to say without my voice breaking. He wrapped his arms around my neck, I zipped up my pants and attempted to breathe after almost losing my mind.

"I don't wanna," he whined slightly as he rocked me from left to right and kissed the side of my face and neck. He sighed, hugged me tight, and then handed my shirt to me which slid underneath the stretcher.

"Callum?" I held my shirt tight in my hand. He just gazed at me. It made me a bit nervous. I got down off the stretcher and pressed my torso against his.

"Sandi," he moaned. He actually moaned my name.

I kissed him. It was quick, but *I* did it.

"Hey, I thought I was calling the shots here!" he said as he laid me back on my stretcher, the one everything happened on.

"Hey, Callum."

"What is it?" he asked as he helped me put on my shirt.

"Come sit with me. Forget that thing. You're all right," I said sweetly.

I had to stop him before he got himself resituated with that oxygen mask.

"I was going to see if you were going to say something or be a wimp and wait for me to," he said with a smile. He sat close, so close I could hear his heartbeat.

He wrapped his arms around me, and I leaned into him. "Sandi… umm…" He paused. We heard the footsteps of people outside. I sat up, put my knees on the stretcher, so I could face him, kissed him, and held him tight in my arms. I pressed his face to my chest. "I can hear your heartbeat… it's weird. Are you nervous?" I couldn't answer him… I *am* nervous. "Umm… Callum."

He sat up, sat crisscross on the stretcher as best he could and put his forehead to mine. I tilted my head and leaned forward. "You're such a coward, little girl." He kissed me roughly, deeply. *God, Sandi, just say it…* I pulled back softly; he grabbed my arm and pulled me between his legs. We hadn't been this close in a long time… a *really* long time.

I sat in the waiting room for hours, staring down the empty hallway. "Sandi, are you ready to go yet?" Dustin asked impatiently.

"Yeah, of course…" I said somberly.

"What's wrong?" he asked.

"There is just something I needed to say… and I haven't said it," I replied.

He sighed.

I felt like sighing, too.

"Why didn't you tell him?"

I looked up at him shocked. "What, Dustin?" I asked.

"You *heard* me," he said sternly.

"Dustin!"

"What? You don't know how irritating it is for a guy to have to wait for the love of his life to let him love her. Sandi, stop putting it off. He won't wait forever."

"Dustin, we're only fifteen… I'm not the love of his life… especially if he won't wait."

"Sandi, it'll hurt him to go, but it hurts more to stay and be rejected because you love him but are too afraid to say it."

I could feel tears streaming down my face. *Why couldn't I tell him? What's wrong with me? God… please help me… please?* Then, I broke down. I'd never been such a mess in my life.

"Sandi?!" he said with concern as he held me. "I didn't mean to make you cry… cheer up," He said with guilt.

"I-I-It's not your fault… it's mine. He called me a coward today… it didn't hurt but now I know why he said it."

"Sandi, GO TO HIM!" he said dramatically.

I giggled. He was right. I need to go, but I was too scared. "Come on. I won't walk you. If you don't do this, he may not be there for you to do it later."

"Fine." I got up, still a little shaken, and walked down the hall. I tried not to look back. I knew I would turn around and run. Crap… I did it. *Why did I?* I felt like the walls were closing in around me, I could feel the sweat trickling off my forehead. My lips were quivering with anxiety. My life was flashing before my eyes. My fingers were trembling with fear. My legs buckled, and I couldn't move, I wanted to run. I needed to run! My heart started beating faster, quickly picking up its pace like a cheetah going after its prey. If only I could run this fast. I felt my head start pounding, and my heart sat in my throat. It choked me up and made my words inaudible.

"Sandi!"

I turned my head and just barely avoided whiplash from turning it so fast. "Yeah?!" I gasped for air. I think I was holding my breath all this time.

Callum walked up behind me and placed his hands on my shoulders. "Are you okay?" he asked.

I couldn't answer.

He put his lips to my ear. "You all right?" he asked with a darker tone than usual.

I couldn't speak. I choked on my words. It felt like my heart was sitting in my throat.

"Ameliana, what's wrong?" he asked as he wrapped his arms around my torso and rocked me. I sighed deeply, if only he could read my mind. He kissed my neck, and I sighed deeply again. "I thought you were asleep, Callum," I said softly, regaining my voice.

"Oh, she speaks!" he said sarcastically.

"Whatever!" I slid out of his grip and into his hospital bedroom. He closed the door behind us.

I couldn't face him.

"Sandi Ameliana Jacobs, look at me," he demanded.

I stood there, hyperventilating. *I can't do it… I can't…* before I even knew it, Callum was in front of me, gazing into my soul. "God, Sandi." He moved in closer. "What the hell?" He took me by surprise.

"What?!" I said hysterically as I pulled myself away from him.

"Sandi!" he yelled angrily. He grabbed my wrists. "Calm down… please?" He stared at me.

"I'm fine… I'm fine," I answered softly. I swallowed hard, took a deep breath, and grabbed his hands. He raised his left eyebrow. It was like his signature move. "Callum… I…" I paused and thought for a second. "Okay, Callum, I need to tell you something… it's important."

He moved in closer and put his forehead next to mine. "Soooo, tell me," he said sweetly. He had an eagerness about him, as if he'd been waiting for this his entire life.

Oh, wait... he has... why do I have to say it first? Sandi? Yeah? I love you... I remembered the way he tightened his grip around me. I wouldn't ever try to live without that. He said it first when we were kids. Now, it was my turn. I moved in close. He wrapped his arms around my waist. Our noses touched. I could feel his heart beating rapidly against my chest. I leaned in to kiss him. He pushed my hair behind my ear, and then I woke up.

Chapter 17

I COULD HEAR MY MONITOR beeping rapidly as I jolted out of my sleep. Jaycelyn and Dustin waited outside the room, anxious to come inside. "Breathe, Miss Jacobs," the doctor instructed as he pulled a mask over my face. I quickly pushed it away, frantically looking around, trying to take in my surroundings. My dream left me in quite a daze. I sat up quickly and walked toward the door. "Miss Jacobs, are you all right?"

"Yes, sir. Sorry… I just need to find someone." I quickly excused myself from the room. I stormed down the hallway to the stairwell.

"Sandi!" Jaycelyn shouted.

Ignoring her, I took off in a sprint toward the staircase door. I couldn't breathe. I felt like I was stuck, running in place. I got to the stairs and ran up. I just knew where to go. I don't know how, but I didn't question it. I flung myself through the fourth floor door, and there he was, standing in the hall, hugging his parents. I sighed, ran my fingers through my mane, and leaned against door. He spotted me multiple times but wouldn't come near me.

His parents just seemed to know what he was staring at. They slowly walked toward the elevator. Callum kept his eyes on me. When his parents were gone, I sprinted to him. I could see the smile on his face. He always had a charming smile. I jumped into his arms and hugged him tightly. I could hear him sigh, as if he was relieved. "Sandi. You were asleep for a long time." He squeezed me tighter. "I was so scared that you wouldn'—"

"Callum?" I said softly, wrapping my legs tighter around him.

"Yeah?"

"I love you… so much… I love you." I could feel a teardrop fall onto my arm. I got down and looked at him. "Callum… what… what's the matter?"

He kissed me roughly. I stumbled back, dumbfounded by the sudden act. *God… why didn't he do this earlier?* He pulled back. "Hey," he said with a soft voice.

"Yeah?" I asked worryingly.

He held my hands tightly, staring at me as if this is the first time we'd been this close. "Sandi." He put his hand on the back of my head and roughly pushed my forehead to his.

"Ow!" I giggled and looked at him.

Even though we'd been through so much together, even seen so much of each other… I'm still a coward. "Sandi… I love you. Like seriously… really, really love you."

"Oh. yeah?"

"Yeah."

"So, then what are you going to do about it?" I asked.

He looked at me, surprised by my choice of words. "Well, Miss Jacobs, first thing I'm going to do is change that name of yours," he said slyly.

"What?" I looked at him with shock. "You don't like Sandi?" He wrapped his arm around me and ushered me toward the elevator.

"Your *last name*, Sandi."

My cheeks turned red with embarrassment. "Oh… hey, I knew that."

"Uh-huh. Sure, you did." He kissed my neck as we entered the elevator.

"I love you," I said quietly.

The doors slowly closed and came to a stop. Callum paid them no attention. "Sandi Ameliana Jacobs, I love you, too."

There was an awkward pause. I could have sworn that I saw something. "Callum, where are we going?" I asked. I was beyond confused.

"The cafeteria, Sandi," he said as he massaged my shoulders. I saw a black shadow start moving frantically at the end of the hall.

"Sandi!" Jaycelyn screamed.

I sprinted out of the elevator.

"Sandi, what are you doing?!" Callum yelled as the elevator doors closed.

I paid him no attention. I just kept running. I felt like my feet were barely touching the ground. I made it to the dark void of a hallway, turned out I walked through an open doorway. There was just no door.

"Jaycelyn!" I yelled. My voice echoed down the hall. I got on my knees and felt for the stairs. "Jaycelyn, where are you?!" I shouted fearfully. I could feel a presence suck the air out of the room.

"Hey, pumpkin! Whatcha doin' in here?" I heard a voice say. It was a man, a familiar voice. *Oh, thank God.* "Here. Let me help you up." I felt a hand wrap around my waist, and then there was nothingness. I toppled down the stairs. The concrete scrapped my arms, and I could feel gravel in my teeth. When I finally stopped falling, I heard a low chuckle. "So how far did you think you'd run?" Kick. My stomach was in agonizing pain. I could feel rough-skinned knuckles hit my face. "Oh, still so fragile, aren't you?" the man said. *Am I imagining this?* I felt *a* man pin me down to the ground, and then there she was. Schizophrenia. The beast, she looked just like me, except older now, like before. "Please don't! No! Help!" I shouted frantically, a towel was placed into my mouth, and water saturated the towel.

Schizophrenia cracked her neck and proceeded to *aid* the man in his dirty work. "Ah!" I screamed, but my scream was muffled by my constant choking on water. I tried to breathe in through my nose, but another man squeezed my nose between his fingers. I felt a foot stomp on my stomach. All I could see was schizophrenia, waiting for the right moment to strike. *It's not real. It's not real. Come on, Sandi. You can get past this,* I thought calmly, but the situation was anything but calm. I tried to breathe, but the towel was choking me. I lifted my torso up, and it was violently forced back down to the floor. *She is stronger than me… too strong. Always has been, always will be. I need to call for help…*

"Jay—"

A man's grimy, swollen fingers shoved the towel further down my throat. My screams were muffled. I couldn't escape this fit, not this one.

"What are you waiting for?" one of the men said. They just looked like dark shadows, but she stood out. She resembled me in so many ways. A smile ran across her face and was gone in the blink of an eye. She stared at me. Then, I couldn't see this, but a cloth bag was placed upon my head and slid over my face.

I could feel a violent twist of my knee and a sharp whack to my collar bone. A few quick jabs to my body, and I couldn't move. I felt rough hands to my face through the scratchy cloth, continuously hitting my cheekbone. I could feel my stomach constantly being pounded on, and I threw up from constantly gagging on water. I couldn't breathe, and my heart was beating rapidly. I felt like a bird, frightened in a cage. I won't get out of this, I thought. I heard a crack, then a crunch. I threw up again and choked. It was thick and sour. Blood seeped past the corners of my lips. *Callum! Rohan-Kyle, Lidianna, Dustin, someone help me!* I thought. Tears stung my eyes. It hit me harder than the abuse I'd gone through with my family. *Jaycelyn… I'm sorry I couldn't save you.* I felt nothing but air whooshing past me. I hit a rail. The stairwell lights came on, but mine went out.

Chapter 18

I COULD FEEL SMOOTH, HEAVY hands run through my hair. I usually could make out voices and hands really well but not anymore. Too traumatized to process things with my eyes closed, I jolted myself awake. Panting, I bewilderedly looked around the room.

"Sandi, Sandi!" I heard Dustin say as he held my face still.

"Let go! Let go!" I yelled with a raspy voice.

Callum squeezed my hand, trying to comfort me. "Sandi, it's us! Sandi!" he yelled. He pushed Dustin to the side and pulled me into his chest. "Sandi, breathe please," Callum said as calmly as he could. I couldn't move my neck, arms, hell I couldn't feel my body. I could feel Callum kiss my cheek repeatedly. I was surprised he did it in front of everyone.

"Callum," I whispered. Everyone was staring at us…at *me*. My heart monitor began to beep loudly again. I glanced at it out the corner of my right eye.

"Breathe, Sandi," he said. He continued to kiss my cheek, my forehead, and then my opposite cheek.

"Your parents are looking… Callum," I said nervously.

"Then, let's give them something to look at shall we?" he gently grabbed my face and kissed me on the lips. *Oh, my God, Callum, what are you doing?!* I wanted to pull him in closer to me. I wished I could move. I could feel him kiss me deeply. I wanted to wrap my arms around him and kiss him forever. But I was too weak and I couldn't breathe.

I slowly pulled away and stared into his eyes. "I love you," I said, still loud enough for only him to hear.

"I want you to say it loud enough for China to hear you."

"I love you, Callum," I said in the loudest voice I could muster up. I had to push the words out a bit to get past the raspy sound. He laughed a bit and had a wide smile on his face. He kissed me and touched his forehead to mine.

"I love you, too, Sandi," he said cheerfully. I could tell I had an emotionless tone of voice. I looked up at the ceiling. I was stuck lying down, paralyzed in mind and body. I looked at Callum, who was still staring at me.

"Umm… could you come and lay with me please?" I asked softly. He nodded slightly and gently *tried* to climb into the small hospital bed. I laughed, "Ouch, Callum! I can't feel my arm!"

"Move over then!"

"I can't, jerk!" I joked. He messed up the bedsheets trying to get comfortable underneath them. "Callum! What's wrong with you?"

"What?!"

"I'm going to be cold!"

"No, you won't. I'll keep you warm." He hugged me as best as he could. My neck cast brace thing was in the way. "Jaycelyn, can I talk to you please?" she looked at me worriedly.

"Alone please," I said to hint to everyone else.

"Callum, exit," Rohan-Kyle said sternly.

"No…" He put his forehead to my left temple. "I'm going to stay here with her. She doesn't mind," he replied.

"He can stay please," I said softly. He gave me a hard glare.

With that, they exited the room and closed the door. "Sandi, what… are you okay?" she asked worriedly.

"Well, I'm not okay… but I…" I hesitated. I have no way to explain how I feel.

"Sandi, what happened?" Callum asked.

"Umm… I just want to go home."

"Why? You need to get better," Jaycelyn said. Her voice broke between her words.

"Jaycelyn, don't cry. I just..." I cried uncontrollably.

Callum kissed my forehead and whispered in my ear, "You're okay, babe." He caressed my face. "I just don't feel safe anymore. I feel like I'm being watched constantly," I cried again. I don't know how to explain myself at all. Jaycelyn clasped my hand and studied me carefully. She sighed. She had a sorrowful expression. It was now worse than before. "The doctor said that... umm, well... what do you remember?" she asked cautiously.

"Jay." I sighed and breathed in sharply, "I specifically remember hearing you scream for me. Then, I ran out of the elevator and to the hallway to get to another stairwell. It was quiet, and I was trying to find the stairs in the dark." I paused to think about that voice. I gasped, and my eyes widened. "Your uncle Tehran, he helped me up!"

"B-b-but how? He and my cousin are in Canada. They just sent a postcard and a picture today," Callum said with disbelief.

"I swear to you, Callum. He was there. I heard him."

"Just because you heard something, doesn't mean it was there. You could have been scared and felt you needed someone that made you feel safe."

"Callum, I swear it. He helped me up, too... but let me go. And I fell down the stairs, I heard... two men where I fell."

I stopped to think, *How did I get out of there?*

"What else?" Callum asked impatiently.

All the voices I heard were processing in my mind. I had a lack of sight, but my other senses were going haywire. "Jaycelyn... Tehran, Rohan-Kyle, and... Lee were there."

Callum sat up and eyed me harshly.

"Dad, Sandi? Are you sure?" Jaycelyn asked with uncertainty.

"I am positive. I've never been more sure of anything in my life."

Callum sat there, staring at me. "After all my family did for you? How could you say that?" he asked sternly.

"Callum, who found me?"

"My dad did, but that doesn't mean tha—"

"Okay…okay. All I'm saying is eventually he was there."

"When though? When he found you, you were unconscious."

"Before then, Callum, he was there with my father."

"Shut up, Sandi. You're delusional."

"Callum, I'm being serious!" I yelled.

"I never heard Jaycelyn call you. Jaycelyn, did you call out to her?" he asked angrily.

"It wasn't a call. It was a scream." Jaycelyn looked down at her feet. A tear dropped from her nose. "Sandi, I…" She sniffled. "I never called for you." She quickly left the room. I could hear her break down outside the door.

"I'm leaving," Callum said as he got out of the bed.

"Callum, please… please."

"You know you're schizophrenic. They were asking us if we thought you should be put back under care." He put air quotation marks around the word "care". "I think I'll say yes since you don't feel too safe."

"Callum!" I yelled. My monitor started beeping loudly.

He ignored me and stormed out of the room.

About an hour later, a doctor entered the room. I didn't care for his looks. What I cared about was getting out of here. Jaycelyn entered the room, followed by the whole crew. Callum stayed in a darkened corner. He wouldn't look at me.

"How are you today, Miss Jacobs?" the doctor asked as he watched me carefully.

"Slightly agitated. I can't move," I replied.

"Well, do you know why?" he asked.

"Umm… you're the doctor, right? You tell me." I sighed at how snappy I sounded. "Sorry. I'm just upset. Well, yesterday, I remember my sister calling me and then… a lot happened."

The whole room fell awkwardly quiet with everyone's eyes on me.

"How long were you…" The doctor cleared his throat. "Asleep, Miss Jacobs?" he finished.

"A day? Okay. A week or two at most. I remember hitting my head really hard."

The room stayed silent.

"Miss Jacobs, what month is it?"

"January?" Now, I was uncertain.

Callum briskly walked over to the window and angrily let up the blinds.

"What year is it, Sandi?" he asked in a punitive tone.

I sighed loudly. I just wanted to go back to sleep now. "I'm guessing I should be saying Happy New Year?"

"Merry Christmas, Miss Jacobs," he said with a very resentful tone.

"It's the end of 2007, Sandi," Dustin said sorrowfully.

"Oh. Well, umm… that makes it a little better I guess." I said as I stared at the ceiling, trying to forget how angry Callum was.

"Miss Jacobs, your sister and your boyfriend to—"

"I'm not," Callum interrupted.

Jaycelyn shifted uncomfortably in her chair. The tension heavily filled the room, making it difficult for me to breathe.

"Best friend," I said.

"Associate, ma'am," he said coldly.

"Okay, well, they told me about what umm… happened." He cleared his throat and looked at Jaycelyn. "Now," he turned away from me to face the "family". "With schizophrenia, one can hear and see things that aren't real. In this instance, hearing you call her and then running out of the elevator to your rescue. This was the first warning sign that something was bound to go wrong. She ended up having a very violent seizure. She broke bones, coughed up blood, and even imagined that her father…" He pointed at Callum. "Your father and your uncle were attacking her. She has a past of being afraid of men. Perhaps, she was abused. That's why that hallucination took place, now…" There was a loud ringing in my ears, I completely blocked the world out. *Hallucination? You've got to be kidding me, right? How could I have imagined that?* I thought. Then, I remembered the first time I saw *her*, that hallucination of a girl. Maybe the doctor was right. It's constantly triggered when I'm afraid. I sighed regretfully. Slowly but surely, I eased myself up onto the wall behind me.

I'm tired of being so helpless, needy. I don't want anybody. I don't need anyone. I just want to go… *I have no home.*

"Sandi!" Rohan-Kyle yelled.

I jumped and, without control of my body, flung myself forward over the guard rail on the bed. My heart stopped. I could feel myself wheezing violently. I had been frozen all this time, unable to respond to anything, like a robot unable to emote. The doctor quickly ran over to help me up, but I gripped the railing.

"Miss Jacobs, calmly let go and sit up please," the doctor instructed.

"Sandi?" Dustin said with a worried tone.

I had no feeling in my hands anymore. They turned purple from how hard I was clinging to the railing. Callum slowly approached me. I couldn't see him, but I knew his footsteps. I started gagging. I felt like I was choking on lumps of dry rice. Blood spewed out of my mouth like a running faucet. I couldn't breathe. Callum ran to me and moved my hair out of my face. "Doc… you've got to be kidding me, right?" Callum said solemnly.

"We're going to run some tests, huh, nurse?" the doctor said as he ran out of the room.

I continued choking. The blood seemed to get thicker. I was clinging on to life by a thread. "Ahh!" I wailed as I held my stomach. I couldn't move from my stationary spot. My throat stung, and my eyes felt like they were bulging out of my head. I felt like a fish out of water. I couldn't breathe.

Lidianna ran over to my bedside, pushing Callum out of the way.

"Mom!" he said with a shocked look on his face.

She pushed my hair behind my ears, grabbed my face, and shook me slightly.

"Sandi!" Jaycelyn screamed. She'd been trying to keep her composure.

"Sandi honey, please, please, please stay with us. Come on. You're a strong girl. I know you are!" Lidianna said as she patted my cheeks with the palms of her hands.

My body became limp, and my torso began to fall toward the guard rail. My arms hung down over the rail, and Lidianna held me upward slightly by my head. My eyes rolled back. I could see the darkness fall over me like a veil.

"Doctor! Doctor!" Rohan-Kyle yelled. "Callum, go find help!" he yelled.

Jaycelyn spotted her boys and their babysitter coming to the room. "No, no!" she yelled as she ran out and closed the door.

"Mommy, what's wrong with Auntie Sandi?!" they both said simultaneously.

"Nothing, boys… nothing. She's going to be…" Her voice trailed off, and she broke into hysterical sobs. I felt myself being thrown back onto the bed. I could feel rough-skinned hands push on my chest.

"Sandi!" Dustin yelled.

I began fighting him, the man with rough-skinned hands, hair on his knuckles, the heavy breathing. I remembered him. I started having convulsions. Something triggered my attack, my fit, my longing to breathe. "Ahh!" I whimpered. I relived my nightmare exactly like it was yesterday, but it wasn't. I could smell him, his scent, the musk he used that masked his clothes.

"Clear!"

I felt a spark, not of life but something dark and sullen. I could feel the man holding me down. *No! Stop!* I could feel my lips move, but my speech was inaudible. *Let go! Stop it! Stop it!*

"Stop it!" I bellowed. I opened my eyes.

Everyone looked at me like I'd torn the walls down. Lidianna, Rohan-Kyle, and the few doctors and nurses in the room were the only ones allowed in. I looked at who had me. It was Rohan-Kyle. I stared at him fearfully, eyes wide, face scrunched.

"Let go please," I said innocently.

He released his grip and slipped out of the room.

"Miss Jacobs, breathe," a nurse instructed as she put a cold stethoscope to my chest.

"Big, deep breaths, Sandi." I looked out the window with concern. I turned my attention to my monitor. It was beeping dangerously slow. "Sandi, you're not breathing, hun. Look at me," the nurse said calmly. I looked at her fearfully. "It's okay." She clasped my right hand. "You're safe here." If she were made of wood, her nose would have hit the wall behind me. Although I didn't believe her, I breathed in sharply through my nose and out through my mouth. It stung my throat. I coughed. "Ouch."

"You're having quite the exciting day today, aren't you?" the nurse asked.

I wasn't in the mood for sarcasm. Instead of answering, I just kept breathing, enduring the pain. I realized that I had full mobility of my neck. I cleared my throat, which hurt more than it helped, and slowly sat myself up. A woman from the front desk entered the room. I hadn't realized how quiet and empty the room was. *Where did everyone go?*

"Miss Jacobs, there is a phone call for you downstairs. Would you like to take it?"

I gazed into the nurse's eyes fearfully. *A call for me. Who would it be from?* I looked at the woman from the front desk, out the window, and then back at her. *Could this be an elaborate plan to catch me when I'm vulnerable?* I didn't trust this nurse. I didn't trust this place, and I definitely didn't trust this desk woman. I felt myself curl up and hold my knees. I was so lost in thought I couldn't hear the nurse yelling, "Sandi Jacobs! Calm down! It's okay!" the nurse said, but just because she said it didn't mean I believed her. I was trembling at the thought of walking downstairs. I didn't even want to get in the elevator with that woman. *Where is my family? Oh, wait… you've forgotten, Miss Jacobs. You don't have family.* I sighed. I knew this was a trap for sure, that there were people out to get me, why not send the call to my room, but no one believed me. No one ever believed me.

"Sandi, I'll go with you if you want," the nurse said sweetly.

I nodded, slid out of bed, and collapsed to the floor. "Why?! What is going on?!" I said, frustrated by my sudden weakness. I couldn't walk and could barely hold up my own weight on all fours.

The nurse quickly ran over to me. "Let me help you up." She seemed to be slightly amused by my rebellious spirit.

I didn't want her to touch me. I wanted to do it on my own. "No, I've got this. I've got this," I said firmly, trying to stand my ground. No pun intended.

"Miss Jacobs, please." She giggled at my struggle. "I am only trying to help."

I glanced at her over my shoulder and then let my body fall limp to the ground. My hands and knees were red from using them as my support beams the entire time. The nurse picked me up and carried me, like a baby, into the elevator.

"I want to get down. I want to walk, and I want to go home," I said angrily while trying to fight my way free, but I didn't have the strength.

"So demanding, aren't we? It'll be a little while before you can do things for yourself again." She glanced down at me and then continued looking forward. She had a smirk on her face.

"Wipe that smirk off your face. It's not funny," I snapped.

"You're right, but it's quite adorable. Redheads are known to be quite… rambunctious."

"Rambunctious? Ha. Ha. I don't even feel like there's life in me anymore."

"Well, obviously, there is. You've just got to get back to living in it."

The elevator doors opened, and I gazed upon the beautiful entrance. The upstairs was so gray and basic. The elevator was just a silvery gray, just like the walls and floors. Downstairs… downstairs was a step into heaven. The floor was a beautiful pale orangey-pink, and the walls were a sunset orange. The main desk had a marble top and a wooden bottom. There was a plant hanging from the ceiling behind the desk. It had beautiful orange flowers blooming, blushing with pink. They had the employee of the month on the wall and pictures of their patients besides the employee of the month.

"Umm… it's beautiful down here!" I exclaimed with joy.

"Yeah, I know, one of the reasons why I love working here," the lady from the desk said as she briskly walked to the phone.

"Sorry for the delay, madame. We had a bit of an issue."

As I got closer, I could hear the lady speaking frantically. She sounded like one of those characters on the phone from Veggie Tales. Specifically the rumor weed episode, no one will ever know what that lady was saying on the phone in the beginning of the episode. Must've been important though.

"Miss Jacobs, Therapist Heinbock here," a woman said as she walked up to me. She held out her hand. I shook it carefully, wrapping only my fingers around three of hers, leaving her pinky and thumb out. Her nails looked dangerous. She had long fake nails that had spikes on them and had been "bedazzled" with rhinestones. I curled up like a cat in the nurse's arms, slowly removing my hand, bending my arm, pulling it to my chest, and frowning my face with slight discomfort.

"Is that allowed in the workplace? Is it safe?" I asked.

"I'm a therapist, Miss Jacobs, not a surgeon. I talk to people for a living, not give them baboon hearts. Now let's go. Shall we?" she said with a snappy tone. She yanked on my arm, and I almost fell right out of the nurse's arms. "Hey! Wait! She can't walk!" the nurse yelled. "Well, then come on, bring her." Therapist Heinbock seemed to be in a rush for some reason.

"Wait, Sandi! Here's the phone!" the desk lady said.

The nurse took me to the counter and gently brought me to my feet. I gripped the slippery countertop of the desk with my forearms and my torso. I felt like a horse trying to walk for the first time. I couldn't do it, and I refused to be put in a wheelchair.

"Hello?" my face was scrunched up with confusion, no one else knew I was there. I had no friends at school; I never went to one except for in my younger years when I stayed with my parents. Being homeschooled definitely wasn't part of the socialite business. I had no family, absolutely none. They all thought I'd lost my mind.

"Sandi? Sandi honey, are you all right?" a weeping woman asked.

What a dumb question.

"Oh, yes, I'm fine. I'm just being rushed to the ER back and forth for no apparent reason. Who is this?" I snapped. I wasn't in the mood for games.

"Talk about schizophrenic, she's quite iconic," Therapist Heinbock mumbled.

The nurse brutally hit her in her chest. "Be quiet, Clarissa," she snapped.

I raised an eyebrow at the name.

"Sandi… you there?" the woman asked.

"Yes, who is this?"

"Sandi, it's your mother," she began; she broke out into a sob. "Do you not remember your own mother's voice?"

"I don't remember having a mother at all," I said coldly.

I slammed the fancy turn dial phone and turned my head enough to see the nurse out of the corner of my eye. "Okay. I'm ready," I sighed heavily and smiled a tired smile. She walked over to me and was about to pick me up when I put a firm hand to her shoulder to stop her. "You know what," I said with my back to the edge of the desk and my left arm bent backward, supporting my weight on the desk as I stood. "I'll walk," I said with a smile.

"How?"

"Simple you will help me." I wrapped one arm around the nurse's shoulder and began my long journey… *around the corner.*

It took me about fifteen minutes. My legs wobbled, and my knees gave out about ninety-seven million times on the way, but I made it!

"I admire her persistence," Therapist Heinbock said as we entered the room.

The room was plain and white. The floor was made of white foam, and the walls were the brightest shade of white I'd ever seen… and these past few years, I'd seen a lot of white.

"So, Miss Jacobs, how are you feeling?" Therapist Heinbock asked. She crossed her legs, put on her glasses that had been hanging from her shirt and sat her clipboard on top of her legs, arms crossed on top of it. She was about five-four. Her torso made her seem taller than she was when she sat down. She was a curvy Hispanic woman with blond hair and green eyes. Her lips were a glossy, glittery pink. She wore a black dress and a white lab coat with two black pens and a number two pencil in her single coat pocket. The pocket was oddly placed at the top of her chest, sitting close to her collar bone. "Miss Jacobs, are you there?" Therapist Heinbock asked sarcastically.

"Where is my family?" I asked worryingly.

"Home, Miss Jacobs," the nurse answered.

"Yes. Now how are you feeling?" Therapist Heinbock asked again.

I held my stomach. it had been making whale noises the entire time. "Actually, I'm quite hungry," I replied.

"Oh, yes, indeed. We shall have lunch brought to us soon," Therapist Heinbock said.

She eyed the cherry wood coffee table in front of us. It was the only thing in the room separating us and was oddly placed perfectly in the center of the room. I realized that I didn't remember sitting down, although I was, and looked at the couch behind me, then the floor. "The couch is the floor. That's so cool! And Therapist Heinbock is just sitting on the other side!" I said, excited by my new discovery.

"Surprised, huh?" Therapist Heinbock asked. She had a smirk on her face.

I crawled around, laughing. "Seriously, I want a couch like this!"

Suddenly, there was a knock at the door, and I quickly sat back down in my original spot, next to the nurse.

"Miss Heinbock?" a man from the cafeteria said.

"Yes, set it there," she said as she pointed to the dead center of the table. Everything was too straight, too centered, too odd. It made me nervous. I felt like I couldn't breathe. "Relax, Sandi. So do you know what happened to you?" Therapist Heinbock asked.

"No, actually," I answered.

"Well, Popper tell her." *Is that how she addresses the nurse? That's a weird name.*

"Well," She turned to face me and rested her hand on my thigh. "You umm… your collar bone was fractured, shoulder separation, punctured both your lungs, broken ribcages, sprained your left ankle, broke your right, and twisted and dislocated both your knees. And you've been in a coma for a year, so it's understandable you may not walk for a bit," Nurse Popper said.

"Thank you. That'll be all, Popper."

With that, the nurse exited, slowly closing the door behind her. She had an apologetic look on her face.

"Eat please. Then, we can begin." She grabbed a salad from the table, even though there was a wider selection than that. "I'm trying to watch my weight," she said.

"Oh. Well, you've got a pretty good figure anyway. There's no need," I said sweetly. "Thank you."

She smiled. "Please eat."

I nodded. There was a choice of salad, yogurt, spaghetti, grilled salmon, spicy boneless wings, mac n cheese, chicken breasts, and chili cheese fries all by their lonesome. "Hmm," I said as I tried to make my decision.

"You may eat as much as you like."

I glanced up at her, eyes gleaming with joy. "Really?" I asked. I couldn't believe it. I was indeed famished. First, I chose grilled salmon and a salad. By the time I picked, she was already finished with her food. "We will be keeping you here for a few days, to keep you under our supervision." Her words practically interrupted my meal. I dropped my fork, and the food in my mouth fell onto my plate. "No. I can't stay here. It's not safe!" I yelled.

"What do you mean?" Therapist Heinbock asked.

"You know what I… never mind, nothing. It's nothing." I bit down on my fork harshly as I continued eating.

She watched me for about thirty minutes as I ate everything but the yogurt. I dipped my last wing in the ranch sauce and stared at it. I sighed and my shoulders slumped. "I feel fat," I said.

"No, no, this is good. You need to eat," She reassured me.

"Can I see what I look like?" I asked.

"Of course." She got up and began to walk down the hall. "Come on!" she said as she trailed off down the hall.

I quickly stuffed my last wing in my mouth, crawled to the door, and stuck my head out the door. I slowly stood up and went out to the right. My legs wobbled, but I used the wall to keep my balance. This time, it only took me thirteen minutes to make it to my destination. She led me to a bathroom with a full-body mirror hanging on the door and closed it behind me.

"Aren't your feet cold, Therapist Heinbock?" I said as I grabbed on to her for balance. She was barefoot, just like I was, and the bathroom floor was freezing.

"No, I'm fine," she answered.

I turned my attention to the mirror. I looked extremely pale. My hair grew to my hips, and it too lost its glow.

My eyes were a deep green for now, and the only color on my face was from me blushing at a hickey I had on my neck. "It's just a bruise, not what you think it is."

She said, "Okay."

I watched my lips move as I spoke. They were a pale pink and terribly chapped. "Don't worry. We'll get you fixed up after therapy."

"All right."

Instead of letting me walk, she carried me this time. I did lose a lot of weight, but I didn't look thinner. "All right. We made it." She *threw* me to my side of the room. I looked at her with bewilderment. "How'd you know I wasn't going hit the wall?!" I shouted.

"She closed the door. I didn't," she replied with a smirk.

"Are you sure you're not the one who needs therapy?" I snapped.

"Maybe." There was an awkward pause. "Do you remember me?" she asked.

"Yes, Clarissa, but you've changed… a lot," I replied.

"I know I have," she answered.

"For instance, your last name," I said.

"Yes, I've married."

"Oh, well, that's nice. I would have mistaken you for a Hispanic woman."

She wasn't always so tan. "Well, my gran is Hispanic."

"Oh, that's cool! Well, you look good."

"Thank you," she said. "Who'd you marry?" she asked.

I laughed. "I didn't marry anyone." I looked at her.

She was eyeing me strangely. "Who is your family?" The playful tone of the conversation turned tense quickly.

I looked down and twiddled my fingers. "I don't have a family. I'm too much of a burden."

"Why do you think that?"

"Because," I tried to blink away my tears, "I'm sick and *no one* can put up with me, at all."

"What about your best friend?"

"I don't have one of those either. They wouldn't care if I stayed here or not."

"Why do you feel like that?"

"Nobody," I began to hyperventilate, I couldn't stop my tears from rolling down my eyes. "Nobody wants me."

"Yes, they do. Mr. and Mrs. Acolola seem to love you. They took you in."

"Who?" I asked. I'd never heard these names before in my life. They were foreign to me.

"Callum's parents."

"That's their last name?"

Hmph. No wonder why they seemed foreign. Callum's parents might as well be a country away. That's how much distance they kept between us.

"You never knew that?"

"No."

"Well, you learn something new every day, huh?"

"I guess, but that still doesn't change anything."

"Sandi, what's your relationship with your parents?"

"Don't have any."

"Sandi," she said sternly.

"What? Does that not answer your question? I don't want to talk about it." I got up and stormed out. The sunlight shining in from the front doors seemed to brighten up my appearance. I got so angry that I gained my strength back *and* ran up the stairs to the fifth floor.

When I got to my room, I picked up a duffle bag that my "family" must've left for me. It had fresh clothes, pajamas, a toothbrush, shampoo, washcloths, multiple pairs of socks, a hairbrush, my coat, a winter hat, boots, gloves... damn! They expect me to stay the whole winter. *Merry Christmas to me, huh?* I got tired of looking like a clown, pulling an endless supply of cloth out their mouth and took the duffle bag into the bathroom. They might as well pack my whole room into a suitcase and mail it to me. I slowly undressed. I had a bruise on my neck, shoulder, stomach, multiple on my thighs, and one huge one spread across my left hip... not too bad. I turned to look at my back in the mirror. With trembling fingers, I slowly moved my hair over to one side. Little by little, bruises were exposed all down my spine. I started crying but stopped myself...I've been doing too much of that. I grabbed a bar of soap out of the many that were in there and stepped into the shower. As I tried opening the Dove box, I lost my footing and hit my head on the glass. "Shit." I could feel a bump forming on my forehead. I rubbed my head and smelled the soap. Shea butter... smells nice.

I realized I forgot a washcloth and stepped out. I slid across the slippery floor even while trying to keep my balance. I reached for a yellow towel at the bottom of the bag. It had rubber duckies on it, one of my favorite animals of all time... not in rubber form, of course. I stood up, and to my amazement, Callum was standing there. I fell on the hard, cold tile floor and hurt my elbows trying to catch myself. "Ouch." I helped myself up, a bit dizzy from standing up too fast. Thanks to my hair being longer, I used it to cover my breasts. He gawked at me, and instead of making me feel special… it was just plain awkward.

"I brought you your key," he said and held out the ducky designed key.

"Toss it," I said as I held out my hand.

Instead, he took off his coat and slowly walked over to me. "Sandi," he said as he pushed my hair behind my ear. I closed my eyes. Tears streamed down my face. He kissed the bruise on my neck, the one on my shoulder, my thigh, my hip… but when he saw my back… when he saw… he cried. "Sandi, I don't know who to believe anymore. I'm confused. I love you, but I don't believe my parents would do anything to hurt anyone, especially you, Sandi. I know my dad's been pretty hostile toward you before, but he'd never try to hurt you." He broke down. He was as much of a mess as I was. He hugged me and fell to his knees. I went with him, sat down, and wrapped him in my arms. I had to get better, not just for me, but for Callum's sake. He had such a good poker face that I never realized how much this was hurting him… *I* am hurting him…

"Shh now. It's okay, Callum. Your dad didn't do anything," *thump, thump, thu…mp.* I could feel my heart sink into the pit of my stomach. I hated lying to Callum. "My therapist and I worked it out. I'm just sick. I'm loopy in the head. We're going to do something, so I get better, okay? I promise, Callum. I promise." I kissed his head. I just wanted him to stop crying, but he wouldn't. I rocked him back and forth, caressed his face, and tried talking to… lying to him again. "Callum, I'm schizophrenic, okay? I just heard voices and things that weren't there. Darkness will trigger my attacks, you know? I get really scared and freak out, and my senses go extremely haywire and…" My voice began to break. I cried but had to speak through it. I didn't just have to convince him; I had to convince myself. No matter what I thought, deep down I knew I was wrong, and I knew I needed help. "I think something is happening when it's not," I finished. "Callum, I'm so, so, so, sorry. I never meant to put you through this. Never," I said solemnly.

"Were you about to shower?" he asked.

I ignored the fact that he finally spoke, and that was what he had to say. If he didn't say anything… him crying was enough. "I was in the shower actually and forgot a towel, so I stepped out."

"Oh, I'm sorry," he said as he wiped his tears. "I'll wait for you out there." He started toward the door.

"Hey! How'd you get here?" I asked, trying to plant my wet feet on the ground… floor… same thing. He leaned against the doorway, slowly walking back toward me. "Unlike you, I have my license." He smirked. We both knew why I didn't have it. "What? You drove?!" He kissed me deeply. Oh, God! I've missed this. I thought he hated me. When I kissed him back, it must've shocked him. *Did he think I didn't love him anymore?* He slid his hand down my back and pulled me in closer. My body soaked the front of his shirt, but neither of us cared. I pulled away from him. "I should shower, Callum."

He looked at the shower for some odd reason. "No, take a bath." He walked over and stopped the water. He drew my bath and helped me…probably more than he needed to. He soaped up my washcloth and washed me slowly and gently.

"Callum," I said as he washed my left arm.

"Hmm?"

"Why'd you come back?"

"To give you your key," he said firmly.

I gave him a slight nod, looking forward at the tile shower wall.

He sighed. "I wanted to. I was wrong to leave… you never left me," he said.

"Oh!"

"Yeah." He walked over to the sink and got my body towel. "Get out now."

I stepped out, but before my foot touched the floor, Callum caught it with the towel and dried it off, doing the same to my other foot. He wrapped me up like a pig in a blanket and carried me to the hospital bed. He seemed to change his mind and carried me with him while he closed the door and the curtains. He sat in a couch-like chair near the bed and held me. He kissed my forehead. "Sandi, how long do you have to stay here?"

I looked down at what would've been my hands if they weren't all wrapped up. "I was up here preparing to go back to the mental institution. I felt like I needed to, like nobody really cared, I wouldn't be missed."

He held me tighter and rested his head on mine. "Sandi, I'd care. That's why I came back. I needed to apologize. I just had a confused moment. I know you'd never lie to me but…" he paused… and so did my heart. Those words felt like needles stabbing my very being.

I pushed myself out of existence. Goodbye, Sandi Jacobs; unfortunately, there won't be a welcome home banner. Not now, not ever. I am nothing but a troubled teenager with schizophrenia and daddy issues. It's all I've ever known… in fact, I've never known anything. "Callum, I told you what happened. Just forget about it, okay?"

He seemed to sigh with disbelief. "I know."

That was the end of all conversation. We just stayed there, admiring the moment. Unless you're me, you're dreading the moment when you find out that your family turned on you and you ran like a refugee with the wrong people. When you find out that you're locked in with the wrong crowd and now you're convicted by association. The people you love have pushed you so, so, so close to the brink that you're running toward the edge, just to get a vacation. All you need is that push, that final push and then they turn you around and reel you back in so close yet so far away. Making you believe you've taken a few steps away from the edge but then that comforting gust of love pushes you over… they flip the script so quick. I'm falling and if I'm not sure of anything, even if I know nothing, without a doubt, I know I'm better off… when I hit the bottom.

Chapter 19

ABOUT TWENTY-SEVEN MINUTES PASSED BEFORE he let me get up. It was a good rest, though.

"I'm going to get dressed now."

"All right. And I want to take you somewhere."

"Where?" I said from the bathroom.

"Somewhere over the rainbow," he sang sarcastically.

I laughed and looked in the mirror. I'd never looked more alive. My hair was bright and had an intense amount of volume. It was soft and bouncy. My hair had loose waves and fell over my right eye. I bewitched myself with my huge, deep-green eyes. I smiled and put clear lip gloss on before I walked out. I wore a white tank top underneath my black T-shirt, with the white showing a bit at the bottom, a pair of dark skinny jeans, and beige flats. Callum looked at me, and once he noticed my shoes, he laughed.

"You are so weird. You know it's cold outside?" He chuckled.

"I know, but I want to feel the cold," I replied.

"You will once you step outside," he said through his laughter.

I grabbed my coat and my gloves and put them on as I walked toward the door.

Callum followed after me. "Do you even know where you're going?" he said as he caught up with me.

"No, but I know that we're getting out of here." I looked at him, smiled, and held his hand.

"Let's take the stairs. We're going out the back." He pulled me toward the right direction, and we raced down the stairs and out the back door.

I slipped on a patch of ice, and before I fell back, Callum caught me. "Haven't learned how to walk yet, huh?" he asked teasingly.

"Hush, kid," I teased back.

"Where's your car?"

"Over there." He pointed at a 2006 air Mercedes, midsized SUV. I took off running toward the truck. He chirped the car and ran after me. I quickly got in the passenger seat and locked the doors. "Really mature. Who's the kid again?" he teased. He unlocked the door, and I locked it back, unlock, lock, unlock, lock, lock, lock… it didn't make the noise. I pressed the unlock button, and when I relocked the doors, Callum was inside the car. I whipped my head around and looked at him. He revved the engine and wiggled his eyebrows. "Hey, there." He said. I laughed at him, "Really now? It's not a sports car." I pushed him gently, then a bit harder because he'd tricked me… and I'd fallen for it. "But it is mine, and I got it for my Christmas present." He leaned in and kissed me. I slowly ran my fingers through his wavy hair. "Hey! Can I tell you something?" I asked.

He touched his forehead to mine. "Anything."

"I love you." He put his hand on the back of my head, pulled me in, and kissed me.

"I love you, too."

He put the car in drive, and we took off.

"Oh, Sandi, shoot!" he abruptly, almost violently stopped the car.

I grabbed his arm as the back of the truck flew up. "What?" I tried to say calmly.

"You need that duffle bag. You're checking out today."

"Huh?"

He turned around and started driving back. Luckily, we were only five blocks away. He parked the car in the front of the hospital, as close as he could get to the entrance.

"How'd you get your license again?" I said as he got out of the car.

"Wait here," he said.

"Right. Because I was planning on going somewhere," I yelled at him as he ran inside.

He turned to me with a smirk and ran into the hospital door. I couldn't help but laugh, even though he sternly pointed at me, telling me not to. A good five minutes passed before Callum came back to the car. He started the car quickly and drove off.

"What's the matter?" I asked.

"They were giving me a hard time, had to check my duffle bag."

"Why?"

"I have no clue, being stupid."

"Oh."

We went the rest of the way in silence and to my surprise, ended up at the house.

"Wait. I can't go in there. I'm not supposed to be here!" I felt extremely anxious. I was going to have a panic attack.

"Says who? It's your house. Now come on."

We slowly walked to the door. As he unlocked it, I heard one of the twins making noise.

"So you're our aunt, too?" Twin One asked.

"Yes," a woman answered. She had a familiar voice but not one I'd heard in person. He opened the door, and there she stood in all her glory. My godmother Emiliana.

Chapter 20

SOMETHING HURT DEEP INSIDE ME. I felt like I had been thrust into another family because the one I had didn't like me. You know how adopted kids can say their parents chose them and yours are stuck with you? Well, apparently, I should've used gorilla glue instead of school glue because they found a way out. I'm a parentless orphan. I know orphan means you're parentless, but I didn't start with any to begin with. I'm an abandoned possum crying out for someone… anyone… just someone to love me. I felt a tug on my heart, and I stumbled over air. I pressed my hand to my chest and caught myself with the help of Amina's dress.

"Oh!" she yelped. She looked at me strangely. "Sandi, are you okay?" she asked as she tried to pull me up.

I had tears streaming down my face against my will. Callum bent down and whispered, "Let's go to the back hall." He pulled on my arm. I knew people were staring. I just dropped in the middle of confirming our reservation…at the restaurant. I slowly got up, balancing my weight on Callum. We passed Jaycelyn and Dustin on the way. She attempted to talk to me, but I assured her I was fine. I was fine some years ago… now, I'm a train and I've lost the tracks.

I'm crying, just crying, I'm going to get sent back. Great, Sandi. Make yourself cry even more. Well done. The minute we got to the hall, I squeezed Callum and started to sob hysterically. Oh, death, where is thy sting? I think you might've misplaced it and life gave it to me. Unfortunately, it was not something I could slap a stamp on and say

"Return to Sender."

"Sandi darling, are you all right?" Sandra asked.

I didn't look up. Of course, I am not okay, I thought. My parents don't love me. My best friend and his family are sentenced to deal with me, and I haven't had a genuine act of kindness shown to me since...I can't even remember.

"If you need time alone, then we can give it to you. The waiter is here, and we need you both," she said.

I tried to suck it up and be a "man," but I couldn't. She quickly bent down, ripped me away from Callum, and thrust me into her embrace. I latched onto her like a leech... the rest was blurry. My tears got in the way.

* * *

"Sandi..." She began to cry. "I tried talking to you at the hospital, but you hung up on me."

I stared at her. I started tearing up. "Emiliana, why didn't you say 'Godmother'? I'd have never hung up on you." I ran to her and hugged her tight. Here I thought I'd dreamed of her and she wasn't real, but she *was*.

"Sandi, you've got to come to Italy. Please," she pleaded. She gave me a look. I knew it was a warning. There was something she needed to tell me, and I was not safe here. She held me by the shoulders. "Your family misses you. Come for a visit." With that, she exited and strode down the stairs, onto the sidewalk, and away from the house. I opened the door and ran after her, I wanted to walk with her to her car but... she was gone. *Wow! That woman walks fast... unless she got in her car and drove off, but there wasn't one when we pulled up. The whole street and a block down looks like a vacant lot.* Rohan-Kyle walked out from the kitchen and glared at me. I slowly stepped off the porch and into the house with my back turned. I could feel his stare making an incision in my back, so I turned around. Lidianna tried to get him to soften his stare, but he paid her no attention.

"We checked you out of the hospital. You will go to therapy every day until told otherwise. You are sick, mentally ill, and what you tell my son affects this family. As quickly as I brought you in, I will gladly get rid of you," he said sternly.

My mouth dropped open, but I covered it and began to cry. I walked toward the door. Callum grabbed my arm tightly and pulled me into him. He quickly wrapped his arms around me. He knew I would try to get away. "Sandi, it's okay. He's just upset. He didn't mean that." Callum tried to reassure me.

"Oh, yes, I did," his father said.

"Callum, let me go… let go!" I yelled.

"Sandi… then, I'm coming with you."

"No, you aren't," his father interrupted.

I jerked away from Callum and ran out the door. Jaycelyn and Dustin were walking toward the house. Dustin grabbed me. "Hey, kid! Where ya goin'?" he asked.

"Away from here. Nobody wants me here. No one!" I yelled furiously. I could feel my face turn red with anger, but as much as I wanted to be angry, I just didn't have it in me.

Jaycelyn stormed into the house. "What did you say to her?" she hissed.

"Where did she go?" Callum asked.

"That way," Dustin said and pointed to his left.

Callum ran out, started the car, and drove after me. Sadly, I didn't get far, and he found me in no time.

"Sandi, come here!" he yelled.

I hopped in. He put the car in park and hugged me. "Sandi, don't do that again," he said.

"All right. All right. Can I go to school with you tomorrow?"

"Yeah, sure… why?"

"I don't want to be at the house anymore. I can't be a burden anymore."

"You're not, Sandi, you're not."

I looked down. I couldn't speak. My heart hurt too much.

He stared at me. I could tell I was hurting him too. "Hey! I have something for you." He leaned over and kissed my cheek. He reached to the back seat, struggled a bit, but finally got what he needed. "Close your eyes. No peeking."

I shut them tight. Then I felt something heavy, like a weight, be plopped onto my lap. My book. I didn't have to write in a stupid diary anymore!

"Callum, thank you!" I had the widest grin on my face ever. "Thank you, thank you, thank you!" I gave him a ton of tiny kisses on his cheek and his forehead.

"Mhm, we are going to go somewhere."

"Where?" I asked.

"Seatbelt, Miss Jacobs," he instructed.

"Fine, Mr. Acolola." I smiled slyly. "Didn't know I knew that, huh?" I teased back.

"Hmph. Smart girl you are." He started driving, and for a moment, the world didn't exist.

"Me? Of course, I am!" I said over dramatically.

"You're such a kid."

"Umm last I checked, you're the kid." I teased.

"You are only a *month* older than me." He stressed.

"Yeah, that whole month makes a difference, you know."

"That's okay. I like older women anyway."

I blushed just a tad.

"Especially this one girl who's older than me. She's pretty hot."

My cheeks flared red. I covered my smile with the back of my fingers, rested my elbow on the armrest, and looked out the window.

"And she has long hair. I love girls with long hair. Oh, excuse me. Young women with long hair." He was making me squirm on purpose. "Yeah," he said with a sigh, "Jaycelyn's pretty hot."

The look on my face had to be priceless. He erupted with laughter.

I hid my face in my hands and laughed. He stopped the car and turned it off. I was still laughing, but he was completely silent. He tried to pry my hands off my face, but I wouldn't budge. "Sandi, stop," he said as he laughed. I turned my back to him. He slowly moved my hair to the right. I could hear him take off his seat belt. He kissed the back of my neck softly. I slowly revealed my face and bit my lip.

He got out of the car and opened my door. I didn't realize where we were. It was just an abandoned alley, somewhat lit, somewhat not. I slowly got out of the car and closed the door behind me. He pushed me against the door and kissed my neck. He slowly unzipped my coat.

"Callum, it's cold outside," I said as I shivered a bit.

"Not for long." He opened the door and ushered me in. As he closed the door, I took off my coat and licked the left side of his neck.

"Sandi." He moaned. He actually moaned my name. He turned to face me, slid out of his coat, and stared at me. "You are beautiful, Sandi, and I love you. Regardless of what anyone else says or thinks, you are perfect just the way you are. Sick and all, I'm sick, too. We'll get better together, okay?" His words eased my pain a bit.

"Okay, Callum." I kissed him. I couldn't believe how much faith he had in me.

"I love you," he said softly. He was breathing heavily.

I kissed him again. "I love you, too," I said. This was it, the person I know I'll spend the rest of my life with.

He kissed that soft spot at the bottom of my neck, the little groove before the collar bone. He worked his way up my neck and massaged my breasts. I ran my fingers through his hair and pushed him into the door. He seemed to get amusement out of my slight aggressiveness. He let out a dark, sexual laugh. I sat on top of him, leaned in, and licked his neck. I closed my lips in once I got to the top of his neck and kissed him softly. "Mhmm." He rubbed my head. I could hear him breathing heavier. It was sexy, a major turn on. He sat up, switched his position, thrust me onto the seat, and put himself between my legs. He took off his shirt and stared at me. Now hovering over me, he just gazed into my eyes.

"What is it?" I asked.

"Just thinking about how lucky I am to have you. That's all." He shot me a devilish grin as he slid my shirt up and off. He groped my breast somewhat aggressively and kissed me. He looked at my pink lace-trimmed bra and slowly slid the left strap off. He kissed my shoulder and down, following the indent my strap made.

* * *

We all ordered and ate in the back hall. I was so embarrassed. People walked by and stared. My cheeks flared red every time someone walked by. "Callum?" I said quietly.

"Huh?" he said from in the hall.

"Just checking."

"For what? You need me?" he asked.

"Maybe later."

He plopped onto my bed. "What's wrong, Sandi? Talk to me please," he pleaded.

"Are you okay, Callum?"

He eyed me, as if I was playing around too much.

I sighed deeply. "I was just wondering if there is actually anyone out there who actually… loves me."

A tear dropped from Callum's face, and he darted out the room. *Gahh,* I thought. *Someone besides you, Callum, someone who can take care of me.* Usually, I'd run after him, but I was too tired. I just sat in silence…well, I laid in my bed all day, but I thought about a lot. I tried not to, but I thought and over thought. What I thought about isn't important. What I cried about… my head hurts so bad I don't remember.

"Sandi, Sandi!" I heard a voice scream. I couldn't wake up. I didn't really want to anyway, but still. My sleep felt…wrong. "You're not asleep," I heard a voice say loudly. I ran and whacked into a wall. "You're dead." The words sent a chill up my spine. I turned to face a faceless man, skin malting, eyeball peeling. Literally one eyeball…peeling away. I felt a brutal whack on my shoulder and saw a disembodied arm. Screaming, I flung myself into my desk, knocking over my book. "No, you need that!" he shouted as he charged at me. He pressed me into the floor, and his eye fell on me. I wailed, arms flailing, hair wild, eyes bewildered. He shook me. My head hit the floor. "Shut up." Bash. "Sandi." Bash. "Shut up!" Slap. "Sandi!" Flash. Flash. "You need to know!" Bash. Bleep! Bleep! I threw myself out of my bed, running… sprinting, fleeing from the man and finding comfort in the rock solid…cobblestone wall? Darkness, absolute darkness. My hands and knees burned. I felt like I belly flopped off a cliff…naked.

I slowly stood up. I felt…no…I didn't. It was an absolute void, a black hole. I didn't feel any walls, barely the floor. I heard huge footsteps thumping down the hall. I slapped a hand over my mouth. I couldn't scream. Period. I was tripped up and hit on the head, vision blurring. The footsteps accelerated. They were…coming toward me. I whimpered and scuffled back. "Will you be quiet!" I gaped, paused. I saw a figure looming in the darkness. Besides that, the only thing I could see was my breath. I couldn't even see my hand in front of my face, and I'd been pretty pale lately. I felt a tug on my ear, a woman's hand.

"Don't play stupid, child. This way," Lidianna whispered.

We walked to a mid-lit, medieval-style room. The torches that lit the room had a darker presence.

"Lidianna, where are we?"

Thwack. The ugly noise made my ears ring. My cheeks felt hot. I was cold. Correction, the floor was cold. I felt blood dripping down my neck. I tried to lift my head. Thwack! My temple hit the floor. My lip bled, head leaking. Knowledge, personality, life…leaking. I survived, except one category, life.

"Sandi Jacobs, you hear me?"

"Who?" I said.

"You…"

"Who are you?" I asked.

"Your…guardian."

"Name?"

"Don't you remember?"

"Do I?"

"Why are you so sarcastic?"

"Why are you so unfamiliar?"

"Child, quit fooling around."

"I'm going back to sleep."

"Sleep? You're dead."

"Am not!" I yelled.

"Are, too."

"No!" I shouted.

"Hmph. Whatever helps you to the grave."

"I'll prove it." I walked to the doorway and gripped the smooth wood surface.

"Child, what are you doing?"

I bashed my head on the doorway. Once, twice, eleven times.

"Stop!" she shouted. "Sandi, knock it off!" she yelled. "Now!"

I was thrust into my dresser. I blinked a few times and saw Lidianna. Callum was staring at the blood on the doorway and the gash on my forehead. I felt a slap across my face.

"Jaycelyn!" I yelled.

She was already in the room…watching. Rohan-Kyle stood in front of me, glaring at me. He yanked me up and dragged me downstairs. He walked into the kitchen…I already knew what number he was dialing.

I stood facing the kitchen doorway, head throbbing, and blood gushing down my face. I stared down at my folded hands. With tears swelling in my eyes, I held back a cry for help, even though I knew I needed it. I ran to the nearest bathroom. I passed Amina and Sandra on the way. My cheeks turned a blazing red. I slammed the bathroom door shut, gripped the sink, and stared at myself in the mirror, blood dripping down my nose. I punched the mirror and crumbled to the floor, glass trickling off the sink like water. Blood stung my eyes. I could only cry out so much. No one understood, not a single person. Someone had been furiously pounding on the door. I rubbed crust from my eyes. I was still lying on the bathroom floor, hugging myself…for warmth? I can't remember.

"Open this damn door, Sandi!" Dustin yelled.

My eyes widened. I'd never heard him talk like that…to me. Of course, I was not me…not at all.

"Jus…" my throat hurt…bad.

"Now!" Rohan-Kyle shouted.

I perched myself up on my elbows. I could barely see. I slithered to the door, slowly but surely. I put my hand on the extremely warm knob and the rest…the rest, I don't remember. The door hit me on *my way out*. Beep…beep…beep…beep.

* * *

I couldn't tell anyone the last time I was sent back to a mental institution. I went back and forth for so long that they started to feel like field trips. I got put in and pulled out like a fishing hook, except this time, I didn't fight everyone's dying need to take me back. I sat up on my hospital bed and dangled my legs over the edge. I grabbed my water cup off a tray in front of me. It had a sticky note attached to it that read: "Concussion. Take these. It'll help." I raised an eyebrow. Where's the nurse? Shouldn't they keep track of these kinds of things? Despite the nurse's inattentiveness, I followed the instructions. I planted my feet firmly on the floor and walked out into the hallway. The receptionist wasn't at her desk either. *Hmm?* I followed the long hallway and stared at the various pictures on the wall as it curved. I could hear voices whispering ahead, and the closer I got, the more familiar they were.

I inched forward against the wall until I made it to where another hallway intercepted this one and I dove for cover behind a bench. "Listen. I did what you asked. This is all becoming more and more convoluted as this entire situation drags on. How much longer are we going to have to do this?" I heard a woman ask.

"Trying to back out now won't help you. You'll only be hurting yourself. You signed your name on the dotted line. No one forced you to do this," Lee said. I held back my surprise as I peered around the bench. There Lee stood in the flesh. The *audacity*. He was speaking to Lidianna, the traitor. I knew it. All this time, I wasn't crazy. She crossed her arms and stepped in closer, trying to keep her voice low. "Lee, I don't know how much longer I can keep this up. It's hurting my boy and that hurts me. You get that, right?" She gave him a pleading look.

What couldn't she do? Were they talking about me? YES, a small voice answered assertively. I knew they were but what exactly?

"Lidianna," Lee started. He gently pulled at the collar of her dark gray cardigan and smoothed it down. "You know you could've been mine so many years ago." He sniffed her hair and exhaled heavily. She put a hand to his chest, attempting to keep distance between them. "No, you were too invested in your studies and your underage violin student," she replied.

"You were, too, when you found out she had just what we were looking for." He paused giving her a long, hard gaze. "And she wasn't that young." He finished.

She backed away from him in astonishment, "She was eight." She hissed.

"Was she? Hmm...Who was paying attention?"

Lidianna scoffed, "You can be sickening sometimes, I swear. You practically... no, you did rape that girl."

"Nevertheless, Janessa never complained. She's always been good about those things."

I pushed my back against the wall next to me.

Did he do... what? None of this was making sense. I decided I was going to confront them. I wanted answers, and I wanted them now. I whipped my body around the corner and beelined for them. "Hey!" I shouted. What was the worst they could do, kill me? People would know I was missing... scratch that. I think I was just beginning to devalue my life. They continued talking, paying me no attention even as I walked straight… through them? I held my hands out to the sides to steady myself. I felt really weird, to say the least.

"Whatever," Lidianna snapped. "Look. I gave her the pills, like you asked. What does this have to do with my son? I told you I don't want him wrapped up in this." She reached for his hand, but he pulled away.

He pointed a finger at her and gave her a stern look, "You know it's already too late for that, I told you to keep him away from her. Attachments happen, I get it, but the minute he falls for her, you have to get rid of the problem." Her mouth flung open, but there was no sound.

I couldn't face them. I held my hands out still like an idiot. I was waiting for the floor to be snatched from beneath me. "You understand me, don't you?" Lidianna nodded her head carefully, dread slowly creeping over her face. "Rohan wouldn't stand for this. That's his boy, Lee. There's got to be something else. We can separate—"

Lee held up a hand to her face, cutting her off. "That boy's gonna stir up a fire in her and when he does…" He took a finger horizontally across his throat.

I mustered up the courage to turn around just in time to miss them leave. Bewildered, I knelt on the floor, trying to grasp a hold of reality. I didn't need to be facing them to know what Lee meant. Whatever business they were dealing with had nothing to do with me, I hoped against my conscience. I shut my eyes tightly, telling myself it wasn't real like a mantra of sorts.

"Darling, are you all right?" an African-American man asked me. He had a shiny bald head and was wearing a blue security uniform. He knelt down next to me and placed a hand on my shivering shoulder. "See something strange?" he asked softly.

I rubbed my eyes with the back of my hands and nodded. "Yeah," I confessed, "they were there. Where'd they go?" I looked at him pleadingly. I wanted him to tell me no one was there, but I wanted so badly for him to assure me I wasn't losing my mind. If they weren't there, I was insane for sure… and I was tired of not believing myself or being myself. He slapped his blue cap on his knee. "I'll tell you what, hon. You come with me, and we'll go look at the security tape." With that, he took off and led me to an elevator.

I had to jog to keep up with his long legs. Four of my steps was one of his. We went up to the fourth floor, one floor above where I was staying. We exited the elevator and walked straight ahead to a stand-alone door at the end of the hall. As we reached it, the security guard grabbed a shiny silver key out of his breast pocket.

"Wait," I said and blocked the door with my arm. "Isn't this kinda breaching your umm… security commitment?"

He raised a brow at my question and placed his blue cap atop my head. He knelt down and pushed my hair behind my ears, revealing more of my face. "There. Now, you're official." He reached for the knob and opened the door. "Go on," he said as he rose to his feet.

I inched forward, skeptical of the dimly lit room.

"Hey! How'd you get in?" a blonde asked me.

"She's with me," the security guard said as he walked over and kissed the woman on her forehead.

I smiled. "Interracial couples are so cute," I said softly.

"Mhmm you think?" the woman asked.

I nodded. "It shows that there's lots of love in the world," I replied. She flashed a toothy smile my way and continued on busying herself. I observed the security guard that guided me here closely and then at the woman and back at him. "You're missing your name tag." I pointed out. He looked down and back up at the monitors. "You are a very smart lady." He waved for me to come over.

"Yeah, I know," I said and trotted my way toward him.

There was a seventy-five-inch screen split up into what seemed like a million different sections. They had a pretty awkward set up in here.

He leaned over the desk as he pushed some random buttons on a keyboard and switched the screen into thirds. "So what is your name, sir security guard?" I asked.

On the far-right side of the screen showed me leaving my room and descending cautiously down the hall. "You can give me a nickname if you'd like, but it's Ellis Hull," he replied.

"Hmm… interesting," I said as I peered at the screen. The middle section showed me crossing into view and then ducking behind the wall. Ellis crossed into view not too long after and watched me from a distance. I hadn't even noticed him. I looked over to the far left of the screen where I shouted at *nothing*.

My heart ached from some untold truth that I forced myself to believe in, but I'd been lying to myself the entire time. What a shame. My heart said one thing, but my mind said another. How tiring. Suddenly, the world turned on its side, and everything went out of focus. I took deep heavy breaths as I got down on all fours, trying to balance myself against the now rocking room. I blinked hard, once, twice. Where was I? Abruptly, I was pushed back into white space. I watched in horror as I saw Ellis and the rest of the room become further and further away. Ellis was moving to my side, but everything was in slow motion. It looked like a frightening movie scene. My heart raced as I watched myself outside of my body. My floating self came to an aggressive halt, and I was dropped out of midair. I hit the ground with a thud. I rolled onto my side, shut my eyes tight, and clenched my stomach, trying to regain control of my mind and breathing.

"You should stand. It makes it better. The quicker you learn it, the better."

I glanced in the direction the voice was coming from. There stood an Asian man. He wore a leather jacket, a blue shirt, black pants, and boots to match. He had a scar across his left eyebrow, which he used his long bangs to cover up. I drew in as much air as I could before it began to hurt. I grunted and whimpered as I strained myself to get up. My legs were wobbly, and my arms were noodles. With this new mysterious man's help, I was able to stand. I dusted myself off and cleared my throat. "Who are you?" I asked as calmly as I could under the circumstances.

"Ah, yes, where are my manners?" He clasped his hands together.

"I'm Mikko. I usually don't introduce myself under these kinds of conditions, but it is very much needed." He sucked in a sharp breath as he circled around me. "What am I missing? I don't get all this stuff. I don't understand what's going on. Can you dumb it down? You know, eight-year-old dumb?" I say out of breath. He stood in front of me, a puzzled look overtaking his face. "You don't have the mind of an eight-year-old now, do you?" he asked.

I shook my head in confusion, "Listen. My entire life has been one huge riddle, and I'm only this many," I say in a child-like tone and hold up eight fingers. "So could we have a normal conversation. Better yet. What is this?" I asked, circling my finger in the air.

"We'll call it your safe space," he said.

I nodded slowly, ignoring the pain slithering down my spine.

"Sandi," a voice called out in a melodic tone.

I hadn't noticed I'd closed my eyes. I opened them to see myself… well, another of me. "Hi…um…me," I said awkwardly. My clone waved back at me with a smile and giggled.

"Wow! I never thought you'd let me out into the limelight," my clone said.

"What do you mean? Are we the same person?" I asked.

"This is your inner you, your intuition, the one that holds your inner truth," he said as he stood next to her.

"Again, with the riddle talk, Mikko?"

"Sandi," my clone said softly, "I want us to be happy. We can't be happy in that house or this hospital. Someone is conspiring against us before we even have a chance to do anything wrong." Her voice became dark the angrier she got. "We can't let them get to us. Lidianna, Rohan-Kyle, Mom, Dad, they're all in on it. You're not safe here *or* in that house," she said.

"What? Why are you… no more, I want no more of this maddening sickness. Stay out of my head, I just want to be normal."

I turned around and ran back in the direction I'd come from, but there was just white space. I could hear Mikko calling out for me, but I didn't look back. He appeared in front of me, and I ran through him like mist from a sprinkler. "S-S- Sandi." He sounded like a dying animatronic. His body faded in and out until he disappeared. I stood alone, staring at where he once was, unsure of how to get out of this place. A hand gripped my wrist tightly and whipped my body around. There Mikko was, with his face dangerously close, blood seeping through the corners of his lips, his face contorted. One side of his head had been scalped, and his neck was skinned enough to see his vocal cords working. "You will be dead!" he shouted and grabbed my shoulders with both hands. I screamed as my body floated upward. I shut my eyes tightly, and when I opened them, I was back in my hospital room. Lidianna had been sitting at my bedside drawing liquid from a container into a syringe… in the middle of a hospital.

She flicked the needle and squirted some of the liquid out. I looked down at my strapped down arms and legs. I could hear my heart monitor beeping loudly… in the middle of the hospital, where not a soul had come to check on me. I tried to wiggle free. I tried to scream, to no avail. My mouth had been stuffed with a towel. "Don't move too much. I don't want to hit something important," she said as she placed her hand roughly against my forehead. I screamed louder as she held my head in place. "Hush! No one will come. It's just better this way, if you don't know." The needle pierced deep into my skin and lulled me to sleep. My heart rate dropped rapidly. My eyes fluttered one last time before the dark void of slumber took over.

I stood facing the kitchen doorway, head throbbing, and blood gushing down my face. I stared down at my folded hands. Tears swelling in my eyes, I held back a cry for help… even though I knew I needed it. I ran to the nearest bathroom and passed Amina and Sandra on the way. My cheeks turned a blazing red. I slammed the door shut, gripped the sink, and stared at myself in the mirror, blood dripping down my nose. I punched the mirror and crumbled to the floor. Glass trickling off the sink like water. Blood stung my eyes. I could only cry out so much. No one understood, not a single person. Someone had been furiously pounding on the door. I rubbed crust from my eyes. I was still laying on the bathroom floor, hugging myself for warmth. I can't remember.

"Open this damn door, Sandi!" Dustin yelled.

My eyes widened. What's the word when you experience something again? Ah, déjà vu. But this hadn't happened… had it? I'd completely lost all memory of my last hospital visit, but why remember it now in a time like this? I put my hand on the extremely warm knob and the rest… the rest I can remember. My heart rate monitor continued to drop as my memory slipped away like rainwater through a drain. Beep… beep…beep…be—uzz…buzz.

Chapter 21

Callum and I pulled into his driveway and hesitated for a minute before we went inside. As we walked up the steps, he kept his hands on my shoulders, his attempt at making me feel safe. I slipped inside, bolted up the stairs, and beelined for my room. I shut the door quietly behind myself and took in a deep shaky breath. I blinked once, then another time, squeezing my eyes shut until I saw dots. Yet I still saw the silhouette of a six-foot man draped in my curtain, staring aimlessly out the window. I tiptoed quietly over to the end of my bed and slid my fingers along the bed frame as I snuck around to the side of the bed near the window. I knelt down and slid my book underneath the bed for safekeeping. A floorboard creaked behind me and sweat beaded on my forehead as I pretended not to notice. Paralyzed, I stayed with one arm tucked away underneath my bed and my other hand gripping the edge of my mattress. A finger trailed down my spine and then across my scalp. "I really don't want to do this right now. Please," I mouthed. I couldn't push any words out. It felt like something was stuck in my throat, and all I could focus on was breathing correctly.

I stared at the door helplessly, praying someone would come in and break me out of this trance. I felt something prickly creep across the hand I had under the bed, and I swallowed hard as the creepy crawly revealed itself. It had the body of a tarantula, but one big veiny eyeball sat in the middle of its body. Its legs made a lot of sharp crooked angles and the creature continuously made a clicking noise. Its "skin" moved in waves from back to front. A handful of my hair had been braided while I was distracted by the spider-like creature. I could hear the man kneel behind me as he grabbed my arm and placed it on the top of the bed. My breath became ragged as he brushed his knuckles up and down my sides. Tears fell down my cheeks as he undid my pants and slipped them down my legs enough for him to work with. I could *hear* him unbuckle his belt, I could *hear* his breathing become heavier. I could *hear* him tauntingly telling me not to scream, even though he knew I couldn't.

My lips trembled as he interlaced our fingers. He was so real… but Rohan-Kyle couldn't see him. The man grunted as he pushed himself inside me. I clenched my teeth and choked back a sob of pain.

"Sandi!" Rohan-Kyle yelled.

I stared at him blankly. I could barely hear him over the slapping sound of flesh. I felt like a cave of rocks just collapsed on to my chest and restricted my breathing. I clasped my hands together and prayed to God, any God that would make this man go away. Tears streamed down my face. I whimpered as my insides began to burn, and he covered my mouth. His sounds echoed off the walls as he threw his head back and pushed himself inside harder. He hit a barrier somewhere deep within me, and I curled my toes so tight I felt cramps dance across my legs.

"Shh," Rohan-Kyle said, looking past me.

No matter how hard he looked he wouldn't see what was bothering me. I screamed wildly, but they were stifled by this man's tight grip around my mouth like a muzzle. Rohan-Kyle turned my face to look at him. I hadn't even noticed that he'd stepped in so close. "I've been calling you from the doorway for a while now. What's the matter with you? Why are you making so much noise?" he asked.

My eyes pleaded for Rohan to help me. I tried to reach out to him, but my arm was yanked back and pinned behind me as my face was stuffed into my comforter. I could hear the others running up the stairs. Lidianna made it into my room before anyone else. The man yanked my hair, pulling my head violently onto his shoulder. With newfound caution, his sounds of pleasure grew into an ominous roar, but this time, it was not loud enough to overpower my muffled pleas for help. I cried uncontrollably as my body was contorted from the inside out, blood seeped down my leg in a small steady stream. Lidianna urged Jaycelyn, Dustin, and Callum to go downstairs and get various random things that were supposed to make me feel "safe", a detail I didn't have enough time to pay attention to in my given state. The man's grunts were a crescendo as my screaming turned into inaudible whimpering and trembling.

"Shh, shh, shh," Lidianna said with urgency, a finger lifted to her lips as if that would keep me calm.

The man finally got off, in more ways than one, and I stayed staring at the doorway. He quickly pulled up my pants and fastened them. Then, he laid himself down on my bed. My hands trembled as Rohan and Lidianna helped me up off the floor. They'd been speaking to me the entire time, but I'd never heard a word they said. The man had his back facing me as they pushed me toward the doorway.

"Y-Y-You don't see him?" I cried. "Y-y… no one saw what… no one," I said in a raspy voice. I looked between the two of them frantically.

"Who, Sandi?" Rohan asked. He turned me to face the bed, but I bucked roughly against them and looked down.

"I don't want to see his face!" I exclaimed, but with shaky hands, Lidianna pushed me to look anyway. She peeled my eyes open one by one with her hands. **No one,** absolutely *no one* was laying in my bed. I ripped myself away from them and looked underneath my bed. Empty. I looked in my closet. Empty. I ran to the window, pried it open, and stuck my head out, searching the streets for him. He wasn't here… he never was. I leaned against the window, sticking most of my frame out of it. *I should jump.* My fingers gripped the window sill as I stretched my body out a little further. Rohan-Kyle snatched my lifeless shell up and out of my room.

Callum held my hand against my will all the way to the hospital I'd just snuck out of. For four invasive hours, doctors poked and prodded and swabbed at me. They gave me medication to "calm me down," but it really just put me under. I could still feel them touch me, spread me open, stick me with foreign objects. I could hear the doctor barking orders to the nurses and the scratching of their pencils on their clipboards. I could hear them mention my schizophrenia and my many made up tales. I could hear the disbelief in their voices, even though I swore up and down that there was another person in my room. I could hear them call my therapist. I could hear… everything all over again. The way my breath shuddered when he touched me, the thoughts in my mind telling me to run and scream for help. The sounds that wet flesh made when they were constantly pushed together. The various screams mixing in with his groans and moans, creating a cocktail of chaos and disgust. How he rocked himself against me as he let me have it.

I said little to nothing to my therapist except, "I thought I was dreaming the entire time up until I'd just gotten up." I cried in the shower later that night as quietly as I could. Trying to wash away the sticky feeling and the bruises he left in his wake. I slept with Callum in his room and cuddled in closed to him. I silently apologized over and over for not giving him my virginity earlier today. Now, it had been stolen from both of us. I slipped out of bed and into my room to look at the bloodstain on my floor. This was all the proof I had that something happened. I went into Callum's room to grab my phone, but it wasn't plugged in on the nightstand where I'd left it. I ran my fingers through my hair. *Did I leave it at the hospital? No. You pulled it out in the car on the way home.* I searched in his drawers, under the bed, under the sheets, in my nightgown pockets, my bra, and under the pillows. Callum shuffled around and turned over. I stomped down the stairs and searched around in the kitchen. No luck.

I went into the living room and pulled the cushions off the couches, but it was to no avail. I saw Mikko standing in front of the doors to the kitchen. He tapped his knuckles against the doors. I glared at him. "I'm not in the mood for anymore of this schizo bullshit, really I'm not. So whatever twisted joke you think you'll be pulling, I'm not having it. I've had enough. I'm done." I grumbled as I angrily put the cushions back in place.

"Hmph. Looks like you need my help," he responded.

"Oh, is that it? Hmm? Is that what this is about again? Was that scene earlier your doing, Mikko? Where were you then? Why are you trying to play a knight in shining armor now with a phone, instead of when I *really* needed you? You're sick," I said, keeping my voice at a low hiss.

He made his way over to me, grabbed my arms, and led me to the kitchen sink. He bent over, opened the cabinet, grabbed my phone, and shoved it in my hands. "Listen. There's only so much I can d-d-do. Around… here." His voice started to sound like a toy using up the last little juice from a dying battery. I hated when this happened. "Sandi," he whispered from behind me. His neck was broken, and his eyes were gaping black holes.

I'd learned to control myself when Mikko was like this. "Tomorrow. School. Talk." He dissipated into the air, and Dustin was standing in front of me with Rohan-Kyle. They were fully dressed, and Dustin had his car keys in his hand. "What're you doing?" Dustin asked.

"I was looking for my phone. I left it on the counter." I stood on my tiptoes. "What are you doing?" I tossed back, I felt defensive for various reasons.

"We're going on a joyride," he responded. "You're still allowed to go to school with Callum tomorrow. It'll give you other things to focus on besides… your illness," Rohan-Kyle said. "Keep your mind super busy," he finished.

I smiled, thanked him, and went back to the scene of the crime to snap a photo. However, the bloodstain was gone. *I saw that coming.*

The annoying vibrating noise my phone made against my night-stand finally made me cave to wake up. In a haze, I answered the phone. "Hello?" I said grumpily.

"Whoa! Someone woke up on the wrong side of the bed," Callum teased.

"Sorry. Didn't get much sleep."

"Oh, too nervous about your first day?" he asked.

"Uh, yup. Yeah." I lied. Truth is I couldn't sleep the rest of the night after the close encounter Callum and I had. That and I kept thinking about my illness and how I'd begged not to be put on medication because I could handle it. I'd been saying that since I was diagnosed *years* ago, but I never really got a grip on it. Every time I thought I had, it slipped through my fingers like sand. "Are you even getting ready, Mr. Grinch?" Callum provoked.

I growled at him in response. I jumped out of bed and whisked around until I made it to the bathroom, hopefully looking somewhat presentable. "I am now," I gurgled, mouthwash dripping down my neck. Jaycelyn knocked on the door gently. It seemed that I, somehow, saw less and less of her as the years went by, even though we stayed under the same roof.

"You all right?" she asked.

I could hear her pacing back and forth beyond the bathroom door.

"Yeah." I turned on the faucet and splashed my face with water. "Just a little nervous is all," I replied.

"Can I come in?" she asked.

"Yes, please."

She turned the knob hesitantly as her slender frame came into view. I never noticed how thin she'd gotten. "What?" she asked defensively, which meant I was bad at hiding my shock. I shook my head and examined my eye in the mirror. "Nothing. Just got something in my eye." I looked back at her. Disbelief was written all over her face. I took a deep breath. "I just… where's the time gone, Jess?" I gripped the sink as I peered into it. Tears swelled in my eyes and mixed with the running faucet as I failed to blink them back. There was so much worry on Jaycelyn's face all the time that it pained me to look at her. The more of a burden I became to her and everyone else, the more of a burden they became on me. My only choice had been to stay away, from her and my nephews. It was better this way for them. I sighed, *So then, why do I feel so guilty?*

"We should hang out sometime, don't you think?" I asked, forcing myself to look at her. I had to prove I was okay, even if I had to fake it until I was.

Her expression lightened a bit. "Yeah, of course. What about today? We could go out to lunch or something?" She grabbed my brush off the sink and gently brushed my wild mane behind my ears.

"That sounds cool. I'm only going half of the day today, so could you pick me up around one-thirty?"

She nodded in response. "There. You look so nice," she said. Her face dropped. "Tehran is in the kitchen making breakfast…they're waiting on you."

I looked at her in the mirror. She was curling her long black locks on her finger. I nodded slowly. *This couldn't get any sketchier, could it?* Jaycelyn spun me around, her face wrinkled up in a serious expression. "You know I wouldn't let anything happen to you, don't you?" My mouth gaped open, but words didn't come out. Instead, I hugged her briefly and made my way downstairs.

"Mornin', pumpkin!" Tehran called out cheerfully as I entered the kitchen.

"Good morning to you," I said as brightly as possible with nerves eating away at my appetite. I slid into a chair next to Kennith and gave his shoulder a squeeze.

"You're looking pretty pale this morning, little lady. You all right?" Tehran asked as he took pancakes from the skillet he was holding and piled them on to a plate in front of us. I imagined a scenario, Tehran asked the guys to go do some mindless task, next thing you know, I'm being branded on the face with a frying pan. *I can smell the flesh now, yuck.* Someone whacked my hand hard and broke me out of my trance.

"Dude, what are you doing?" Dustin asked while he looked over my hand.

I furrowed my brow. "What?" I countered. Clueless, I had reached for one of the steaming skillets of veggies on the table and stayed there. Dustin raised an eyebrow at me. I already knew what he was thinking.

He had I'm-not-so-sure-this-is-a-good-idea etched all over his face. I didn't blame him. If I spaced out like that in a classroom setting, who knew what I'd do.

"Sandi, are—"

I patted his lips, shushing him. Even if this was the most dangerous idea of the century, Mikko needed to speak to me, and he'd get a mouthful to hear from me.

"Don't worry. I just spaced out… in a daydream sort of way," I assured him, but his face remained firm on his position.

"Seriously, Dustin, I'm not gonna go around screaming bloody murder the entire time I'm gone. Only when I'm home," I joked.

Still he remained unmoved. Instead, he started preparing a plate for me. He stacked it high with blueberry pancakes. There was also an omelet and two slices of pineapple on the side. After decorating the omelet with various veggies from the table, he sat the plate in front of me. He gave me a peck on the cheek. "I love you, kiddo. You'll do great." He squeezed my cheek and then tended to Jaycelyn and Lidianna as they joined us at the table.

I expected breakfast to be anything but silent, and it definitely lived up to my expectations. Everyone was rowdy and laughing and talking about their plans for the day. Tehran showed us a few pictures from their visit to Canada, and just when I had gotten comfortable, there came the interrogation. "Anywhere specific you'd like to visit, Sandi?" Tehran asked.

I shielded my mouth with my napkin, so no one could see my food. "Oh, I dunno." I swallowed hard. "I kinda want to go to Italy to visit my godmother." A piece of egg dropped out of my mouth and on to the table. Whoops. Callum's cousin started chuckling at my mishap. Leave it to Kennith to laugh at *everything*.

"Sandi, don't talk with your mouth full. It's piggish." Lidianna started and smiled at me. "No boy at school is going to like you if you're not lady like," she said gleefully.

Callum pointed his fork in my direction and pieces of syrupy egg stuck to Kennith's face. I held my head down and laughed silently. "I like her." My head jolted in his direction. He stabbed his scrambled eggs. "She doesn't need to worry about other guys." He brought his fork up to take a bite but hesitated. "As a matter of fact, be as gross as you'd like, ward off all the other guys." He glanced at me while finally tending to his fork.

The excited look on Lidianna's face was overtaken with sorrow. She gnawed on her empty fork and tapped her fingers on the table gently. She caught my stare, but hers never wavered. I opened my mouth, clasped it shut, and raised an eyebrow at her. I sighed, "Callum, you know what Stockholm syndrome is, right?"

Although I spoke to him, Lidianna and I kept our gazes locked. She began tapping her foot impatiently.

"Yes…what does that have to do with…" He paused, thinking for a minute. I could feel him glare at me, but that was it. "W-What's wrong with you guys?" he asked Lidianna and me, but neither of us jumped at the opportunity to explain. I wouldn't be the one to tell him if she wasn't. She'd be responsible for breaking his heart. I could never hurt him like that, the pain she must feel watching him do the exact opposite of what she'd prayed for.

Tehran cleared his throat. "Lidianna," he said once, then twice before he tossed a crumpled up napkin at her. She snapped her gaze to Tehran. "Huh?" She was visibly shaken up. "Come on."

Tehran rose to his feet and went to hold the kitchen door open for her as she followed him out. "You have a problem with us being together, don't you?" Although he questioned her with an accusing tone, Callum already made up his own answer. "Honey, it's complicated… it's not that. That's not it."

Tehran placed a hand on her shoulder, shook his head, and whispered something to her. "Callum, I don't think any parent would want their son with me. The whole psycho thing is kind of stressful." I shot Lidianna a knowing look. I remembered now, the last time I was in the psych ward of a hospital. I was so close, so close to the brink of truth,

I just can't remember exactly what happened. "It's okay," I mouthed to Lidianna. Tears formed in her eyes, and she took off.

I clenched the straps of my backpack as Callum and I cascaded through the empty halls. "Shouldn't we just head straight to class? You're already super late," I said nervously.

He wrapped his arm around my waist and pulled me in close. "You're way too nervous for nothing. High school sucks really," he replied.

"Wow! You're barely in and already sick of it. Maybe I should turn around."

He gripped me tighter. "I don't think so. Barely in? I've been going to high school since the ninth grade. Where've you been, hmm?" he teased and kissed my forehead. He opened up his locker, stuffed our coats inside, and grabbed a few books he needed for the day. "What's wrong?" he asked. I scooted closer to him, attempting to hide my body inside his locker.

"You see that woman right, the one walking toward us?"

He peeked past his locker and jumped back so hard I fell into the locker the rest of the way. I gripped the sides of the lockers to try to stop myself from falling any further inside what seemed like a void at this point. "Mrs. Strickland, you scared us," Callum confessed as he pulled me out. Mrs. Strickland walked around him to see me.

She extended her hand. "Hi. I'm Libby Strickland. I'm the school counselor." I shook her hand, "Sandi Jacobs. Nice to meet you, Mrs. Strickland." She enveloped my hand with hers. "Oh, please call me Libby, you kids are so formal," she said.

"Okay, Libby it is then," I replied with a smile.

"She's also the school therapist," Callum warned.

I could feel the life in my face deadpan as I withdrew my hand, disgusted I'd been so friendly with her. She grabbed me by the shoulders and looked me over, apparently missing the hint.

"Yes, we should talk soon." Her voice had a sense of urgency. "How about right now?" She gave Callum a strange look. Her grip became overprotective, and I wiggled my way free.

"Later," I said, finally freeing myself.

She nodded. "Extremely soon. It's important if you're going to have a good year here."

Callum shut his locker, and we strode off, leaving Libby watching us like a hawk.

"That was weird," I said.

Callum was so tense he looked like his eyes might pop out of his sockets. "I've never seen her get like that," he replied.

"Maybe it's because I'm starting in the middle of the year?" my voice squeaked. I prayed she didn't already know about my illness. He looked at me apologetically and pulled me in close. "I doubt it," he said and ushered me into our first destination of the day. *It'll never be my story to tell.*

The first couple of hours flew by as we shuffled from room to room. Around lunchtime, the psycho tracker caught me up in conversation and, somehow, lured me to her office. I sat down cautiously on her faux fur couch. I wiped the sweat from my hands onto my pants as I sat down. She leaned on her desk eagerly, awaiting my attention as I scanned the room. She cleared her throat, "Well, this usually doesn't happen this quick," she said and folded her hands together.

I raised a brow at her. "What do you mean? Kids coming to see the counselor?" I asked.

She nodded and reached for her coffee mug. She held the cup to her lips. "So tell me about yourself, things you like, previous schooling." She took a long sip.

"Umm… I don't know where to start." I hesitated, but she egged me along with a hand motion.

I slouched. "Oh, I dunno… umm… I'm learning how to speak Italian. I like dogs, but Callum's dad doesn't want another one since theirs died." I paused.

"Go on."

I looked around the room. My nerves were eating away at the office as I imagined myself in a dark room. I was under unflattering light and a microscope, being prepped to be dissected.

Sweat beaded on my nose. She snapped her fingers. "Hey!" She sat her mug down. "It's okay. No one's going to do anything to you here."

My eyes snapped to her, everything slowly coming back into focus. Just as I opened my mouth to speak, I saw the outline of a man, his threatening aura extremely familiar. He waltzed right through the door. Frozen, I stared at him, waiting for him to turn around, so I could see his face.

"Sandi?" She tried to get my attention by clapping her hands a few times. He glanced at me over his shoulder, his eyes dark and condescending. He held a finger to his mouth and shushed me. Even though I hadn't seen his face before, I knew this was the man from the other night in my bedroom.

"What do you see, Sandi?" The question was so foreign to me that it drew me in like a moth to a light. Ignoring my warning, I opened my mouth to speak. Swiftly, he brought his hand to my neck and squeezed enough to put some fear in me. His eyes began to glow a dark amber as he spoke in some dead language.

Annoyed, I rolled my eyes. If he wanted to take me out, he could just do it. My life wasn't of much value anymore anyway. He chuckled. "Now we both know that's too easy." His tone churned up something maniacal and awful in my very being. I soaked up as much of his appearance as I could emotionally handle, and then I lunged for him. Ignoring his tightening grip on my airway, I grabbed his head and jerked it one way as hard as I could. He receded in pain, double checking to make sure his neck was still intact. I clenched and unclenched my fist. I could feel sparks surging throughout my veins. I wasn't sure what I was going to do to him, but I wanted him to bleed. I wanted everyone to. Mikko appeared in my blind spot. "Sandi, calm down a bit. You don't know what you're about to do." He inched in carefully. I turned my attention back to my victim now. Someone was going to pay up. If not him, I'd find the next best fit and bathe in their vital fluids.

Mikko stood in front of me, snapped his fingers, and my dear prey was gone. I glared at him. "Ugh." I stomped my feet. "Mikko, you never let me have any fun." I groaned.

"Who's Mikko?" the school nurse asked and came to gently stroke my back.

I closed my eyes and sighed. I held my wrists out to the nurse. "Just take me away or whatever you've got to do," I said casually and clenched my eyes tight.

"You're used to this kind of thing, aren't you?" she asked politely but also poking fun at the situation. Finally someone who wasn't so uptight about everything.

"Yeah, it's fine." I opened my eyes. "Where we headed?" I asked.

"Just stay here. This is fine," the counselor said. "You called me for her, though, didn't you?" the nurse asked. "Yes, but only to make sure she was all right, not to haul her out of the office." She gave the nurse a bothered smile. "She's fine now. We can continue on," she finished. *What's with this woman? Why is she pushing to talk with me so bad?* I couldn't figure out what this woman's deal was, but she seemed a little too eager to get to know me.

I let the nurse go about her day and plopped back on to the cozy little couch. "Stretch out. You'll be here a while," she said and stepped outside to stick a "do not disturb" note on the door. She locked the door behind her. Tentatively, I positioned myself to be able to book it once things went down. She sat on her desk and grinned at me. "Now I know you're scared but settle down. You're safe, really." She urged. With due consideration, I listened. I did so reluctantly, but nothing about her stuck out. Mikko appeared on the left side of the couch and took a deep breath. "I think now's the best time we're gonna get, babe," he said.

"I know. I just don't know how to go about this exactly without scaring her," she replied.

"You can forget about that. Too late."

I looked between the two of them, eyes wide.

"Spooked," I interjected.

Mikko grabbed my hand and pulled me in close. He rubbed my

shoulders. “Relax, wild child. We’ll get to explaining stuff in a minute or so. You just plug your ears and try to stay calm,” he advised.

“Are you stupid? I’ll still be able to hear you if I—”

“Hey! No back talk. Plug ’em.”

I sighed and pushed my ears closed with my fingertips.

“Well, she’s the wildest one out of the batch, huh?” Libby said. “She’s got a few screws loose, but nothing we can’t handle,” he replied.

“This is literally the dumbest shit I’ve ever done. I can still hear you.” I squeeze in.

Mikko grabbed hold of me and started tickling me. “Cut it out. I’m not five. This isn’t funny.” I blurt out between constant laughter.

“Enough already, you two,” the counselor said.

“What do you mean ‘you *two*’? *He* did it, not me,” I clarified, while getting out one last giggle. I rested my head on Mikko’s torso, taking note that he felt different. Not just like a wall of energy that I could lean on to or interact with. “Bad news first, guys,” I demanded.

She cleared her throat and took a long pause to think before she said, “You ever heard of the Truman Show?” My jaw dropped, it barely took a second for me to make the connection. I looked up at Mikko, his face affirming every doubt I had in my mind was false. “Now the only problem is how fast can we get little scaredy cat on a plane.” He teased, “Yesterday.” I stated firmly as I shot up and paced around the room.

My mouth started spewing out the things I wanted to do to humanity. All the pain and suffering was going to end in a blood bath. I wanted revenge so badly it should’ve been my first name. I would do terrible, unspeakable things. The rest of the world and my ramblings became almost completely inaudible. There was nothing but loud ringing in my ears. Satan would cower in my presence and beg to kiss my feet. If he didn’t know my name by then, he would. I felt something prick my skin and pinch my neck really hard. I blacked out for, at least, a few seconds, I opened my eyes to my head bleeding a little and the nurse fixing me up. The counselor knocked and came in with a mug of coffee. “Here you go. It should help with the headache,” she said.

"Sorry, hon, ran out of aspirin," the nurse confessed.

"Would you mind checking to see if the office has any before her guardian comes to pick her up?" Libby asked.

The nurse nodded and swiftly exited the room. "Are you okay?" she asked and handed me an ice pack.

I tried to nod, but it hurt too much. "Uh… I dunno, after hearing you tell me that my life was pretty much a bunch of people out to get me like I thought so all along I'm pretty wound up."

Perplexed, she squinted her eyes at me. "Sandi, you kind of umm… you just fell back on to the floor motionless for, at least, fifteen minutes."

Our conversation ended when the nurse left, and then she turned right around to help me assist you." She said. Great, *of course*. Why not imagine this? "I'm sorry, sir. You can't barge in here. You were supposed to wait in the office." Our eyes snapped to Rohan-Kyle. I grabbed my belongings and headed for the door.

She followed closely behind me. "Oh, Sandi!" she called out with urgency. "Be sure to stop by again, so we can finish getting you situated." Rohan-Kyle towered over me and placed a hand on my shoulder. "That won't be necessary." He stared at her icily, making both of our cores shiver.

"Be careful," she said, still looking up at him. He tugged me away and luckily let me sleep in the car.

* * *

"You're very special, little Miss Sandi," Mother said as she spun me around in our great room.

I giggled. "Higher and higher, Mommy. Straight to the moon!" I yelled excitedly.

"Okay. Straight to the moon! Here we come!" she said and lifted me so high I could've swore the butterflies in my tummy took flight and spread out across the room. She set me up for a smooth landing and gently touched my feet to the floor.

"Whoa! I'm dizzy," I said with my hand pressed to my forehead and my body teetering side to side.

Mother laughed, and after a while, a stern look gradually took over her face. "Honey, come here a sec," she ordered.

And I followed. "Is everything okay?" I asked, worried I'd done something wrong.

She gripped my shoulders tightly. "Honey, I need you to listen to me, really listen."

I nodded my head and steadied my body, bracing myself for horrendous news.

"Sandi, someday, when you're older, Mommy might not be around, and you might wonder why." Tears swelled in her eyes. "Mommy's so sorry, baby." She cupped my face in her hands and wiped my tears away. "I'm waist deep in quicksand, and I can't get out. But you can, baby. You can run so far away from here," she said.

"Even to the moon?" I asked between short breaths.

She wiped her nose. "Yes, even to the moon." She paused, grabbed my hands, and looked deep into my eyes, "Sandi, promise me that, no matter what it takes, you'll run as far away from your father and me as possible." She wiped her eyes with the sleeves of her sweatshirt. "But why? Don't you want me to stay? Don't you love me?" I asked, disheartened.

"Oh, of course!" She pulled me in and hugged me tightly. "Have I ever told you the story of the Lion and the Mouse?" she asked.

I shook my head. I listened as I sniffed her hair as if it was the last time I would be this close to her. A foreboding feeling of loneliness consumed me as my poor little mouse continued on. "Well, to sum it up, a lion was trapped in netting and a mouse came by. The lion begged and pleaded for the mouse to chew through the netting to set him free. He swore he wouldn't harm the mouse, that they were friends. The mouse believed him and chewed until the lion was free. When the mouse finally freed him, the lion killed her."

I clung tightly to my squeaky friend as she finished her story.

"A lion is still a lion, Sandi. Never fall for the deceit of words."

With his mane well-groomed and his teeth so bright, his majesty emerged from his den. Ravenous and seeking to devour anything in his sights. If I'm not mistaken, I dipped my head low, eyes beaming a red dot at his forehead. My mouth curled into a snarl, and my eyebrows knitted together. I let out a growl that rumbled deep in my belly and used my body to shield my quivering friend away from the jaws of death. That was the first time I felt the lion in me stand up brave and tall. Father, however, had his eyes set on his new acquired target, and I was right in the line of fire, a perfect bullseye. My mother slipped something in the pocket of my jeans, something I'd lost and never seen at all. "There needs to be a new king of the jungle, Sandi. The old one's gone rotten. You've got the power to make him tremble at your feet and beg for pardon. Snack on his bones." Silly little mouse, you protest too loud for your own ears.

I followed some little girl through thick brush. The wind swept our hair backward and stung our gullible faces. I stepped on a twig, and the sound rang like a crack of lightning. The girl's icy blue eyes shot back at me. "You've got to be quieter, or they'll catch you," she said sternly.

"Sorry," I mouthed and continued to follow her. A branch wacked me in the face and cut my cheek.

Swiftly, she turned around and examined my wound. "Oh, boy, you really know how to be a distraction, huh?" she asked.

"Huh? Yes." I replied. "It's fine. You can speak you know. They either hear us or find the scent from your blood. We can redo the course later, yeah?" She grabbed my hand and stood up. "Come on." She guided me through the bushes and held my hand all the way until we reached the wood line.

Mother ran up the hill from the facility and scooped me up in her arms. "Sweetie, are you okay? What happened?" she asked as she carried me back the rest of the way. As we entered the electric fence that towered well above the adults in the facility, Ms. Strickland removed her shades and chewed on them nervously. "You aren't supposed to do that, Jacobs," she barked.

"My baby is hurt. I authorized myself," Mother retorted.

I eyed Ms. Strickland, all bark and no bite. "Moriah, head inside, hon. We're gonna take Sandi to the medic hall."

Moriah nodded. Her black hair bobbing up and down. Her yellow sundress swayed side to side as she sashayed away. Yellow always made her brown complexion light up. She waved as she entered the eerily white building. I squeezed my mother tight as Ms. Strickland reached out for me. "Give her to me. The medics will take care of her." Mother lurched backward. "They'll reinstate her. She shouldn't have to do this. Jaycelyn doesn't."

"Jayci doesn't participate anymore because there was no reasonable suspicion." Mother groaned disapprovingly. "She's only gotten a small scratch. We can just take care of it." Mother protested.

"Enough, Janessa." Ms. Strickland said and snatched me away.

A blonde-haired teen waltzed into my clinic room with a clipboard and a stack of papers that piled up as big as the Oxford dictionary. She was 5'3" and no more than one-hundred and ten pounds. She caressed my face. "Hey! You up for another round of tests today?"

I shook my head frantically.

"Oh, don't fret too much. I won't let them bite." She shot me a smile and continued fumbling around with her clipboard. She had the ends of her bobbed hair cut curled inward with a pencil on one side and a pen on the other. I raised a hand. "Yes, HXXV8?" she answered sweetly, her smile vibrant. It helped aid to her innocent air. I pointed to the writing utensils twirled around her hair. "Aha! It stops me from losing them. After my last test, I've been experiencing some memory loss." My eyes widened. "Don't worry, XV8. Your tests will be far less rigorous than mine."

There was a knock on the door, and shortly after, a man poked his head inside. "Dr. Gertrude, we're waiting on you," he said.

"Oh, right. Come on now." She rounded me up, along with a few other kids like a shepherd to their sheep. She led us to what was known as the "group testing room" among us kids since you wouldn't go alone.

The room was bright and creatively disgusting. Each one of the four walls had been painted a different color, one green, another blue, the third pink, and the last yellow. There were objects scattered in every corner of the room, all of them varying in shapes, sizes, and obscurities. I rolled my eyes as the rest of the children dispersed. I, however, looked for the coziest corner I could find and tried to nod off, but I kept hearing someone call my name. "Sandi, you can't be sleeping in here. What's gotten into you?" Ms. Strickland asked.

I sighed loudly. "Tired. I am very," I said. It had been two entire weeks, and I still sounded stupid when I talked. She rubbed my head, and Moriah popped out from behind her. "I thought I heard a familiar voice," Moriah joked.

I laughed. "Stupid. I still…sound." I grinned wide.

Moriah always knew how to help me feel better. "Kind of humorous," she replied and scooted in close to me.

I wrapped my arms around her and snuggled her tightly, afraid she might be forced to leave me at any given moment. "How'd it go today?" Ms. Strickland asked Moriah. She kissed my arm lightly before she spoke, "Besides the mission, everything went well." She started playing with my fingers.

"HXWJ8, you are showing very inappropriate behavior." Ms. Strickland warned.

Moriah scrunched up her face. "Love is not an inappropriate behavior. In fact, it's very appropriate to let someone know you care about them. And Sandi is my best friend." She smiled up at me, but my face was filled with dread.

"Don't get yourself into trouble, HXWJ8. Where did you learn that word? We don't use those types of terms," Ms. Strickland asked.

"I heard it from one of the other lab coats. They were talking about Sandi and I. It makes perfect sense describing us with it."

I wanted to warn her to keep her mouth shut, but I couldn't find the will to speak; instead, I clenched my stomach and swallowed hard.

Trouble seemed to follow both of us everywhere, and for some reason, Moriah couldn't figure out when she was getting wrapped into it.

I gave her a little pinch, and luckily, she took the hint. "Listen, as a top percentile candidate for the outlier, you know you shouldn't be making such strong attachments to others. Am I correct?" Moriah nodded her head slowly. "Now off with you. Your presence is not needed at this time." Ms. Strickland demanded, and Moriah reluctantly took off. I sighed. This was the story of my life. *What are we even doing in here?* I thought I was being tested alone. This just looked like a bunch of orphans making a sad attempt at recess. I shook the negative thought to the back of my head and closed my eyes lightly. I thought I'd drifted off to sleep, but when I opened my eyes, I felt exhausted, and the room was dark and desolate. I turned around to see myself slumped in a corner, eyes fluttering gently as I "*slept*." I took one step forward and then another and another until I made it to the door. Each step took a lot of focus and felt like I was waist deep in water with weights in my shorts. The hallway had a single light flickering on and off, drawing me to its presence and out of the unflattering harshness of the sun beaming in through holes in the ceiling. I shielded my face from the seemingly visible UV rays and avoided walking into them as if they were laser beams.

Gravel caught between my toes as I continued inching my way down the hall. "Janessa, you know what happens to those who disobey, don't you?" I could hear Father say. My heart sunk to my stomach, and I sprinted as best I could down the hall. Carefully, I peeked through the key hole where I heard the voices come from and spied. "Darling, please, I don't want to be a part of this anymore. Please," Mother begged. Father strode over to her as she backed herself up onto a wall. My lips quivered, I could feel my fingertips become itchy with anticipation. *You don't have to watch this. You don't have to be the hero every time. You can walk away, walk away.*

He kissed her deeply. "And where will you go? What will you do without this? You've spent your entire life knowing nothing but this way of life," Father responded.

With my body still on edge, I jumped forward and accidentally cracked the door open. I gasped and covered my mouth. Unmoved by my fatal mistake, my parents continued on, "I love you, Lee. I stayed for you. I obeyed for you. Come with me. This doesn't have to be the way we live anymore. Don't you love our daughter, at least?" she asked.

His facial expression remained as hard as stone. "Have I given you reason to believe otherwise?"

Yes.

He countered. He wrapped his arms around her waist tightly, controlling her breathing. My legs began to shake as I watched what seemed like a loving gesture being turned into something so sinister. "This corporation has—" she sucked in a sharp breath and tried to push his arm away. Her face cringed with pain. "We've all fallen under the spell of this corporation. This wasn't the way this was supposed to pan out, and I want to put an end to it. I don't want my daughter to be a part of this anymore." She confessed. Quickly, he grabbed her by the shoulders, looked her sternly in the eye, pulled her in for a deceivingly loving hug, and dipped her toward the floor. "Oh, baby, I do this because I love you." Just like that, he'd pinned her to the ground and struck her face. I let out a yelp as she fought to get away from him. I backed away as she ran toward the door and flung it open, but Father caught her and slammed it shut. She let out a bone chilling shrill, and I could hear her body bang against the metal door.

Her fingernails scrapped the concrete as she tried to stop him from dragging her further in. "Mommy!" I bellowed. I bound through the door, leaving it unmoved, and stood inches away from it. There were streaks of blood along where she'd been clawing so hard. She was shielding her face with her arms, which were bloody from her fingertips. "Lee, please!" she pleaded desperately as he stood and cuffed her to a table. He walked to one of the shelves in the room and grabbed a wooden rod.

"Stop it!" I yelled over and over, using the doorway to balance myself. My vision went blurry from how hard I was crying.

He struck her once to the ribcage, a loud crunching noise echoing back at me from the other end of the room. I fell to my knees, feeling hopeless as he struck her again, this time to the face. A smile crept across his as he continued to *submit* her. She let out a side splitting wail and lurched over on to her stomach, blood spewing from her mouth.

My blood boiled as I dipped my head low in defeat. Somehow, I rose to my feet and found the courage to step in between them. With all of the strength I could muster, I let him swing down at me, and the energy around me reverberated around like someone rang a gong. Shocked, Father stared at his broken rod and noticed a little eyeball peeking through the keyhole. In his amazement, he sprung toward the door and caught Moriah before she could run off. My head felt like it'd been split in two, and I pressed my hands against it to try and stop the pain. I watched him struggle with Moriah until she finally escaped. I melted into the earth like liquid on unthawed meat and found myself waking up to medics and test administrators ripping wires off my body. Everyone was moving with a sense of urgency. The top of my hair was stained deep with blood that had been leaking from my ears and nose while I was slumped over. Disoriented, I lurched further away into the corner, the hard thwack noise resounding off the walls and threatening to bring the building to gravel with its unyielding force.

Moriah was claimed the outlier. They poked, prodded, and submit every ounce of innocence out of her until she became as brittle as bone in front of me, painted up nicely in a casket. While my mind began to drift backward to think of the last time I saw her before her untimely death, my breath hitched. The guilt of me getting her killed was finally enough. I woke myself.

* * *

I awoke in a panic. I was laying on the living room couch with Jaycelyn watching over me. "Heard you had a tough day at school today," she said.

I disregarded her statement. "Jessie, when I was five, Mom and I had been out playing around in the leaves sometime around the fall, right?" I asked.

"You guys used to do that all the time. How should I know which specific time it was?" she retorted.

I raised an eyebrow. I didn't need her snarky attitude right now. "Yeah, school. Tough. Normal life tough. It's over. Now there was a specific day, Mom was crying with me in the house. Do you—"

Her face lit up and then saddened. "Oh, yeah, I remember that day. I'm pretty sure Dad beat the shit out of her, too," she replied.

"Do you remember why, or what pushed it to that point?" I pressed.

She looked at me curiously. "Something about her telling you that you could keep a rock. It was always the stupidest little things with him. She just wanted you to remember the day someday when you could look back and reflect on life."

Tears streamed down my face. "Do you have any idea where she might have put it?" *Come on, Jaycelyn. What do you know? What aren't you telling me?* She pretended to think for a long time, and I ushered her to be quick about it with jerky hand motions.

"Somewhere she knew you would find it, but you haven't found it yet, have you?" There was a lot of caution in her voice.

Picking up on that, I calmly shook my head. "That's okay. It was a stupid rock anyway. Probably at our old house."

She looked back at the kitchen doors and pretended to be surprised to see Rohan-Kyle standing there. I excused myself, claiming to be wiped out and headed upstairs as slow and as calmly as I could. When I was out of eye and earshot, I sprinted to my room and closed the door. I pulled my book out from my hiding spot and jerked it around as well as I could, but nothing fell out. I flipped the pages over and over time and time again until I noticed a page thicker than the rest. This particular page had a slit running down the edge of the page. I stuck a finger inside and pulled out a diamond-shaped piece of paper. I unfolded it. "*Quindi ora sei più vecchio*." "So you're older now," it read.

Chapter 22

I PULLED OUT THE FIRST shape to reveal a bunch more all connected together like an accordion. I hid my book again and sat on my bed, facing the door. My head was spinning from the dream, but now my stomach was doing summersaults. There was no way this could actually be happening. This had to be a set up. I looked around the room before continuing on reading the itty bitty papers with small Italian scribbles on them. "I know this will seem like a lot. Believe me. My first experience was a rough one, but I fear that they have something even more grotesque in mind for you. Without the slightest doubt in your heart, you must go to Italy. It is as safe as we can get you from this mess. I hoped and prayed for days on end that they wouldn't bring you or Jaycelyn in to this. He made promises upon promises that he wouldn't if he found out one of you were the outlier. But I think he knew, even before you were born, you are something of a marvel, Sandi. Educate yourself. Learn about what the human body does and does not do and ask yourself why *you*. I cannot give you all the answers, not any. But you can find them. They are out there. There are hundreds of people watching you by now, waiting to see what you can do. But none of them want you to be anything better than they are. Their thrones are made of glass, weak and easily shattered."

I raised an eyebrow. "He" must mean my dad, but who is *they*? I continued on reading: "Don't let them turn you into a China doll. Go to Italy, speak to my sister, find a way out of this. Look through the eyes of people and into their souls. There, they hide nothing. It is easier to tell lies to others because they are above the surface, but deep below in the recesses of souls… no one can lie to themselves. Only failed attempts to convince themselves. Trust no one, make no new friends. Did I ever tell you the story about the man who made a deal with the devil? Well, the moral of the story is, he always comes to collect. *Go kicking and screaming if you must… but you MUST run.*" That's it? Riddles and parables? I flipped the note over to the back: "P.S. The stone I gave you is safely hidden away. Only your godmother knows where. I assume that we're separated by now. At least, I hope so. I love you dearly, and I am truly sorry." I went to put the note away where I'd gotten it from and stuck the corner out a little to mark the page. I could hear Callum walk through the front door and all I wanted was to be with him. There was no way he'd betray me.

As I made it to the stairs, I could see Rohan-Kyle speaking to Callum in a hushed tone. Life had this amazing way of making me paranoid all the time. Callum flashed a smile my way, and without looking back, Rohan-Kyle ordered me downstairs to join their conversation. I inched my way toward them, afraid I was in trouble. Or worse, I'd gotten Callum in trouble. "Don't be scary, Miss Jacobs," Rohan-Kyle said and placed a hand on my shoulder. "Today was a hiccup. We aren't mentioning this to your mother, okay?" He looked between Callum and me. "She's been worrying a lot lately over trivial things, so we won't trouble her further." He turned his attention to me, "You'll get the hang of it, and you'll do better tomorrow, yes?"

I nodded. "Of course, crazy counselor kept asking me questions about my life. I don't know how it all even happened. I can't remember… barely remember coming home." I confessed.

Rohan-Kyle eyed me cautiously. "Turn around, Sandi."

I froze.

Callum looked just as shocked as I did.

"Okay," I said, the simple response getting tripped up by my tongue on the way out.

As I turned around slowly, I could feel his gaze analyzing every fiber of my being. At least, it seemed that way. He walked over to me and had Callum hold my hair up to reveal my neck. Something inside me racked around and jolted my body backward onto the couch. I'd hit the arm of the couch hard enough to knock the air out of my lungs. I gathered myself as best as I could before getting off the couch. My surroundings were moving in a lethargic state, but it was even worse than that, and it made me extremely nauseous. I groaned. *Not this again,* I thought to myself.

Just as he did at every possible opportunity for bad timing, Mikko materialized in front of my physical body. He warded off Rohan's fingers and took a good gander at my neck. "Geez! Stupid spot," he said. Then, he turned his attention to the other me. Well, the "me" that was still me but outside of the real…me?

"My head hurts," I verbalized. I fell back onto the couch and carefully watched Mikko as he made his way over to me. He seemed to be on guard.

"What the hell, Mikko?" I asked, becoming more unsettled by his suspicious behavior. "Is it the house again? We can talk outside." I grabbed his arm and made my way to the door. He pulled me away and grabbed hold of me tightly. Swiftly, he managed to "change the setting" to my room. Breathless, I said, "We could've just walked."

He went to sit on my desk chair and studied the room for a minute. "Heard about your day, need me to come with you tomorrow?" he asked.

I raised a brow at him. He *was* there for— "Weren't you supposed to—" *oh.* The counselor's office "hadn't happened". I rolled my eyes at what I now knew was a concrete lie, "Never mind. Yeah sure, come with. I'd like it if you did." I finished. He nodded and played with a pencil. "Why are you so quiet?" I asked. Irritation masked my voice. He turned his back to me as he continued to nod to himself and tapped the pencil on his index finger. I walked over to him and put a hand on his shoulder. I didn't want him getting all creepy on me again. I'd had enough to deal with that day.

He glanced over his shoulder. "Hmm?" he said.

I hugged him. "You okay?" I asked him, becoming more worried about his mind state.

"We're friends, right?" he asked.

I nodded. Was this about to turn into one of those awkward, unrequited love scenes? I hoped not.

"So that means you trust me and my judgement, right?"

Again, I nodded. "Mikko, where is this going already?"

He let out a frustrated sigh. "Stay away from Callum. It's too risky of a situation."

His words stung me like a slap in the face.

"What? Why?" I let go of him as he spun around to face me.

"Don't you think it'll be hard, up and leaving? Doing what your mom said and running off to another country." He paused and glanced at me, guilt graying his beautiful eyes. He couldn't look me straight in the face. "You can't carry his love with you. It's weighing you down."

Tears swelled in my eyes. "I can't do that. We can figure something out. I know we can."

"Sandi, that boy is gonna get you killed, or you'll get him killed. You can't be together. It won't work. They won't even let that happen."

I shook my head. "I don't want to talk anymore." I said.

"Wait a second. Listen to everything I'm about to tell you."

"No, thanks." I stormed out of my room and back into my body.

I felt a stinging sensation. "Quit moving. We're trying to get the bug out," Callum demanded.

"What? Like a tick?" I asked and jerked my neck away, freaking out. The pain I felt when Rohan finally squeezed it out affirmed it wasn't that type of bug. He spun me around and held out the tiny tracker on his finger for us to see. "Any idea who might have put this on you?" I thought for a second. "Stay away from that counselor. Do you hear me?" All I could do was blink. What the hell am I in the mix of? Why would she bug me, and how does Rohan know it was her? Find out next time on "wow just how fucked up can this get?" The nauseous feeling I'd gotten from shifting bodies unfortunately followed me back into this one. I kneeled over, sweat dripping off my forehead. "Callum, go pull up the truck." He bent down to me and lifted my head. He wiped the sweat off with the bottom of his T-shirt. I never expected that Rohan-Kyle had a dad bod, but he skyrocketed those expectations. Not that I ever wanted to picture it in my mind, but now I don't have to. *Gross.* "Sandi, can you go change into something you can get in and out of quickly? And I need you to pack an overnight bag," he said calmly.

"Dad, what's going on?" Callum asked and grabbed my hand.

Rohan helped me stand up straight. "I think she might've been drugged. Now go get the truck. We've only got so long to catch it," he ordered. I let out a yelp at the idea, and just like that, we were running around like chickens with our heads cut off. Breaking law after law, we made it to the hospital with our limbs intact.

Callum carried me in, even after I protested a countless amount of times. I kissed his cheek as discreetly as I could. He smiled halfheartedly. "I'm sorry. I don't mean to be such a burden," I said.

"I love you, sunshine," he replied.

As they ran a few tests and poked at me, I wondered how much money I was costing Callum's parents. Had to be a fortune. The doctor came in to let me know I was staying overnight and that I'd been subjected to a strange experimental drug that was supposed to induce memories. He brought Callum and Rohan in the room and explained it to them, "She might experience a lot of déjà vu and paranoia. It'll be hard for her to decipher some of her memories, so, Dad, if you could help her, that would be a great ease on her. She was given a really high dosage."

"Any idea where a drug like this would come from?" Rohan asked.

"Oh, yes, it's pretty accessible on the black market. There are undercover drug pharmacies that'll carry something like this, too. It's usually in the hands of therapists and doctors since drug addicts have no use for it, but it's not FDA approved and has a lot of side effects. So the use of this could end in someone losing their license."

Callum's face lit up with shock. "What are we gonna do, Dad?" he asked.

Rohan calmly replied, "I'll take care of it. Feel like staying with her for the night?"

Callum nodded eagerly. "Yeah, of course."

"You rest up now. Callum will drop me off and be right back." His voice was sweet, and his words were caring. It almost made me forget about him disapproving of the way I breathed every five seconds.

Sweat dripped off my body like it had been through a torrential downpour, and my eyes went in and out of focus on multiple occasions. I had the strongest urge to sleep, even though I wasn't tired. My overnight nurse dropped off a glass of water and began dabbing sweat off my face. "You need to take small sips of water, or else you'll be here for dehydration," she joked.

Laughing hurt my aching insides too much, so I flashed her a toothy smile. "Will do," I said as she exited the room. I tried lifting my arms numerous times already, and every time, they became heavier than the last. Eventually, my entire body seemed to be weighed down into the mattress, and I fell into a deep sleep.

* * *

My hand cascaded down the cobblestone wall as a shadowy figure led me through the dark halls. "Where are we going?" I asked. I received only gurgles in return. "Can't you speak?" I questioned. Still silence. I remained quiet the rest of the walk until we made it to an exit near the back of the building. The figure ushered me to follow. "I'm not allowed to go out there," I responded, but the figure continued to urge me to follow. "No, I won't do it. I'm sorry." I turned to walk away, and suddenly, I was whisked away and into the forest that hid the building. Branches from the contorted forest scarred my arms, but the adrenaline rush kept the pain at bay. As we neared the end of the forest, I was thrust forward and scraped my hands and knees on the ground. I whimpered as I rolled off my hands and onto my back, moss cushioned me from the rough surface underneath.

"Stand up," a rough, husky voice commanded.

Shakily, I managed to stand and face away from whomever was speaking to me.

"Move," the voice demanded.

I inched forward, trying not to let the thorn-like rocks puncture the bottoms of my feet.

Suddenly, I was propelled forward and fell, face first, into a stream of water. Before I had the chance to regain my footing, I was held down and submerged in water. No matter how many times I told myself not to freak out, I could only flail my arms and gasp and scream when I was let up for air. I could hear heavy hooved footsteps coming closer, too close. The noise trotted through the water, skimming past my fingers every now and then. My head was raised from underwater, and I let out a cry for help. Water stung my eyes and nose as I was held back down. The hoof of the animal came crunching down on my pinky finger, and immediately my lungs filled with water. I writhed and flailed my body, trying to break free but slowly started losing consciousness. I pushed upward with as much might as I had left in me, but I couldn't get away. I was ripped from the water, coughing and gasping, and thrown back onto the ground. I rolled onto my side as water seeped out of my mouth. Hands grabbed my arms and legs and spread them outward. A needle pierced my thigh and threaded its way through to my stomach. My mouth was covered. Then the thread was pulled until my skin pulled away like meat falling off the bone.

The shock sank in like a weight. I couldn't move. I couldn't see. I couldn't feel the hands pinning me to the ground. I felt an intense itching sensation start to creep across my body and outward. I tossed my body side to side as hard as I could trying to get a hand free to scratch the skin off my arms. Just as I couldn't take much more torment. I was rolled over onto my belly and branded like a cow. I screamed so loud I threw up, and when I did, I was force fed it back to me. My head throbbed, and my vision blurred. My ears rang so loud I couldn't hear the bark of a tree crack and tumble down my way. I was graciously kicked out of the way before the tree toppled over and hit the ground next to me with a thud.

I woke to bright lights and a loud ringing in my ears. There were shapes around me that I assumed were the outlines of people. "Sandi, can you hear me?" Ms. Strickland asked. All the ringing made everything else seem extremely quiet.

"Loud," I shouted and pointed to my ears.

Mother came into view and snapped her fingers to grab my attention. "Your ears ring?" she asked me.

I nodded. "Very. Ache… head. Lots," I responded.

Mother went to grab a cold compress and placed it on my forehead. "Libby," she started, but Ms. Strickland turned away from her. Mother went and grabbed her arm. "Libby, help us please," she begged.

"Janessa, do you understand what you're asking for? You want me to lend you thousands of dollars for a down payment on a house," Ms. Strickland replied.

"Yes, but in cash," Mother responded.

"A secret house," Ms. Strickland added.

"Call it what you want, but I have to have my best interest in mind. You don't have kids. You don't understand."

"But I do have family, family that I'd prefer to stay out of your drama."

"I can pay you back just as soon as I get my own accounts, please," Mother begged.

Ms. Strickland looked her over carefully. "Do you even know how to do that? Lee wouldn't have let you learn," Ms. Strickland responded.

"It can't be that difficult. I've been researching. Plus, I'm great at math."

"You're great at equations and formulas. You don't know a thing about money." Mother ran her hands through her hair, trying to hide her frustration and soothe the panic that was slowly creeping up on her.

"Why can't you help me? You're the closest person I have. He's going to kill me," Mother whined and stomped her feet.

"Us… if we get caught, Janessa. There can't be a paper trail at all. If this ever comes back to me, I'm going to be pissed. After this, we're done," Ms. Strickland warned.

"Elizabeth, you can't just give me the money and walk. You said so yourself. I have no idea what I'm doing," Ms. Strickland scoffed. "Janessa, I'm trying to help you within reason, and right now, you're not being very reasonable. Where are you even going to go? If you buy here, I'm sure he'll find you."

"It won't be here," Mother responded.

Ms. Strickland raised an eyebrow at her. Mother sighed. "Wisconsin."

Ms. Strickland huffed, "You're going to need more than a down payment. A mortgage means a paper trail. You need to find a place first and then come back and talk to me."

Mother sighed. "You're stalling. You're not going to give me up, are you?" she questioned.

Ms. Strickland pounded her fist on the metal table next to her. She laid her head down on the cool surface and took slow deep breaths. "One-hundred and fifty thousand is the most I'm going to donate you," Ms. Strickland said.

Mother furrowed her brow. "Donate? You're just going to give it to me?"

"Yeah, but you're going to do something for me." Mrs. Strickland pointed at me. "You and Jaycelyn can go, but she stays." Ms. Strickland finished.

Mother's eyes widened, "Absolutely not. She can't stay here. Once he finds out what happened, he'll never cut her a break. He's going to wear her out. She's going to die here." Mother whimpered. "Look you have to be reasonable, you've got to wo—"

"Fuck," Mother yelled. "She's eight! She's eight years old. Why don't you get it?" she stressed. "Because her and all the other kids here are her age. Most of them even grew up here, they didn't have the luxury of being able to go back and forth. You only care about it now because it's yours."

Ms. Strickland jabbed a finger into her chest. "That's why you're never allowed to see her. You knew what would happen when you got involved with this. You've been here since the beginning. You let him have Jaycelyn, and the same goes for Sandi. You don't get to pick and choose, Janessa, just because you feel like acting as if this isn't what you married into. You signed your name on the papers like everyone else," Ms. Strickland said as she snapped in my ears.

"You have some fucking nerve telling me what I married into when I didn't have a choice in that either. You ask him about the pilot of the company and how I signed my name when I didn't even learn how to write in cursive yet." Mother pounded her fist against the desk. "Ask him, and watch the look on his face when he tells you." She shouted. "Then you can come back to me and tell me all about the man I married, but until then, I need one-hundred fifty-five thousand so that my daughters and I can get out of here." She pushed Ms. Strickland's head back with her finger. "And it better not be a penny less."

* * *

I never knew it was possible to feel seasick on dry land, but here I was with Callum holding my hair back. "Are you going to be okay? To go to school, I mean?" he asked me.

I groaned in response.

"Sandi," he started and sat down next to me, "What's going on?" he asked.

"What do you mean?" I said into the toilet bowl.

He let go of my hair. "Sandi, nobody in their right mind would just bug and drug someone for no reason. On top of that, my dad seemed to know way more about it before the doctor even said anything. He found the little thing so fast and now here we are," he said.

"Callum, what are you talking about?"

"He didn't seem surprised in the slightest. At all. Sandi, I was trying to ask him questions in the car, and I've never seen him so distracted, like he was calculating something."

"He probably was just—"

"Stop. I've seen it. I've seen them whisper about you—"

"I'm si—"

He put his up his finger. "Don't try to talk over me and don't try to sell me that." He demanded.

I nodded. "I'm sorry," I said to him.

He held my hand in his. "Listen to me. If you lie to me like everyone else, I'll never be able to trust you or anyone else again. Why would all this stuff be happening to you? Does someone have it out for you?" he asked.

I laughed a lot harder than I should have. *Is he serious?* "Yeah, my dad, that's kinda the reason I'm around," I responded.

He squeezed my hand tighter. "What if that isn't the case? What if we didn't find you by accident?" he asked.

I snatched my hand away from him and shot out the door. All this time, I had been tired of hearing I was so sick, sick of hearing the word schizophrenia. The countless amounts of annoying times I brought it up to remind myself or someone else. I was tired of hearing it, yet it was in conversation so frequently that I'm just a sick girl with great stories. For so long I believed it to be that way, and here Callum was, reminding me of the opposing side.

"You're crazy," I blurted out.

He turned me around and waved his arms around frantically. "Sandi, did you just see what you did to me? Do you get it?" he asked, stressing every word.

I shook my head slowly. "I think this whole situation has you a little paranoid," I responded.

"That, there," he said and pointed at my mouth.

"What are you—" He put his finger on my lips and shushed me. "Listen. Don't speak. When I tried to explain something to you, something I think you know is the truth… you told me I was crazy. To keep lying to me. Then you told me I was paranoid, you would have kept going."

I sighed and looked down at my feet. "What if I'm trying to protect you?" I asked.

He cupped my face in his hands. "What if they're trying to protect themselves? It's called gas lighting, Sandi. It's a form of mental abuse."

Tears streamed down my cheeks. *Why would he want to mess up everything he has? Destroy it all in one conversation. Why?*

"Your parents love you. They would do anything for you. Anything," I whimpered.

"Like continue to abuse you after that was exactly what you ran away from?"

"Why? Why would they just lie? What could they possibly have to gain from it?" I just wanted him to stop. I needed him to believe that I would get better, that we would get better together.

"Come here." He grabbed my wrist and led me to the bed. He dumped a bunch of files out of his backpack and spread their contents across the sheets. "I found these after I did some digging. How old was Jaycelyn when she got her first job?" he asked.

I crossed my arms and rolled my shoulders back. "I don't know, fifteen or sixteen. She was pregnant then, so, at least, fifteen. I remember she needed to make money in order to get out on her own," I replied.

"Where was the job?" he questioned.

"Why do I get the feeling you already know the answer? Haven't I told you before?" I said, and he squinted his eyes at me. "I need you to say it," he said. "At a library in Wisconsin, I believe. She was an assistant or something." He nodded his head and laughed as he pulled out a piece of paper for me to see. He waved his finger at me, letting me know I was incorrect. It had yellow highlighter all over it. "Sandi, I remember you mentioning to me that Jaycelyn worked at some library and made a killing. She made thousands of dollars by mopping floors and dusting off books?"

"Some guy gave her his check. Plus, she worked so much overtime that she practically lived there," I responded.

He pointed to the paper. It had a copy of a check on it written to Jaycelyn with the back of it signed by her. "Not possible. One, because of child labor laws. You don't let a fifteen-year-old girl work forty hours a week, let alone *overtime*. Two, these checks are all written out to her from that library, which by the way is here in New York. All these are pretty decent-sized numbers. Jaycelyn wouldn't have to work until retirement with stuff like this. There's no way some librarian was making enough to add *thousands* to her check every two weeks."

I hesitated for a moment and looked at the checks. "She said—"

"Sandi, that is the entire problem here. She *said* this, your parents *said* that, the doctor *said* this. Look who the check is made out to, all of them are directly to her. Unless he gave it to her in cash or something like that or put his money in with the revenue for the library, then he couldn't have reflected it in a check which means she lied."

"Callum I saw her go to work, and it was at that library," I responded.

He looked over his documents in an organized frenzy. "This check was written off checks belonging to a technology company. See here?" He pointed to another piece of paper with the same color highlight. Then, he pulled out another paper with green markings all over it. "This company *owns* a library, three hospitals, one of which specializes in psychiatric care, and the technology company, of course. All of these places *you have been* to expect for here."

He pulled out pictures of a fortress-looking cream white building. "It looks like just a two-story building, but it's surrounded by a forest covering the rest of it. It's almost like it was built strategically, so it could conceal the bottom levels. There's been countless rumors that they do weird stuff down there. Weird illegal stuff," he rambled.

"Okay, what does this have to do with Jessie and how did you get all this stuff?" I questioned.

"I'm getting to it." He sifted through his documents. These had the matching green highlight as well. "Years ago, around when we would've been four or five, a woman named Amanda Carpenter wrote a book about a technology company called Highbreak Productions. She had explicit details about how she was promoted to work in the lower level operations. She even had pictures of documents and supposed experiments to support her claims."

"All right. I think I'm following… but you aren't answering my question."

"Hold your horses. This woman was so scared she had to write under the pen name Amanda Carpenter. Her real name is Luisa Rodriguez." He pulled out another copy of a check with her name and the company name highlighted in the matching colors.

He pointed to even more documents he frantically turned green. "The company sued her for defamation of character, slander, stealing company property, and breaking her non-disclosure agreement, and all of her profits went to the company. On top of that, they told her they'd let her re-release the book if she told the press the truth and let them know that it was apart of a new set of video games soon to be released called *All in the Mind: the Psychosomatic Series.* She told everyone she could that those files and documents and pictures were all for that video game series. A series that *never* came out." He pulled out copies of the original book and showed me where they'd changed it to say it was a work of fiction. "Then, there were a bunch of people claiming their original copies weren't the ones saying it was a work of fiction and that the photos were way more graphic and grotesque than the new copies. Somehow, it got around that everyone who believed they'd seen differently were tricked by the good old Mandela effect." He pulled a copy of the book out of his bag and shook it violently. "But here is an original copy, Sandi," He flipped it open and showed it to me.

I nodded, gently took the book away from him, and placed it on the bed. "Why do I care about a book and a lawsuit?" I asked kindly. "Are you listening to the biggest coverup story to fall in your lap? This company that this Rodriguez lady and your sister got paid by, did backflips to cover their asses because this is what they do. They experiment on people." He looked me over carefully and sighed, "Okay, you've been to a hospital in D.C. and New York both owned by this company." He pulled out two documents, one with home purchases made by his parents and one from mine. He started comparing the two. "New York, New York, Wisconsin, Wisconsin, D.C, D.C, and the company is based in New York. This is the birth certificate that my parents used to prove your identity or whatever to the school. When I looked you up, I—"

"You searched for my birth records?"

"Sandi, listen! It's fake!" he exclaimed. "All of it! Everything. You weren't born in Wisconsin. You were born right here." He pulled out another birth certificate and pointed to the name of the hospital which was highlighted in purple along with another document. "Clearwater Lake Hospital Center, owned by Highbreak Productions, owned by our parents. They also have Hillsdale Medical Center and Rosewood Trinity Medical Center." He finished.

"You…" I couldn't say anything. I turned away from him and tried to collect my thoughts. "I bet they have all of your records—"

"Right here." I cut in. "But that doesn't make any sense. I remember living in Wisconsin. I remember growing up there. Jaycelyn met Dustin there. She went to school there. I was a baby, and that was the only house I'd been in," I protested. "What if your timeline is off and this entire time you've been missing bits and pieces of your life, so your brain just helped you put something there? You know, like how we can't actually see our noses so we unknowingly put together the rest of the picture." *Why on earth didn't I trust Callum to help me in the first place? What if my memories I did have were false, that would mean I lie to myself just like everyone else? No wonder why I've been so gullible.* Ignoring his last statement, I said, "Maybe Jaycelyn didn't know… maybe she just innocently—"

"I need you to say it, thousands to a library assistant. And you took her word for it."

"I need to find out." Callum nodded. "They're going to release you tomorrow night. You've got to get back here."

Chapter 23

I LET DAYS GO BY before I went to confront Mrs. Strickland about what happened. I left out what Callum and I talked about. That was between us, but everything else that I was seeing in my dreams were all suppressed memories. She drafted up a fake field trip slip for me, and I presented it to Callum's parents.

"Absolutely not," Rohan said.

"Why not? It sounds like it'll be fun. Plus, I won't be around forever. I'll have to leave for college someday," I said.

"Well, college is one thing but this… you'll be away from us for a while," Lidianna added.

"I plan to go to college out of state anyway. This is my family. I'll always come back home. Please." I begged. "How are you going to go to an out of state college when you can't even functio—"

"I think it's a great idea. You'll make new friends. Sometimes staying close to home gets boring. You should explore." Lidianna interrupted. "But just not Italy?" Lidianna sighed, Jaycelyn weighed in, "Who's going, the class?"

I nodded. "So we can make better use of our Italian. We'd be with a host family for a little while. I'll be safe. I promise." I pulled out a "homework" sheet. "Hey, Jessie, quick side note. For my project, I have to make a poster board about where I'm from and where the family is from, so I was born in Wisconsin, right?" I asked and wrote on the worksheet.

Jaycelyn folded her hands together and sat up straighter to get a look at the sheet. "Yeah, we both were born there." She replied.

"Did we live anywhere other than there?"

"Nope, not until after everything happened. We have family in Italy, though, and Mom is from there. I don't remember exactly what part of Asia Dad is from, though."

"Great," I said. Now I can't even believe my own sister. "So, is it a yes to Italy?" I asked again.

"No." Rohan answered.

I turned to Jaycelyn and Dustin. "Guys, come on. I'll go on medication then."

Jaycelyn laughed. "Sandi, medicine doesn't work instantly. You need time to adjust and figure out the side effects. Starting a medication away from home is risky business." She said.

"Plus, medicine won't cure stupid." Rohan said in a condescending tone and shot me a strange look.

"Maybe I'm not as stupid as you think." I snapped back and slid my report card across the table. "Maybe I'm just waiting for the right time to blow you out of the water." I know he meant that I hadn't seen what's been going on all this time, but I wouldn't let him be too sure.

Callum knocked on my bedroom door. "Are you alright?" he asked through the door.

"Yeah, you can come in." I mumbled and stuffed my face back into my pillow. He sat down next to me and patted me on the back. "We'll get you to Italy. You just need to give me some time. I'll talk to them," he said.

I laughed. "They don't care about you trying to vouch for your sick friend," I said.

He laid down next to me. "What if I say I'll go with you?" he asked.

I scoffed, "You know how weird that'll sound? Plus, I don't need a babysitter. I should be able to go on my own."

"Hey, don't get mad at me. Do you wanna make it to Italy or not?" He ran his fingers through my hair. "Just relax, I'll figure it out." He said and left the room.

He stopped his mom in the hallway and went with her to his room. "What's on your mind honey?" Lidianna asked.

"I'm thinking about going to a different college than the ones we talked about before." He said.

"Oh, well that's fine. Did you think I was going to be upset about it?" Lidianna asked.

"No, I want to go to an out of state college… with Sandi." He admitted.

Lidianna scoffed and threw up her hands.

"What? I think it'd be fun going together." He said.

"What's the purpose of going with that girl? You have so much more to look forward to than following her around like a puppy." Lidianna said angrily.

"I'm not a puppy. I can make my own decisions, Mom. It's not like I'd get distracted or anything."

Lidianna balled her fists up and groaned, "Callum, you do get distracted. You've been distracted this whole time. That girl is no good for you. You'll find someone else."

"What's wrong with her having friends, huh? You always treat her like she's got the plague. She's actually a decent human being, you know."

Lidianna paced back and forth. "Callum, don't you see she's sick? She's not worth your time. You're so much better than that. You can do better than that. You shouldn't settle for less than what you are." She snapped.

Callum stood. "I see, so because she's sick, she's beneath me. So then, I must be the same way then? That's how you and Dad look at me, too?"

"You're sick, sick. It's different."

"It's not different, Mom," he yelled. "Sick is sick. It doesn't matter where it is," he said and left the room.

I heard the front door slam, and I looked out into the hallway. Lidianna stormed down the hall and barged her way into my room. "Close the door now," she demanded.

I closed the door and rested up against it. "Did I do something?" I asked.

"You always do something." She stressed and looked up at the ceiling. Tears rolled down her face. I grabbed a tissue and cautiously went to dab her eyes dry. She glared at me, "Get your hand away from my face." She snapped and snatched the tissue from my hand.

I backed away. "Sorry. It was out of line." I said as she eyed me up and down.

"Come here," she sighed and opened her arms wide.

"Ah, I see. You're having a meltdown or something." I said and pressed my back against the closet as she walked toward me.

"No, Sandi, I want a hug." She retorted.

"You've clearly taken something, show me your eyes." I said but she got closer, to go for the hug, I shrieked and slid underneath her arms.

"Sandi, just give me a hug, I'm trying to apologize." She groaned.

I hopped across the bed and hid. "Lidianna when have you ever wanted to hug me, let alone apologize. I understand if you're upset but I don't want to be choked out today." I said.

She laughed, "Hug me and I'll let you go to Italy." She whispered.

I popped my head up just enough to see my eyes over the bed. I squinted at her, "I'm calling you on your bluff, there isn't actually candy in your big white van." I joked.

She giggled, "Sandi, just come give me a hug for crying out loud."

I pulled the slip out of my back pocket and slid it across the bed. "Sign the slip." I demanded.

"Jesus, you sound just like your dad." She blurted out. She bit down on her lip hard when she realized what she said.

I tried to change the subject, "Thanks for doing this, I'll take plenty of pictures and—"

"Don't try to pretend like you didn't hear what I said. I know you're not stupid." She said.

"Well I wasn't going to draw attention to it but since you brought it up," I hesitated, and she stopped writing and looked up at me. I twiddled my thumbs, "I'm not going to keep writing if you just sit there in silence,"

She started, "What were you going to say?"

Why is she being so civil towards me? It has to be a trap. She must've found out that Callum went through their stuff the other day and now she's pissed. Definitely trying to pull a good cop routine and then Rohan-Kyle is going to bust in and threaten to beat me until I tell them what I know. She knelt down, rested her head on the bed, and stared at me. "Do I look more friendly like this? What do you want me to do?" she asked. I couldn't do anything but look at her and assume the worse. There's no way she was just going to let me ask whatever I wanted. "Speak now or forever hold your peace." She said and pretended to tear the slip.

I rolled my eyes and glared at her. "You're not going to tear that slip, Lidianna, because you want me gone." I said to her.

"Maybe, maybe not. Now what were you going to say?" she said and held the pen over the paper.

I sighed, "Let me consult the audience." I said and pretended to whisper to someone next to me. I looked over at her, "Must not be a funny joke." I said to the air.

"No, not funny." She said.

"Well maybe she needs a sense of humor." I whispered to myself.

"Sandi, I won't sign the freaking slip if you don't cooperate." She hissed.

"Well what do you want from me? You come barging in here acting like a mad woman with your hugs and false sense of love. Just tell me what you want Lidianna." I demanded.

"Continue your statement and quit stalling." She hissed.

"So, you've known him all this time?" I asked.

"Unfortunately." She said and signed the slip.

I took the slip back to Mrs. Strickland with a smile. "How'd you managed to get it signed?" she asked.

"Callum's mom… she's in the hospital." I responded.

"What?" she asked.

I slid my backpack off and sat onto the couch. "She and Callum had an argument because he was applying for a college that I said I wanted to go to. He kept saying he didn't understand why I couldn't have friends and I guess she ended up saying that I was beneath him or something because I'm sick. So he asked if he was beneath his parents because he's… physically sick. With all the lung stuff. He didn't go home for a few days and when he did finally show up, she just… snapped." I explained.

"Snapped how?" Mrs. Strickland asked.

"Started saying stuff about the three of us skipping town and living under new names. I think she told him a lot of the other stuff, too. I'm worried something is going to happen to her because of it, which means Callum gets hurt, too," I whispered.

A police officer knocked on the door and let themselves in. "Ms. Jacobs, we need you to come with us." The police officer said.

"I'm sorry is Sandi in some trouble?" Mrs. Strickland said.

"Who are you?" The officer asked.

"I'm the social worker for the school. I keep a close eye on Sandi here."

I nodded, "If something happened, she needs to be informed." I responded.

"We've temporarily placed you at a hotel per your guardian's request. Their son's DNA came back on your kit that was done some weeks back." He said,

"No, there's no way. Callum would never, he wouldn't, he didn't. I know he didn't." *That kit came back and made me look like a fool, now it comes back positive for his DNA?* "Ma'am, you described the man as," he pulled out a report from his file, "A six-foot-tall man, with a hazy frame and you couldn't quite see him because your mind started hallucinating. Maybe you don't want to believe he did it and you made yourself see someone else because that hurt you, that's okay. However, the facts are with the DNA, he's been taken into custody. Sometimes people we love use that to do bad things."

I cried every night I was in that damn hotel. I kept trying and trying to get someone to hear me out, but no one passed "How could he do that to a sick girl?" I pounded my fists against the wall and screamed. Rohan-Kyle entered the room.

"You really must be one sick bitch." He snapped,

"That's funny coming from you of all people." I snapped back.

"Why my son? What did he do to you?" he yelled,

"Nothing, Callum is my friend, why would I say he did this?" I yelled back.

"Because you did, you told the police he did." He raised his voice even higher.

"No I didn't, they said it came up on the freaking kit," I stepped to him, "Unless there's some reason why someone had a reason to lie and fabricate the entire thing I don't know how—"

He slapped me across the face, threw me against the wall, and pinned me, "He's not your friend, you're never going near him again. Once this is over, I want you out of here. I don't care where you go, but if I see you near my house again, I'll kill you myself."

"Rohan-Kyle, I didn't do this. I don't know what's going on, so you need to tell me." I pleaded. This was the first time I ever tried to reason with him, and I didn't know what else to say to strike a chord. "Help me help you, but I need answers. If not for me, then for Callum. I don't want to hurt him and hurting you hurts him."

He hesitated for a moment; I could see in his eyes his spirit wavered for a moment, but he was able to gain back his resolve. "I'll see you in court and then after we win, I'll let them throw you in the system for all I care." He stormed out of the room.

I screamed as loud as I could for as long as I could. I curled up in a ball on the floor and sobbed. *I didn't say that he did it, did I? No, I didn't. I wouldn't have said that, I wouldn't have, I wouldn't have. So then why do I feel the need to convince myself I didn't?* My vision started to blur, and I could only see what was right in front of me. I could feel goosebumps stretch across my skin. I pulled at my hair and smashed the lamp against the wall.

"More, more," a voice said in a low tone. I went to the bathroom and smashed my head against the mirror until it shattered into pieces. I used one of the thicker pieces to shred the bedspread into as many pieces as I could. The phone rang, I ripped it from the wall and used the lamp to beat it until it broke in half. The voice grew louder and louder the more I obeyed. Demanding more demolition until there were things, I couldn't do by myself and my body was no longer my own. I was whisked around the room and debris flew left and right, but I couldn't make out what any of it was. The room became scorching hot and I burned an ankle in one of the flames.

I stripped down to my underwear to beat the heat. I was guided by a force beyond me to face myself in the half of the mirror that was still attached. I was so outraged I could feel it consume my limbs and the ground seemed like it shook beneath me. I pressed down on the porcelain sink and broke off the edge with the pressure building inside my head. I felt like I was diving too deep into the middle of the ocean and the weight would crush me if I didn't release it. I grabbed the biggest chunk of glass I could find and pulled down my bottom lip. I pushed into the soft wet skin until I carved thick, bold, blood-stained letters into the skin. Blood dripped down my mouth like a faucet. I dragged the glass down my wrists and crumpled to the floor. The sprinklers came on and sounded the fire alarm. There was a loud thud on the bathroom door after a few minutes, but I ignored the noise. "Go away, I don't want to be bothered." I said, still the thudding continued, "Leave me alone." I yelled weakly. If being mental was a sports competition I'd be number one and I was the best at being just that.

Chapter 24

My latest stunt didn't go over so well with the judge, and that meant I couldn't go anywhere near the courthouse. I didn't even have a say in pressing charges or not because I technically wasn't able to take care of myself and if Jaycelyn protested she'd lose me to the system. Being too unwell to withstand trial meant I had to find a different way to clear his name. I tiptoed across the hall and slid into the hospital's records room. I went to the J section and flipped through the folders until I found one with my name on it. "You're fucking kidding me. What does this mean?" Inside on a red slip of paper read *follow protocol for red-letter patient.* "Sandi Jacobs and all records are to be held in paper copy only, due to red letter status. Conditions of treatment inclu—"

The door creaked open, and I hid on the side of the file cabinet. "Sandi? I know you're in here."

"Callum?" I called out.

"Where are you?" I peeked around the cabinet.

"Over here," I responded.

He ran over and hugged me. "My lawyer got your letter to the courthouse. The tape, too, but my dad told me what he did. He kicked out Dustin and Jaycelyn and the kids. I don't know what that means for them, but I promise I'm not going to let them make me leave you. I'd never leave you." He said.

"Callum maybe we shouldn't be together, maybe I really am si—"

He kissed me slow and passionately. "What happened to your lip?" he asked and stuffed his finger in my mouth.

"Ew! Gross! Get away!" I giggled and slapped his wrist.

"We'll talk about," he looked down at the scars on my wrists and arms, "all of it later. In the meantime, you need to take pictures of this file and everything else you can find." He said and handed me his phone. He flipped through the pages and shriveled up his face, "What's project Almanac?" he asked.

"Let me see." I said and got in close. He stood behind me, slid his arm around my waist, and up my hospital gown. My knees buckled, he stood me upright and pressed me against the file cabinet. He kissed my neck softly, "What if there's cameras?" I said and held him at bay.

"So what, my dad owns the place." He said as he propped my leg up on his hip and slipped inside me.

▶ Present

"AUNTIE SANDI!" TWIN ONE CALLED out.

"Give me a minute, Declan," I answered. I put the family diary away semi-content with most of what I'd written in there about my life. I hid the book in the secret compartment of the desk and went over to the crib to check on the baby. She mirrored a lot of my features, "Someday, I'm going to have a cute little girl like you."

My phone chimed. It was a text from Callum. "Hopefully sooner rather than later." I whispered as I responded to his message. It's funny how you can feel a threat before you can even lay your eyes on it. The way fear drags a finger down your spine, taunting you with what's to come. I turned to face a slender woman with honey blonde hair and lips as red as a fire truck. Her eyes shown gray through her elaborate masquerade mask that was covering her face.

"Sandi?" Jaycelyn called out.

Then again when I didn't answer. My phone rang. The woman signaled with her hand for me to pick up.

"Hey lovely, are you excited to celebrate your golden birthday?" Callum asked enthusiastically.

I laughed as the woman pulled out a pistol.

"Sandi, are you upstairs?" Jaycelyn called out, then footsteps.

"No need to come up. I'll be down in a minute." *Click.* "Twenty-three seems so old, don't know think?" I asked Callum.

"No, it's not. I've been waiting to make this the best birthday you've ever had." He responded.

The woman's hand trembled, she didn't want to do it. She knew me. "Sandi, would you hurry up?" Jaycelyn said. I kept hearing a clicking noise coming from downstairs. "I love you so much. We're going to—"

A sharp swirling noise came through the phone and then the sound of two cars meeting. The woman pulled the trigger, and the baby started wailing. The woman took off as I bled out on the floor. I slid my way to the desk and wrote shaky letters underneath it the best I could with blood trailing on the floor. I could still hear that stupid clicking noise twitching in my ear.

"Sandi," Jaycelyn screamed, but she never made it up the stairs. I could hear sirens not too far from the house. I guess someone had triggered the emergency alarm downstairs. Someone would see her run down the stairs and out the house, through the yard, and down the street. I was just a sick girl who made up stories and materialized monsters from thin air. Nobody believes in ghosts, I thought, and they damn sure won't believe in this one. Sometimes I used to believe that Jaycelyn and me were destined to be twins but separated by time. Like strong twin intuition, Jaycelyn panicked for me before danger knocked at my door. Two bodies, one heartbeat, right?

www.ingramcontent.com/pod-product-compliance
Lightning Source LLC
Chambersburg PA
CBHW021827090426
42811CB00032B/2049/J

9781535617840